DAILY
WISDOM
for
Women

"To one of my cherished Sisters and Best friends."

This book belongs to

~~Donna Pitcher~~

"Given To You from A Heart of Love."

Sincerely Your big Sis! Liz Bramble

DAILY WISDOM

WISDOM
for Women

Practical, Biblical
Insight for
Today's Woman

Carol L. Fitzpatrick

BARBOUR
PUBLISHING

Published by Barbour Publishing, Inc., P.O. Box 719, Uhrichsville, Ohio 44683, www.barbourbooks.com

Member of the
Evangelical Christian
Publishers Association

Printed in the United States of America.

In Christ alone we find the wisdom we seek:

"*But by His doing you are in Christ Jesus, who became to us wisdom from God, and righteousness and sanctification, and redemption, so that, just as it is written, 'Let him who boasts, boast in the Lord.' "*

1 Corinthians 1:30–31

Preface

Woman was lovingly and uniquely created by God to be not only a helpmate to man, but to have her own special influence upon the earth. I must admit, I didn't always see my own life this way.

When I was young, women were seen only in the "shadow of man." While we married for love, marriage was clearly expected of us, perhaps before we'd even pursued a career. And then we had families.

Only when I came to Christ, in a Christian commitment of faith, did I finally realize the importance of being a woman. All of the talents and resources God has built into each of us are essential—to love a husband, maintain a home, nurture children so they exhibit godly behavior, and perform specific tasks here on earth (Ephesians 2:10).

These devotions are designed to acquaint you with every book in the Bible. My hope is that you'll come to know how much God loves you and, at the same time, gain a better understanding of yourself as a woman.

As we journey together this year perhaps I'll even touch your heart. If so, it is simply because the powerful Word of God has embraced my own so profoundly.

CAROL L. FITZPATRICK

Created by God

So God created man in his own image, in the image
of God he created him; male and female he created them.
Genesis 1:27, NIV

A whole new year stretches out before you, like a crisp carpet of newly fallen snow. What kind of footprints will you leave? Maybe your strides will be gigantic leaps of faith. Or perhaps you will take tiny steps of slow, steady progress. Some imprints might even be creative expressions, woman-sized angels in the snow.

You are a woman; you were created in God's own image. But that isn't the message our world peddles. So what does it mean to be created in God's image? For starters, you have imagination, intellect, and most importantly, a soul. That's the deepest part of your being, where you long to feel whole, loved, cherished, and understood.

But hold the phone: God made you so that He might have an ongoing relationship with you. You need Him and He's promised to always be there for you. Isn't that the kind of life companion you've searched for?

On her fifty-fifth birthday a close friend confided in me that she's never felt really loved by anyone. "That's not true," I told her. "God loves you." Hopefully during this year she'll understand that God has been there all along. She just didn't take time to look in His Word. She didn't take time to feel His love.

Prayer — Lord, Psalm 139:14 says, "I am fearfully and wonderfully made." Thank You, not only for purposely creating me, but for loving me perfectly.

In the Garden

When the woman saw that the tree was good for food, and that it was a delight to the eyes, and that the tree was desirable to make one wise, she took from its fruit and ate; and she gave also to her husband with her, and he ate. Genesis 3:6

On a day she'd never forget, Eve stood beside the "tree of the knowledge of good and evil" and began listening to the seductive voice of the crafty serpent. How could she know that this voice desired to entice her and Adam away from God and the security of the Garden of Eden? She innocently chose to ignore the truth of God's Word and obey that new voice.

And Adam, who loved her, listened to her voice. He then accepted her invitation to join her in partaking of the fruit of the tree. As a result, cloaked with garment skins of animals sacrificed to cover their sin, Adam and Eve were forced out of this physical garden paradise. Yet the echo of God's loving promise lingered in their ears. . .a Redeemer would come.

Two thousand years later, Jesus returned to another garden, choosing it as His place of prayer. Kneeling there, He would accomplish for men and women this task of abiding in the Father and obeying His commands. And on the cross the sacrifice of His life provided forgiveness, once again allowing access to God's presence. . .now within a spiritual garden of prayer.

Prayer — Lord, I know I have walked away from You at some point of sin. That's why You sent Jesus to be my Savior. Forgive me, and enable me with Your strength to run from sin and toward prayer.

Seeking Wisdom

*To receive instruction in wise behavior, Righteousness, justice
and equity; To give prudence to the naive, To the youth
knowledge and discretion, a wise man will hear and increase
in learning, And a man of understanding will acquire wise
counsel, To understand a proverb and a figure, The words of
the wise and their riddles. Proverbs 1:3-6*

When asked by God what he wished for, Solomon answered,
"Wisdom." Looking back over your life, if you'd been afforded
this same opportunity in your early twenties, what would your
response have been?

Like most of us, at that age wisdom probably wasn't
high on your priority list. Instead of asking God or your
parents for direction, you more likely turned to your peers.

Natalie, a strikingly beautiful girl who'd just turned
seventeen, found the advances of an older man extremely
difficult to resist. Disregarding all the precepts she'd learned
from years of Sunday school, Natalie turned instead to a
non-Christian girlfriend for advice. "Go for it!" the friend
encouraged with gusto.

A decade later that friend has been married and di-
vorced. Natalie herself found out too late that her "boyfriend"
already had a wife and baby.

Satan may be out of the garden but he still finds his
way into vulnerable areas of our lives. But God is with you,
even in times of sinful temptation. He's promised to give
you the power to withstand such moral crises.

Prayer — Lord, surround me with friends who know You
and Your word. Surround me in a crisis so I can still hear
Your voice of wisdom and reason.

The Rainbow

I have set my rainbow in the clouds, and it will be the sign of the covenant between me and the earth. . .Whenever the rainbow appears in the clouds, I will see it and remember the everlasting covenant between God and all living creatures of every kind on the earth. Genesis 9:13, 16, NIV

Before sunrise the rain beat furiously against our trailer, rousing me from a deep sleep. Once it subsided the birds chirped sweetly and I raised the window shade to peek outside. Stretching boldly across the gray clouds lay a vibrant semicircle of color. And slightly above it arched another, more muted bow. "God, You really outdid Yourself this time!" I shouted, waking my husband who reluctantly nodded and then threw the covers over his head. A minute later I flew out the door for a better vantage point.

Every day God freely displays His blessings. Are we too busy or disinterested to appreciate their wonder? Even if we've forgotten He's there, reminders are all around for He is the God of covenants. In a world where promises (or covenants) are disregarded routinely, I need God's kind of stability.

Have you ever made a covenant or a vow to God only to find that life's circumstances prevented you from keeping it? Perhaps it was a marriage vow. In my own marriage there have been times when just honoring that vow have taken every bit of courage and strength I have. Without God's intervention my stubborn flesh would never stay one more day and watch for His miracles of change and hope.

Prayer — Lord, only You can renew my weary spirit and fill me with fresh expectation. Keep my eyes on Your rainbows!

Fishers of Men

"Come, follow Me," Jesus said, "and I will make you fishers of men." Matthew 4:19, NIV

Walking beside the glistening blue waters of the Sea of Galilee, Jesus saw two brothers casting their fishing nets. When He spoke the words recorded above, Peter and Andrew must have been intrigued. But Jesus didn't invent the phrase "fishers of men." Philosophers and teachers of that day used this term to describe those who captured men's minds.

The passage goes on to say that Peter and Andrew immediately left their nets and followed Jesus. But this wasn't their first invitation to follow Him. They had gone with Jesus to Capernaum and Galilee and later returned to their trade of fishing. However, this particular invitation was to full-time ministry and they responded wholeheartedly.

But why did Christ want these fishermen? Peter and Andrew were men of action who knew how to get a job done without quitting or complaining. Their tenacity would be an asset to Christ's ministry of soul winning.

Jesus came not only to save but to teach men and women how to have true servants' heart. The substance of ministry is service. When the apostles agreed to follow Christ, they accepted the call on His terms, not theirs.

Prayer — Lord, show me clearly where I can be of service within my local body of believers. Perhaps there's a small hand in the Sunday school just waiting to be held.

Our Prayer Requests

*In the morning, O Lord, you hear my voice;
in the morning I lay my requests before you
and wait in expectation. Psalm 5:3, NIV*

When my children were young the only way I could ensure having a special quiet time of prayer was to get up earlier than anyone else in the house. On weekdays this translated to 5:30 A.M. Settled into one particular chair, I read my Bible and then prayed for each member of our family. Although I never made a big deal about this habit, occasionally the kids would catch a glimpse of me there as they began their own busy days.

On Sunday evenings I would ask my husband and children for any particular things they'd like me to pray about that week. Such concerns as tests, projects, or schoolwork that were due, and once in a while class bullies or teachers were voiced. (Whenever "teachers" came up, I figured my child had been given a great deal of homework and resented it.)

Often in the morning I'd find little folded notes on my prayer chair. Now that our children are raised, I wish I'd saved some of those crumpled "last-minute additions" always written on notebook paper. But I do have memories of the celebrating we did when one of those prayers was answered.

Are you laying your own requests before the Lord?

Prayer — Lord, I wander around like those who have no hope, forgetting to ask You for wise solutions to my dilemmas. Help me remember to come to You before I start my day.

A Child of Promise

*"Then I will bless her, and she shall be a mother of nations;
kings of peoples shall come from her." Genesis 17:16*

Long past childbearing age, Sarah had given up hope of
ever cradling a babe of her own. And then when her husband, Abraham, was ninety-nine years old, the Lord made
a covenant with him concerning his future heir. Sarah
laughed as she listened at the entrance to their tent. No way
did a pregnancy appear to be within the realm of possibility!

I also remember listening to a conversation outside a
doorway. However, my doctor's pronouncement to my husband held out no hope, and offered no laughter.

After I carried our first child for seven and a half
months, she was delivered stillborn. Apparently during the
fifth month I had survived pneumonia but she hadn't. Lying
there in physical and emotional anguish, my hope had been
literally ripped away from me. "The baby has been dead for
over two months," stated the doctor. "I seriously doubt that
you'll ever be able to have another child."

Too deeply wounded to cry and unable to pray for the
miracle I desired, a long period of "numbing out" began.
However, the very next year God blessed us with a healthy
son, just as He had Abraham and Sarah. How gracious He
is, even when we see no reason to hope.

Prayer — Lord, only You have the power to override an
earthly pronouncement. I pray today that no matter what
appears to be impossible in my life, I'll be able to surrender
it to Your care and trust.

Vocalizing a Prayer

And when you are praying, do not use meaningless repetition, as the Gentiles do, for they suppose that they will be heard for their many words. Matthew 6:7

Remember kneeling beside your bed and praying when you were a kid? Why did it all seem so simple then? We just talked to God like He was really there and kept our requests short and simple.

Then, as you got older, the lengthy and spiritual prayers of the "older saints" became intimidating. So, where's the balance? Reading a little further in this passage from Matthew, at verse 9, Jesus gives us His own example for prayer. If you can remember the acrostic ACTS, you'll have an excellent formula for prayer: Adoration, Confession, Thanksgiving, and Supplication.

As we come before the Lord we first need to honor Him as Creator, Master, Savior, and Lord. Reflect on who He is and praise Him. And because we're human we need to confess and repent of our daily sins. Following this we should be in a mode of thanksgiving. Finally, our prayer requests should be upheld. My usual order for requests is self, family members, and life's pressing issues. Keeping a prayer journal allows for a written record of God's answers.

Your prayers certainly don't have to be elaborate or polished. God does not judge your way with words. He knows your heart. He wants to hear from You.

Prayer — Lord, Your Word says that my prayers rise up to heaven like incense from the earth. Remind me daily to send a sweet savor Your way!

Turn Your Ear to Wisdom

*For the Lord gives wisdom; From His mouth come knowledge
and understanding. He stores up sound wisdom for the
upright; He is a shield to those who walk in integrity,
Guarding the paths of justice, And He preserves the way
of His godly ones. Proverbs 2:6-8*

Every family has at least one relative who cannot get his act
together. (Meanwhile the rest of us scratch our heads and
wonder how he can miss the obvious, every single time.) It's
as though these people have to fall in every pothole in the
street because it never occurs to them to go down a different
road.

Are you smiling yet? Is someone in particular coming
clearly into focus? Now, hold that thought.

God's Word says wisdom is truly a gift since it comes
from the mouth of God, from the very words He speaks.
And all God's Words have been written down for us, through
the inspiration of the Holy Spirit. Therefore, those who
refuse to accept God's guidance, who refuse to ask for His
wisdom—those hapless relatives, perhaps—will never see the
light of reality.

Know that if you hold fast to the precepts contained in
the Bible, you will walk in integrity. Instead of gravitating
toward potholes, your feet will be planted on the straight
and narrow road.

Prayer — Lord, I can't change my relatives but I can change
myself. So, if my head is the one peeking out of the pothole,
please pull me out!

Sodom and Gomorrah

And the Lord said, "The outcry of Sodom and Gomorrah is indeed great, and their sin is exceedingly grave." Genesis 18:20

This grave sin of which God speaks is homosexuality. While the world may refer to this behavior as a "lifestyle," God says that it is so vile as to cry out for punishment. And when His judgment did fall on the wicked cities of Sodom and Gomorrah, it was swift and terrible.

Reading further in this passage you will notice an interesting dialogue between the Lord and Abraham. God promised that He would not destroy the cities if Abraham could find fifty righteous men there. Well, Abraham knew in his heart that there couldn't be more than a handful of good people left. Abraham finally got God to put the bonfire on hold if he could locate as few as ten righteous men. Can you imagine being unable to find ten people who obey God within your entire city?

And what was Abraham's nephew, Lot, doing living in this place? Flirting with danger, that's what. Lot lived on the edge of all this sin, pretending it wouldn't contaminate him. Even the men who were to marry his daughters didn't believe Lot concerning the pending destruction. Even Lot's own wife was consumed by the evils of Sodom and Gomorrah. As she looked back longingly at her former home, God turned her into a pillar of salt.

When God says flee, don't try to hold on to sin.

Prayer — Lord, if I know someone caught in the deadly snare of sin, please remind me to pray for her. Only through You and Your Word can she be truly set free.

A Narrow Gate

*"For the gate is small, and the way is narrow that leads to life,
and few are those who find it." Matthew 7:14*

During the first cold week of January, my husband and I suffered the loss of his mother and my grandfather within the space of four days. By the end of the next month I assumed that my powers of concentration had returned. It was time for me to take the written driver's license renewal test.

As the man began scoring my test I looked at the sheet in disbelief. Many of the questions I thought I'd answered correctly were wrong. In fact, I missed so many that I flunked the test. Confident that this had been a fluke, I grasped the DMV study book he extended to me. "You can retake the test, but read the book carefully," the examiner cautioned.

After skimming through the book, and feeling in possession of the critical concepts, I returned for another test sheet. To my dismay, I flunked the test again. This time the man at the window said I'd have to wait a month to retake the test, and if I didn't pass it, a driving test would also be required. A month later I returned, having read the book from cover to cover and survived the quizzing my husband initiated. The license was finally mine.

Knowing the right answers and then taking them to heart is critical in our spiritual life as well. You can't get a driver's license without passing a test. You can't get to heaven unless you are truly born again.

Prayer — Lord, Your Word teaches that no one comes to the Father except through Christ. Give me Your light that I may respond.

False Prophets

"Beware of the false prophets, who come to you in sheep's clothing, but inwardly are ravenous wolves. You will know them by their fruits. Grapes are not gathered from thorn bushes, nor figs from thistles, are they?" Matthew 7:15-16

While working within a Christian cult awareness ministry—a real barometer of what's happening in present-day society—I began to wonder about a person's ability to discern truth.

Perhaps the authors of the letters I read just went about the process backwards. Those seeking answers tend to try everything, like sampling dishes at a buffet brunch, and then choosing which to accept and to reject. The main problem with this approach is that life only affords us so much time. What if you run out of time before you find the one thing that does work? Pretty risky, isn't it?

That's why God gave us a way to recognize the true teachers from the "wolves." "You will know them by their fruits," Scripture says. Those who abide in Christ preach the message that is consistent with the one Christ Himself taught. That salvation comes to us by the grace of God, and is obtained through the belief that Christ's blood, shed on Calvary's cross, has cleansed us from our sin.

Don't be afraid to ask questions. True teachers will always be pleased to give straightforward answers.

Prayer — Lord, there are so many voices. Please help us to hear Yours, so that we won't be led astray by the wolves in sheep's clothing, who make a mockery out of Your great sacrifice for us.

A Furious Storm

*And when He got into the boat, His disciples followed Him.
And behold, there arose a great storm in the sea, so that the
boat was covered with the waves; but He Himself was asleep.
And they came to Him, and awoke Him, saying, "Save us,
Lord; we are perishing!" Matthew 8:23-25*

One evening my husband and I attended a meeting for
Adult Children of Alcoholics. This particular group was for
Christians, who shared hope and inspiration from the
Scriptures. We read verses on a certain subject and then
attempted to derive strength from principles we could then
apply to our lives.

When we read this Scripture, the Lord reminded me of
some previous difficulties I'd encountered. The disciples were
in the midst of a storm, just as I had been. Yet Jesus was with
them in the boat. They woke Him, in the throes of panic,
sure that the waves would swallow them up. Many times in
the past I succumbed to this same degree of pandemonium,
sure there was no way out or through the problem.

With sudden clarity I understood this passage. Jesus
took the disciples to the height of the storm's raging fury,
yet all the time He was with them. Later on in this chapter
Jesus rose up and rebuked the winds and sea and everything
became perfectly calm. Yes, the storms of life will attempt
to ravage me but Christ is there, amid the frenzy, ready to
deliver by just the power of His Word. He will carry me
safely to the other side of the shore.

Prayer — Lord, keep my eyes focused not on the storms of
life, but on Your incredible power to deliver me from them.

King Forever and Ever

*The Lord is King forever and ever; Nations have
perished from His land. Psalm 10:16*

When my sisters and I were young we lived in a huge,
newly built, custom home. My father's pride and joy, as a
part-time carpenter, was the gleaming oak staircase going
to the upstairs.

One day several of us got into a fight over who should
have control of a bottle of india ink. As one sister attempted
to carry the glass container downstairs for a parental pronouncement, another sister knocked it from her hands. The
bottle crashed down the stairway, its thick black ink
cascading furiously all the way to the first floor.

My father looked as if he were going to have a stroke
when he saw the mess. During the next few years he tried
everything to eradicate those angry stains but nothing would
take them away, short of rebuilding the entire staircase.

Satan, whose dominion is the world, has devoted all
his efforts to eradicating Christianity. Yet, while the evil
one's influence can seem as ugly as any ink stain, Satan's
mark on this earth will not be permanent. The reason?
God's Son, Jesus Christ, lives forever within those who call
upon His name. And despite the efforts of the evil one,
Jesus will remain King and will one day soon come back to
claim this earth for His own, forever and ever.

Are you assured of your place in Christ's kingdom?

Prayer — Lord, as this world becomes increasingly evil,
reflecting the one who holds its "title deed," remind me that
You're coming back to claim all that is rightfully Yours.

The Lord Sees Us

The Lord is in His holy temple; the Lord's throne is in heaven;
His eyes behold, His eyelids test the sons of men. The Lord tests
the righteous and the wicked, And the one who loves violence
His soul hates. Upon the wicked He will rain snares; Fire and
brimstone and burning wind will be the portion of their cup.
For the Lord is righteous; He loves righteousness; The upright
will behold His face. Psalm 11:4-7

God is watching His creation. I am grateful my parents and grandparents instilled this concept in me as a child. This knowledge, which has created an awareness of His presence in my life, has certainly prevented me from walking down many pain-filled and dead-end roads.

Did you catch what comes next? It's the age-old question, "Why do bad things happen to good people?" Our life on earth is one big test. And contrary to those who like to promote the idea of reincarnation or past life regression, Hebrews 9:27 states emphatically that we all get just one go-round and after we die comes judgment.

Thanks to a judicial system that protects criminals rather than victims, punishment for evil done upon the earth no longer seems to exist. But do not mistake this to mean that the wicked will not pay for their deeds. For to those who choose to obliterate from their minds any notion of a "real hell," God says it *does* exist.

The flip side of hell, of course, is heaven, the place where the righteous will behold His face. Life is not only a test, it is a choice. Where will you choose to spend eternity?

Prayer — Lord, remind me of Your presence throughout the day. Help me to reflect Your Son Jesus Christ.

Who Are the Faithful?

Help, Lord, for the godly man ceases to be, For the faithful disappear from among the sons of men. They speak falsehood to one another; With flattering lips and with a double heart they speak. Psalm 12:1-2

Who are the faithful? They are the ones who continue to follow God, no matter what obstacles are thrown in their path. One of the faithful, a dear friend who has debilitating multiple sclerosis, is one of the most joyful Christians I know. Jo must be assisted to the podium, but once seated on a wooden stool the weakness in her legs is forgotten. The songs which emanate from her wondrous spirit are a radiant tribute to her Savior, Jesus Christ.

Another friend, Sue, has led a Bible study for years, despite the fact that her husband is frequently out of work and their finances are at times nearly nonexistent. She continues at her post, knowing that God is not out of resources. And each time their family stands on the brink of impending disaster, God rescues them.

By now you have probably decided that it doesn't pay to become one of my friends. But I must reassure you that neither of these women consider shrinking back from following Christ. Instead, they agree with the apostle Paul, that these present circumstances and trials are but "light and momentary" compared with the peace we will have in Christ for all eternity.

Prayer — Lord, I have watched people carry burdens that humanly speaking should be unbearable. Yet with these trials You give them incredible joy. I praise You for all You are!

A Great Light

The people who walk in darkness Will see a great light;
Those who live in a dark land, The light will shine on them.
Isaiah 9:2

Shortly after four o'clock in the morning, the students at California State University at Northridge awoke at the jolt of an upward-thrusting earthquake. Forced into blackened hallways, they groped along the walls, attempting to locate the exit doors from their dormitory buildings. Thick clouds of plaster dust, shaken loose from the interior walls, had filled the air, making it impossible to see. But escaping their physical confines did not bring them into the light. The sun had not yet risen and massive power outages had shut down all outdoor lighting. Only the first murky rays of daylight could expose the extensive destruction to the area.

Like the students of this university, the Israelites had no idea that such a great depth of darkness had overtaken them until they were in the midst of it. God previously had provided them with great light, for He communicated directly with their leaders. But the Israelites chose to act as though the switch of truth had never been turned on. They were caught up in the dark snare of idolatry.

Are you refusing to act on God's insight, insisting on pursuits that distract you from worshiping Him? How we spend our time is but a habit, and habits can be changed, by repatterning our actions. Walk in the light, as your Father intended.

Prayer — Lord, change the desire of my heart to seek and know You better. Take my life and use me for Your purposes.

Our Advocate and Defender

"Every one therefore who shall confess Me before men, I will also confess him before My Father who is in heaven. But whoever shall deny Me before men, I will also deny him before My Father who is in heaven." Matthew 10:32-33

My sisters and I attended private schools for most of our lives but that did not render us immune to rowdies or bullies. And since we walked a few miles to school each day, we were at times easy prey.

Busy with friends her own age, my older sister didn't usually accompany my younger sister and me on our morning trek.

However, when we returned home one day relating that two big kids from the nearby public school had threatened to beat us up the next day, she rallied to the cause. As she instructed, we traversed our normal route while she lagged watchfully a short distance behind.

Suddenly the two boys jumped out of the bushes ahead. And just like a superwoman, our sister pounced on them, easily overpowering both and giving them bloody noses in the process. I'll never forget that scene as long as I live. It felt so incredible to have an invincible defender!

If we know Jesus Christ and have responded to His invitation to receive Him as Savior, Jesus remains forever our advocate before the Father, saying with love, "She's mine." Know that you are so precious to Jesus that He gave His life for you. Doesn't it feel incredible to have Jesus as your defender?

Prayer — Lord, how reassuring it is to know You mightily defend not only my body but my soul against attack.

Joseph Honors God

Now Joseph was well-built and handsome, and after a while his master's wife took notice of Joseph and said, "Come to bed with me!" But he refused. Genesis 39:6, 8, NIV

Perhaps you remember this account from Sunday school, as it's often used to reinforce God's expectation of purity. A young woman told me the other day that in the nineties the notion of celibacy before marriage is definitely passé. But for Joseph the very future of Israel teetered on his decision.

Joseph could neither dishonor Potiphar, an Egyptian officer of the Pharaoh, nor disobey his God. But day after day Potiphar's wife kept after Joseph, hoping to wear down his resistance. Can't you just picture this "thirtysomething" woman, doused with perfume and decked out in the latest sheer fabrics, grasping Joseph's biceps? But when Joseph's outer garment falls away as he flees, she proceeds to act like a scorned woman, and has Joseph thrown into jail.

But God had a plan. Through an incredible chain of events Joseph is found innocent and released from prison after he correctly interprets the king's disturbing dream. Eventually Joseph's position is restored and he creates a stockpile of grain which sees both Egypt and Joseph's restored family through a great famine—the one he had predicted in that dream.

Joseph's moral stand preserved the very ancestral line leading up to Jesus Christ.

Prayer — Lord, I can't look ahead to see how a critical moment of obedience fits into Your overall plan. Please give me Your strength when my human desires threaten to overpower me.

Why Jesus Spoke in Parables

And the disciples came and said to Him, "Why do You speak to them in parables?" Matthew 13:10

Jesus' main purpose in coming to earth was to communicate God's love by His perfect words and actions. Certainly He could clearly articulate a point when He desired. So why did He shroud many of His teachings behind a veil of curious stories?

Jesus Himself explains: " 'Therefore I speak to them in parables; because while seeing they do not see, and while hearing they do not hear, nor do they understand' " (Matthew 13:13). Who was Jesus talking about? Only moments before He'd been conversing with the scribes and Pharisees. And although they had great knowledge of God's Word, they refused to see its very fulfillment before their eyes. Everything Jesus did and said confirmed that He was their long-awaited Messiah. Yet they closed their eyes and stopped up their ears.

Then Jesus spoke to the great multitude that had followed Him to the seashore. How well He knew that just because they followed didn't mean they desired to hear His message or respond in faith. Therefore, He spoke in parables, or words of truth hidden under an imaginary net. Only with the hand of faith could these followers lift a corner of the net and view the truth.

Yet to those whom He knew would respond, He provided plain words. How open have you been to God's Word?

Prayer — Lord, Your truth surrounds me. Please lift my eyelids to see it and stir my heart to respond to Your Word.

Wisdom Comes from God

*And coming to His home town He began teaching them in
their synagogue, so that they became astonished, and said,
"Where did this man get this wisdom, and these miraculous
powers?" Matthew 13:54*

The toughest critics you'll ever encounter are family and
friends. The reason is simple: They know you best. When
vulnerability swings your trapeze with such speed that your
grip loosens, they watch as you fall. At that moment you
can stand there gazing at your flattened imprint in the dirt
or climb up the ladder and try again.

Yes, some will continue to stare, waiting for you to
stumble once again, but there will be new faces in your
crowd of onlookers. They believe you can reach your goals
and make a difference in our world. They do not see a little
girl living next door; they see you as you are *now*.

Jesus encountered these same narrow-minded pessi-
mists, those who claimed they knew Him from way back.
Ridiculing Him, they said, "Isn't He just a carpenter's son?"
Yes, He surely was, but that carpenter was the Master
Builder! For Jesus wasn't Joseph's son, but God's Son.

He came from God, full of wisdom. Those who stood
with Him during His earthly ministry had true wisdom
and understanding from God. They made up His true
family of believers. Today, you obtain wisdom through a
personal knowledge of Christ and by studying His Word.
For only then can God's Spirit fill you with the wisdom
you'll need to find and live out your God-given purpose.

Prayer — Lord, even if my earthly family rejects me, You
have promised to be there for me.

Rescued from My Enemies

*He reached down from on high and took hold of me; he drew
me out of deep waters. He rescued me from my powerful
enemy, from my foes, who were too strong for me. They
confronted me in the day of my disaster, but the Lord was
my support. Psalm 18:16–18, NIV*

David wrote this psalm at a time when he was being pursued
by Saul. Imagine David's terror as he and his band of loyal
followers clung within the concealing walls of caves for
shelter while Saul sought to slaughter him. During this time
of desperation, David learned to lean on God's power, convinced in his heart that He alone could rescue him from
harm.

Have you ever known such desperation? A time when
even the ground beneath you seemed unable to support
you? Perhaps you were exactly where God wanted you, just
as David was, and yet untold trials and tribulations were
heaped on you anyway. Did you doubt God's presence? Did
you realize that He could act in your behalf, despite the
obvious circumstances?

The very nature and character of God demands that
He rescue those whom He loves. When confronted with a
crisis, like David, you can put your life in His hands.

Prayer — Lord, when all is lost I thank You that You reach
out to me with Your mighty hand of rescue. Your welcoming
hand is a lifeline in any storm.

So Much Promise

*"I am God, the God of your father," he said. "Do not be afraid
to go down to Egypt, for I will make you into a great nation
there. I will go down to Egypt with you, and I will surely
bring you back again. And Joseph's own hand will close
your eyes." Genesis 46:3-4, NIV*

The same "I Am" who spoke to Jacob's forefathers is also
speaking to him. Next, the Lord confirms the Abrahamic
covenant to Jacob. For although Jacob and his family go into
Egypt as a remnant of only seventy, they will become "a great
nation." God even promises to be with Jacob there, giving
him the assurance that he's not only in God's will but that
God's presence will accompany him to this new homeland.
And then comes a promise which most assuredly warms
Jacob's heart: He will never be separated from Joseph again
during his lifetime. God says that Joseph will be present with
Jacob as he passes from this life into the welcoming door of
eternity with God.

And as Joseph honors Jacob's request that he be buried
in Israel, the last part of God's promise is fulfilled. Jacob,
renamed Israel by God, is brought back again into his land.
His life ends with the promise of Messiah coming through
his line.

The promises of the future will be filled with futility if
God has not claimed His rightful place in your home.

Prayer — Lord, You are a God who fulfills promises. I
praise You!

Trials Have a Purpose

Then Joseph said to his brothers, "Please come closer to me."
And they came closer. And he said, "I am your brother Joseph,
whom you sold into Egypt. And now do not be grieved or
angry with yourselves, because you sold me here; for God sent
me before you to preserve life." Genesis 45:4–5

How many of us could forgive as Joseph did? His jealous
siblings had kidnapped him, thrown him into a pit, and
then allowed him to be sold into slavery. Yet Joseph trusted
that from God's perspective, not his own, his trials had a
purpose.

Joseph walked through his humiliating ordeal with his
eyes focused on the Lord. He continued not only to love his
brothers but to find forgiveness in his heart for them. Studying his life has enabled me to look at my own situation
differently: God can accomplish miracles in the midst of
trials.

Is there a hurt so deep inside that you have never shared
it with another human being? Perhaps someone in your own
family has rejected or betrayed you. Remember the pain
suffered by Joseph; remember the anguish of Jesus Christ,
who was betrayed by one as close as a brother, Judas Iscariot.
God knows your pain and He is strong enough to remove
any burden.

Prayer — Lord, sometimes I want to enjoy my agony a
while longer. Show me the brilliance of Your forgiveness
that I might trust You in the trial and not miss the outcome
You've planned.

Of Little Faith

"How is it that you do not understand that I did not speak to you concerning bread? But beware of the leaven of the Pharisees and Sadducees." Matthew 16:11

It never fails! You take a "mental health day" off from work and get the whole house cleaned up. You even make a nice dinner. Then your son invites his Little League friends over after the game, your husband says he'll be home late for dinner, and the dog takes a playful romp through your garden, tracking his big paws across the kitchen floor. You feel like crying, but you settle for trying to get them to understand how hard you worked all day. Do they care?

This is how Jesus felt after He had healed the lame, given sight to the blind, miraculously fed 5,000 from five loaves, with baskets leftover, and on another occasion fed 4,000 with only seven loaves. And yet when He warns the people to "beware of the leaven of the Pharisees and Sadducees," they conclude that He's speaking about bread.

Jesus used a physical reality to get across a spiritual truth. But they missed the point. His warning concerned the teachings of their religious leaders, men who knew the Scriptures and yet denied Jesus as the Messiah. Although the people marveled saying, "No one has ever made a man born blind see," they failed to have enough faith to realize that Jesus Christ was in fact "God with them."

What miracle has Jesus accomplished in your life? And yet do you see with the eyes of faith who He really is?

Prayer — Lord, please expand the little faith I have and provide me with real comprehension. Please help me know Your truth.

A Life Turned Around

The man said, "Who made you ruler and judge over us? Are you thinking of killing me as you killed the Egyptian?" Then Moses was afraid and thought, "What I did must have become known." Exodus 2:14, NIV

Moses had killed an Egyptian. And the action he thought he'd taken in secret had been observed. Why had he killed the man? Because Moses as a Jew, miraculously delivered by God from certain death, could not stand by and watch an Egyptian beating a fellow Hebrew. Was it right? No. God Himself administers true justice, in His own time, to those who deserve punishment.

Later, on Mount Horeb, Moses encountered the living God when he saw a burning bush. " 'Moses! Moses!' " called God's voice from the fiery bush. " 'I am the God of your father, the God of Abraham, the God of Isaac and the God of Jacob' " (Exodus 3:6, NIV).

Then God revealed His plan to Moses, a plan to bring the Israelites out of Egypt. So when Moses asks God, " 'Who am I, that I should go to Pharaoh and bring the Israelites out of Egypt?' ", it comes from the heart of one who has murdered and knows His guilt before God. But instead of rebuke Moses hears, " 'I will be with you. . .I am who I am' " (Exodus 3:11-12, 14, NIV). This is the same "I Am" who calls you to serve Him today.

Prayer — Lord, Moses felt unworthy to serve You because of his great sin. Forgive me of my sins and focus my life on You.

Who Is Christ to You?

"But what about you?" he asked. "Who do you say I am?"
Simon Peter answered, "You are the Christ, the Son of the
living God." Matthew 16:15-16, NIV

Jesus repeatedly asked this question to those who followed after Him. He knew that in a short while He would be gone from the face of the earth and all these fledgling Christians would have to bolster their faith were His words and actions. Jesus wanted to be sure they understood.

Jesus knew that once He was gone His followers would be scattered and most would die for their faith in Him. Therefore, it was crucial that they understand exactly who Christ was.

Six days after this conversation with Peter a miraculous event occured. Jesus took Peter, James, and John up a high mountain. And there He was transfigured before them. "His face shone like the sun, and his clothes became as white as light" (Matthew 17:2). Moses and Elijah appeared with Jesus and spoke with Him.

A bright cloud overshadowed them and a voice from heaven said, " 'This is My beloved Son, with whom I am well-pleased; hear Him!' " (Matthew 17:5) Just the awesome sound of God's voice caused the disciples to fall on their faces in fear.

Jesus Christ: Son of God, Son of Man, Redeemer, displayed His glory to these disciples. Do you know Him as Savior?

Prayer — Lord, if I have allowed the world's viewpoint to diminish who You are, let me now see the truth. Let me declare as Peter did, "You are the Christ, the Son of God."

Forsaken by God?

My God, my God, why hast Thou forsaken me? Far from my deliverance are the words of my groaning. Psalm 22:1

Have you ever cried out to God with such despairing utterances as these? I have. Amid the deep black void of a moonless night, my loneliness threatened to pull me into a swirling, spiraling eddy of emptiness. The sound of my own raspy voice screamed out from my inmost being: "God, if You really exist, show me how to find You! I don't know where You are!" Church hadn't met my needs. People who promised love only provided pain. While my clenched fists beat against my bedroom wall, twelve years' worth of tears, a maelstrom of anger, hurt, and frustration, flowed freely.

He showed me the cross. The year was 1973. I left my knapsack of grief on the bloodstained ground beneath His wooden cross. And I never looked back. He has met my every need in surprising, miraculous, and incredible ways.

Jesus, separated from the Father because of our sin, reached the ear of God with His own desperation. He experienced for us this ultimate terror. . .that we would never be forsaken or walk alone the road which leads to Calvary.

Where are you today? On the road, walking toward Him? Sitting down, too bewildered to even formulate questions? Or are you kneeling, as I did, right at His bleeding feet?

Prayer — Lord, no matter what hazards are down the road, You've got a signpost ready to hang on whatever misleading marker is already in the ground. And the Son is shining ahead!

Fit for Service

Then Moses said to the Lord, "Please, Lord, I have never been eloquent, neither recently nor in time past, nor since Thou hast spoken to Thy servant; for I am slow of speech and slow of tongue." Exodus 4:10

Poor Moses, he still hasn't grasped the point. God didn't appoint him spokesperson for the Israelites to watch him fail. So what was the problem? Moses heard God's voice clearly calling him to this position. Why was he balking at the task?

But remember that Moses was nothing but a murderer with the best of intentions when God first met him at that burning bush. Perhaps he took a momentary look back at his life before the Lord got hold of him. The previous Pharaoh had wanted to kill him. That could definitely have caused him to quake in his sandals.

The passage continues: "Then the anger of the Lord burned against Moses, and He said, 'Is there not your brother Aaron the Levite?. . .he shall speak for you to the people. . .'" Now if this were God's plan all along, why was He angry with Moses? Because the Lord wanted Moses to understand that He could and would meet all of his needs. Moses needed to understand that God's power is limitless. Instead, Moses settled for allowing Aaron to speak for him.

Do you give the Lord part of your problem and then halfway through start solving it yourself?

Prayer — Lord, I am inadequate to understand Your perfection. Please help me see that Your help is like owning a store that has everything I need, in utterly limitless supply.

Pharaoh Admits His Sin

Then Pharaoh sent for Moses and Aaron, and said to them, "I have sinned this time; the Lord is the righteous one, and I and my people are the wicked ones." Exodus 9:27

One would think that with an admission like this, especially from an unbelieving ruler, the man had finally seen the light. Pharaoh sounds ready to commit his heart and soul to the almighty God. Wrong! Although the Egyptians had already suffered through seven plagues, brought on by Pharaoh's stubborn refusal to allow the Israelites to leave, Pharaoh still wasn't really convinced of God's power.

Even Moses wasn't so easily fooled: "As soon as I go out of the city, I will spread out my hands to the Lord; the thunder will cease, and there will be hail no longer, that you may know that the earth is the Lord's. But as for you and your servants, I know that you do not yet fear the Lord God."

However, because Pharaoh's heart had not yielded to God's authority, as soon as the storm passed he became predictably relentless, again refusing to allow the Israelites to go. Three more plagues would come upon the people because their leader refused to honor the true God.

Pharaoh would pay a terrible price for his sins. In the end his stubbornness would cause the loss of his own precious son. This would be the final curse in Egypt, the death of every firstborn son.

Prayer — Lord, it's so easy to see Pharaoh's obstinate streak. Give me strength to admit when I'm wrong. Give me strength to come to You in repentance.

Renewal of All Things

*Then Peter answered and said to Him, "Behold, we have left
everything and followed You; what then will there be for us?"
And Jesus said to them, "Truly I say to you, that you who
have followed Me, in the regeneration when the Son of Man
will sit on His glorious throne, you also shall sit upon twelve
thrones, judging the twelve tribes of Israel."
Matthew 19:27-28*

Peter, always so practical. Here's what he's really saying:
"Lord, when we get to the end will it have been worth it to
follow You?" And Jesus reassures him with a gigantic yes!

How it must have broken Jesus' heart to know His
treasured follower would be martyred one day. Perhaps Peter
had an inkling about this too. We see he wanted desperately
to know whether life really went on eternally. The Lord went
a step further and related that Peter would not only be with
Christ, the Son of Man, eternally, but he would have work to
do once he arrived in heaven.

None of us will just occupy space in heaven. Our God
is always productive. And this job to which Jesus refers,
that of judging the twelve tribes of Israel, will be given to
the disciples.

Have you ever speculated as to what you might do in
heaven? Well, don't worry, it's not going to be anything like
what you've done on earth. Your "boss," after all, will be
perfect. And the tasks you perform will be custom-tailored
to you. "Job satisfaction" will finally fit into our vernacular.

Prayer — Lord, I can't even imagine what You have in store
for me in heaven. Please keep me faithful to complete the
duties You've called me to on earth.

Signs of a Scoundrel

A scoundrel and villain, who goes about with a corrupt mouth,
who winks with his eye, signals with his feet and motions
with his fingers, who plots evil with deceit in his heart—he
always stirs up dissension. Proverbs 6:12-14, NIV

In old movies facial tics, winking and darting eyes, handlebar mustaches, or too much makeup helped us identify crooks and scoundrels. In real life they're not so easy to recognize.

Modern-day charlatans may wear nice clothes. But underneath their carefully groomed exterior lies a dangerous and destructive personality, one captured beautifully by wise King Solomon.

This same proverb goes on to list seven things the Lord considers an abomination: ". . .Haughty eyes, a lying tongue, and hands that shed innocent blood, A heart that devises wicked plans, Feet that run rapidly to evil, A false witness who utters lies, And one who spreads strife among brothers" (Proverbs 6:17-19).

Well, if we didn't find ourselves among the first list, it is almost impossible to escape membership in this last group. We're well aware of body language today. By simply analyzing a person's posture we can anticipate our competition's next move. But, true scoundrels devise other methods of subterfuge. Whom can we trust? The Ancient of Days, who always remains the same. He alone continues to guide and direct our paths.

Prayer — Lord, all around me are those who seek to divert the path of my life. Help me stand firmly on Your unchanging Word.

The Passover Lamb

"Slay the Passover lamb. And take a bunch of hyssop and dip it in the blood which is in the basin, and apply some of the blood that is in the basin to the lintel and the two doorposts; and none of you shall go outside of his house until morning. For the LORD will pass through to smite the Egyptians; and when He sees the blood on the lintel and on the two doorposts, the Lord will pass over the door and will not allow the destroyer to come to your houses to smite you." Exodus 12:21-23

This Scripture passage paints a comprehensive picture of the Passover.

Each year this symbolic Passover meal is re-created. The man of the house reads Exodus 12:14. Then his wife puts on her head covering and lights two candles. Using circular motions with her hands above the candles, she then closes her eyes and says a specific prayer.

Four cups of wine or grape juice represent sanctification, the cup of plagues (visited on Egypt), the cup of redemption by Messiah, and the cup of praise to God as the King of the Universe.

Other symbols include parsley, which represents produce, likened to Israel as a seed and growing to maturity; a hidden matzoh bread, denoting Christ in the tomb; the shank bone of the Passover lamb; bitter herbs, commemorating their slavery; and karoset, an apple mixture akin to the mortar of the bricks they made in Egypt as slaves.

We can celebrate the Passover with joy and thanksgiving, knowing for certain that the long-awaited Messiah has come, and will come again!

Prayer — Lord Jesus Christ, I thank You for being my promised Messiah and Passover Lamb. I thank You for Your sacrifice so that my sins could be forgiven.

A Pillar to Guide Them

Then they set out from Succoth and camped in Etham on the edge of the wilderness. And the Lord was going before them in a pillar of cloud by day to lead them on the way, and in a pillar of fire by night to give them light, that they might travel by day and by night. He did not take away the pillar of cloud by day, nor the pillar of fire by night, from before the people. Exodus 13:20-22

Finally the Israelites were on their way. They had lived in Egypt for 430 years. Can we even fathom the logistical nightmare of moving millions of people? And don't forget, they took the sheep, all the livestock, and even the silver, gold, and clothing they managed to wrangle from the Egyptians.

Now talk about fanfare! As they leave, their mighty God positions Himself before them, leading them in a pillar of cloud.

God did not lead them through the land of the Philistines, even though it was a more direct route, because He didn't want them to be involved in a war and long for Egypt again. So instead, He led them around the wilderness to the Red Sea.

Following a few quiet days of reflection and recovery from all the plagues, old Pharaoh has a change of heart. Six hundred chariots and drivers were made ready, and the chase was on for the Israelites. But God was prepared. He's prepared today to move mountains for you.

Prayer — Lord, let me not forget that I have seen Your power. Help me to continue walking in obedience to You.

An Invitation to Dine

"The Kingdom of heaven may be compared to a king, who gave a wedding feast for his son. And he sent out his slaves to call those who had been invited to the wedding feast, and they were unwilling to come." Matthew 22:2-3

Have you ever given a dinner party only to have your guests cancel at the last minute? Perhaps they didn't even offer a decent excuse. You're seething inside. You've worked all day long to prepare your home for these "ungrateful people," who will surely never be invited again.

When God sent His Son to earth, He invited all men and women to a wedding feast. Those who accept the invitation become part of the Church. And the Church is the bride of Christ. But there are many who have offered feeble excuses for their lack of faith.

The Son is the Bridegroom for whom the wedding feast is prepared. God Himself has laid the groundwork in the hearts which will respond to His Son, Jesus Christ.

There will be an appointed hour in the future when the guests will come to the banquet. And Christ will call them forth to be His Church when all is made ready, after His Resurrection and Ascension and the coming of the Holy Spirit at Pentecost.

Also, those in attendance receive "wedding clothes." Jesus Christ now clothes them in His righteousness. Those not wearing these garments are cast out because they refused Christ's invitation, and in so doing, have rejected His salvation.

Prayer — Lord, You've invited me to dine with You. Let me graciously accept my "wedding clothes."

Remember the Sabbath

"Remember the Sabbath day, to keep it holy. Six days you shall labor and do all your work, but the seventh day is a Sabbath of the Lord your God; in it you shall not do any work. . . For in six days the Lord made the heavens and the earth, the sea and all that is in them, and rested on the seventh day."
Exodus 20:8-11

During the 1950s in Missouri, where I grew up, blue laws virtually shut down the city on Sundays. You could see whole families, dressed in their Sunday best, walking toward the nearest big intersection, where you'd find a different denomination on each corner. The rest of the day might be spent enjoying picnics, bike rides, or "visiting Grandma." I loved those relaxing times with the extended family.

Merchants finally managed to get these laws overturned and the stores opened on Sunday. Sales were timed to begin early on the Sabbath, enticing people to make a choice between church and shopping. On a Sunday morning compare the number of parked cars in the mall with those in the church lots. This worldly strategy has certainly been effective.

In the very beginning of our marriage my husband and I made a decision to honor God on Sunday. He has blessed our family over and over for this faithful commitment, providing not only the weekly spiritual guidance we desperately need, but also giving our bodies and souls the rest they require.

Prayer — Lord, please help me to remember that Your commandments are always for my good.

Mourning Turned Into Dancing

Thou hast turned for me my mourning into dancing.
Psalm 30:11

If you've never read *The Hiding Place* by Corrie ten Boom, it might be difficult to understand how God could turn mourning into dancing. For hiding many Jewish people in their home during World War II, Corrie and her family were imprisoned in a Nazi death camp. Corrie alone survived that ordeal and went on to travel the world, sharing one message: Jesus can turn loss into glory.

Years ago I was drawn to watch Corrie ten Boom one day on television. She spoke about a meeting, long after the war, with the S.S. soldier who had stood guard in the showers at her concentration camp. When I heard her speak about extending her hand in a gesture of forgiveness, her words pierced through my soul like a dagger. How could she offer the hand of friendship to him? Lacking her own strength, Corrie prayed to God for Him to give His forgiveness to this man. And when Corrie's hand touched the former soldier's, she likened it to love's lightning going through her arm, to the man, and then back again.

At the time, there were many people whom I felt incapable of pardoning. God's name topped the list.

Corrie's words lingered in my mind and heart, making me miserable. But I finally surrendered my life to Christ. And God's power of forgiveness has turned my own mourning into dancing.

Prayer — Lord, Your "merry saint," Corrie, knew joy was a condition of a heart filled with forgiveness. Help me see this too!

Wisdom Calls Out

Does not wisdom call, And understanding lift up her voice?
On top of the heights beside the way, Where the paths meet,
she takes her stand; Beside the gates, at the opening to the city,
At the entrance of the doors, she cries out: "To you, O men, I
call. . .For wisdom is better than jewels; and all desirable
things can not compare with her." Proverbs 8:1-4, 11

"Dream books," that's what my grandmother called catalogues. When I was young we'd view them together, imagining that we'd buy all sorts of jewels and trinkets. As I grew older I realized that none of those things we had circled really meant anything to Granny. This wise woman valued people, giving generously of her time to anyone in need.

Although she never went to college, Granny had a natural wisdom about people, an understanding of their hearts, that doesn't come from most books. Her wisdom came from knowing and living out the precepts in one book, the Bible, God's Word.

Wisdom calls to all of us, but some of us are just better listeners. Notice in this passage that wisdom is found "on top of the heights beside the way, Where the paths meet. . ." Wisdom is a choice. We can walk right past it.

Wisdom is also "beside the gates, at the opening to the city, at the entrance of the doors. . ." Wisdom is at the very precipice of every decision.

Prayer — Lord, You lay before me a path of righteousness. Please help me desire to walk with You!

Aaron's Priestly Robes

*"Then bring near to yourself Aaron your brother, and his sons
with him, from among the sons of Israel, to minister as priest
to Me—Aaron, Nadab and Abihu, Eleazar and Ithamar,
Aaron's sons. And you shall make holy garments for Aaron your
brother, for glory and for beauty. . .And these are the garments
which they shall make: a breastpiece and an ephod. . .and they
shall make holy garments for Aaron your brother and his sons,
that he may minister as priest to Me."*
Exodus 28:1-2, 4

Notice that the priests were appointed by God to minister
directly to Him. God didn't want them to forget whom
they served.

The original priestly vestments had a significant purpose. The ephod, with the breastpiece attached, symbolized
seeking wisdom or judgment from God. It was fastened on
each shoulder by two onyx clasps which had the names of six
tribes engraved on each clasp.

This stunning breastplate itself was fashioned of pure
gold, along with blue, purple, and scarlet material and fine
twisted linen. Even more extravagant, it was mounted on
four rows of precious gemstones in gold filigree settings.

As you come before the Lord today, in whatever garb
and setting, reflect on these Old Testament times. Thank
You, Jesus, for teaching us simply to talk to You.

Prayer — Lord, Your Majesty is incredible. I know that the
things of beauty on earth are but a glimpse of all that's in
heaven.

Peter's Denial

*Then Jesus said to them, "You will all fall away because of Me
this night, for it is written, 'I will strike down the shepherd,
and the sheep of the flock shall be scattered.' But after I have
been raised, I will go before you to Galilee." But Peter
answered and said to Him, "Even though all may fall away
because of You, I will never fall away." Matthew 26:31-33*

Peter was convinced that his faith in Christ was so strong
nothing could cause it to crumble. Yet only a few hours
later he cowered when a young servant girl accused him of
being one of Jesus' followers. And then he openly denied
his Lord.

How boldly he had declared, " 'Even if I have to die
with You, I will not deny You' " (Matthew 26:35). And all
the rest of the disciples verbally agreed with Peter. A little
while later they accompanied Jesus into the Garden of
Gethsemane, where He requested that they pray with Him.
Instead, they fell asleep.

Later that night, Peter would know without any doubt
that Jesus had tried to warn him. Then he would look into
those intense eyes and understand that because Christ went
to Calvary even this sin of denial could be forgiven.

There have been times when you have disappointed
Jesus. Have you asked for forgiveness? Have you realized
that upon asking the burden of sin will be lifted forever?

Prayer — Lord, I have, at one time or another, acted as if I
could live any way I wanted. Yet it cost Christ everything
to purchase my redemption. Let me willingly come and
pray to You.

Before He Set the Heavens in Place

"The Lord possessed me at the beginning of His way, Before His works of old. From everlasting I was established, From the beginning, from the earliest times of the earth. When there were no depths I was brought forth, When there were no springs abounding with water. . .When He marked out the foundations of the earth; Then I was beside Him, as a master workman." Proverbs 8:22-24, 29-30

What existed before anything else? God. And now woman and man come along, filling in a narrow blip of time, and state that all of creation "just simply evolved." Get a clue! God designed, planned, and implemented all that we do see and everything we can't comprehend.

We've already discussed how Solomon asked God for wisdom that he might rule more fairly. In answer, the Lord imparted to him a veritable wealth of knowledge about this extraordinary creation.

In questioning Job, God provides more information about the creation. " 'Have you ever in your life commanded the morning, and caused the dawn to know its place; that it might take hold of the ends of the earth, and the wicked be shaken out of it?' " (Job 38:12-13) Or, " 'Where were you when I laid the foundation of the earth?' " (Job 38:4)

Somehow we have turned around history. Humans are not in charge. God is. And He's still commanding the dawn to happen and the earth to keep spinning and the stars to remain in the sky. Aren't you glad?

Prayer — Lord, keep me from taking Your magnificence for granted. Let my heart overflow with gratitude for all You are.

Offerings for the Tent of Meeting

*Then the whole Israelite community withdrew from Moses'
presence, and everyone who was willing and whose heart
moved him came and brought an offering to the Lord for the
work on the Tent of Meeting, for all its service, and for the
sacred garments. Exodus 35:20-21, NIV*

When was the last time your whole community agreed on
anything? Imagine everyone's talents, skills, and resources
united for a common purpose!

The hearts of God's people were stirred to erect the Tent
of Meeting, following the Lord's command. Leaving all selfish desires behind, they pooled their brooches, earrings,
signet rings, bracelets, and other offerings of gold for the
Lord. From these articles gemstones were extracted to make
the ephod and the breastpiece.

Women spun goats' hair cloth and fine linen. Silver,
bronze, and acacia wood were also contributed, along with
spices and oil for the fragrance, light, and anointing within
the traveling temple. Then the Lord raised up those who
would skillfully engrave, design, or embroider materials. In
the hands of the Master Builder, our human talents soar!

As those in Moses' day brought all they possessed, we
can surrender our own time and talents. A dear "saint" at
my own church writes notes of encouragement to all who
request prayer. How blessed we are to receive her "wisdom
from the Lord" when we're depleted by life's challenges.

How is God using you in His church?

Prayer — Lord, You've created within me something to be
used to further Your Kingdom. Please enable me to open
my hands willingly in service.

True Love Means Sacrifice

And they spat on Him, and took the reed and began to beat Him on the head. And after they had mocked Him, they took His robe off and put His garments on Him, and led Him away to crucify Him. Matthew 27:30-31

Years ago the popular movie *Love Story* coined the unforgettable phrase, "Love means never having to say you're sorry." What a fallacy, and more is the pity for those who bought into this lie!

For love demands that we always say we're sorry. How else can relationships be restored?

Those two words, "I'm sorry," have the power to keep families and churches together. I once knew a pastor whose refusal to recognize his humanity caused almost half of the church family to seek membership elsewhere. In his eyes he had done nothing wrong, but what harm would have been done to admit the possibility of poor judgment?

To admit fallibility is to make a sacrifice. To have done nothing wrong and to offer the ultimate sacrifice is an act only possible by God's Son. Jesus' offering of His body at Calvary gave eternal life to all who believe in Him.

Is there someone from whom you are estranged who is waiting to hear those two little words? Say you're sorry.

Prayer — Lord, You sacrificed all You had to provide my eternal salvation. Help me today to express true sorrow for my sins.

The Spirit Confirms the Son

Jesus came from Nazareth in Galilee, and was baptized by John in the Jordan. And immediately coming up out of the water, He saw the heavens opening, and the Spirit like a dove descending upon Him; and a voice came out of the heavens: "Thou art My beloved Son, in Thee I am well-pleased." And immediately the Spirit impelled Him to go out into the wilderness. Mark 1:9-12

John the Baptist prepared the people to recognize Christ when He came on the scene.

John would proclaim Christ as the very "Lamb of God who takes away the sin of the world!" (John 1:29). His training ground had been the sand-swept, arid, hostile surroundings of the desert.

Decked out in "a garment of camel's hair, and a leather belt about his waist" (Matthew 3:4), John preached: " 'After me will come one more powerful than I, the thongs of whose sandals I am not worthy to stoop down and untie. I baptize you with water, but he will baptize you with the Holy Spirit' " (Mark 1:7-8, NIV).

And then Jesus Christ walked into the cool, refreshing waters of the Jordan River to be baptized by John. As He came up out of the water, the heavens were torn open and the Spirit of God descended on Him like a dove. " 'You are my Son, whom I love; with you I am well pleased' " (Mark 1:11, NIV).

Prayer — Father, the picture can't be any clearer. Jesus is Your Son and You are pleased with His perfect life and His perfect Sacrifice for my sins.

Offerings to the Lord

*"Speak to the sons of Israel and say to them, 'When any man of
you brings an offering to the Lord, you shall bring your
offerings of animals from the herd or the flock.' "*
Leviticus 1:1-2

God communicated His Word and His desire for proper
worship through His chosen leaders. These spokesmen then
communicated His message to His chosen people. Before
the coming of the Holy Spirit, at Pentecost, this chain of
command was vital so that God's flock was not misled.

God required proper and orderly worship. Only an
unblemished male animal could be used as the burnt offering.
Down through the ages men and women were to make a
connection between this sacrifice and the one Christ would
willingly make on Calvary's cross.

The priests carried out God's specific requirements for
slaughtering the animal, sprinkling its blood against the altar
and cutting and arranging these pieces in a certain order.
Finally, the sacrifice was burned upon the wood. And when
these instructions were carried out they made a "pleasing
aroma" to the Lord.

There have not been any animal sacrifices since the
temple in Jerusalem was destroyed in A.D. 70. Since Christ
made His atoning sacrifice on the cross, our sins are forgiven
based on His shed blood.

———————————

Prayer — Lord, how grateful I am for Jesus, Your unblemished Lamb. Might I willingly become a living sacrifice
through service to You as I take the Gospel to this needy
world.

Peter's Mother-in-Law

Now Simon's mother-in-law was lying sick with a fever; and immediately they spoke to Him about her. And He came to her and raised her up, taking her by the hand, and the fever left her, and she began to wait on them. Mark 1:30-31

I mean no disrespect to the way this incident is recorded in Scripture. However, each time I read this passage the tendency is there to view it as a woman.

Now here's Peter's mother-in-law sick in bed with a fever. House guests have just arrived. Somebody needs to get this "party" organized and yet the poor woman is too ill to function.

Notice that the disciples told Jesus "immediately" of the older woman's ailment. It was time for the Sabbath meal and Peter's wife was probably tending to the needs of her mother rather than making dinner. As soon as they arrived in the home, the disciples told Jesus about this problem. It's a high-priority, crisis-magnitude predicament! Dinner is not ready!

Jesus tenderly takes the woman's hand and instantly heals her. None of this "weakness after a fever" stuff. The dear old saint gets up and prepares the meal!

Jesus meets every need for every situation if we come to Him in faith.

Prayer — Lord, thank You for always going well beyond what I expect or ask. I appreciate Your attention to priorities.

A Woman of Folly

*The woman of folly is boisterous, She is naive, and knows
nothing. And she sits at the doorway of her house, On a seat by
the high places of the city, Calling to those who pass by, who
are making their paths straight: "Whoever is naive, let him
turn in here," And to him who lacks understanding she says,
"Stolen water is sweet; And bread eaten in secret is pleasant."
But he does not know. . .the depths of Sheol.*
Proverbs 9:13-18

This woman is beyond sanguine. She *is* the party, not just
the life of it! But how did she end up this way, sitting at the
doorway of her house and calling out to those who pass by?

Perhaps life has just sort of happened to her, and she lost
the battle before she even knew what the war was about.
When she was young, all the road signs appeared to be filled
with possibilities. But now that she's getting older the
options are fewer. She's sitting on a suitcase in an abandoned
train station, waiting for the whistle to blow again.

This woman is not only content to wreak havoc on her
own life, but she entices those who wanted to go the right
way to join her on this road to nowhere. The passage
describes her "naive," because surely if she'd known better
she'd have chosen more wisely.

Have you ever felt like this woman? Did you start out
with endless options and then begin purchasing tickets to
oblivion? With Christ it's not too late to cash in that pass
to nowhere. With Christ your life will have direction.

Prayer — Lord, please provide me with a true picture of
myself. Guide me to the place You envision for me.

Jesus' Earthly Family Reacts

A multitude was sitting around Him, and they said to Him; "Behold, Your mother and Your brothers are outside looking for You." And answering them, He said, "Who are My mother and My brothers?. . .For whoever does the will of God, he is My brother and sister and mother." Mark 3:32–33, 35

Mary and Christ's half-brothers, James and Jude, had come looking for Him. Everywhere Jesus went such a crowd gathered around for healing that He and the disciples couldn't eat a meal in peace. His mother was worried out of love. From the perspective of His siblings, Christ's ministry had become more important than sustenance. They were saying, " 'He has lost His senses' " (Mark 3:21).

The Pharisees, on the other hand, reasoned that Christ's ability to cast out demons was because He was obviously " 'possessed by Beelzebub' " (Mark 3:22). Jesus Christ, the Holy Son of God, was in their midst and His family and the learned religious leaders all missed what He was about.

As women, are we using our precious moments to further the Gospel, or are we involved in trivial pursuits? Do we stand alongside those in our families who dare to make a difference? Or have we added to their burdens by missing their obvious purpose?

Prayer — Lord, instill in my heart a bond with those who seek to bring the Good News to others and show me how to assist them.

To Touch Jesus' Cloak

And a woman who had a hemorrhage for twelve years, and had endured much at the hands of many physicians, and had spent all that she had and was not helped at all, but rather had grown worse, after hearing about Jesus, came up in the crowd behind Him, and touched His cloak. For she thought, "If I just touch His garments, I shall get well." Mark 5:25-28

This woman is frantic. Each time she's received the report of a gifted healer, she's traversed far and wide to find a cure. The wonder is that this dear woman could survive for twelve long years. For that phrase, "endured much," means she "suffered something or experienced evil." She'd become a challenge to physicians of that day.

In one last-ditch effort she reaches out to touch the garment of Jesus as He passes by. She doesn't bother to call out to Him or even ask for help. Somehow she knows that His very holiness can heal her physically.

"And immediately Jesus, perceiving in Himself that the power proceeding from Him had gone forth, turned around in the crowd and said, 'Who touched My garments?' " (Mark 25:30). The disciples think He's "losing it" for sure.

"But the woman fearing and trembling, aware of what had happened to her, came and fell down before Him, and told Him the whole truth" (Mark 25:33). She's been miraculously healed and now she demonstrates her faith by worshiping at Jesus' feet. Does your faith shine through even in small gestures?

Prayer — Lord, You heal me when I come to You, by renewing my spirit and deepening my faith. I worship Your majesty and power.

The Lord's Diet Plan

"Speak to the sons of Israel, saying, 'These are the creatures which you may eat from all the animals that are on the earth. Whatever divides a hoof, thus making split hoofs, and chews the cud, among the animals, that you may eat.' "
Leviticus 11:2

Ever gone on a diet? As soon as you start one, the compulsion to eat things you never desired before becomes an overpowering beast! We know that the right foods are good for us, but we can't block out the joyfully intoxicating flavors of the ones that are off-limits.

Since Moses was chosen by God to deliver these dietary restrictions to the Israelites, we can well imagine the rousing response he received. Leviticus 11 goes on to list creatures that fall into the categories of "clean" and "unclean."

The one meat you probably already know about is pork. God didn't even want the Israelites to touch it. He told Moses that although it has " 'a split hoof completely divided, does not chew the cud; it is unclean for you' " (Leviticus 11:7, NIV).

Unlike the cow, the pig doesn't take time to ruminate. So what in the world does this have to do with anything?

In those days prior to refrigeration and pasteurization, if the Israelites hadn't obeyed God's dietary laws most if not all of them would have died from bacterial infections, food poisoning, and so on. God was preserving a nation from which the Messiah would be born.

Prayer — Lord, Your call to obedience may not always make sense, but help me remember that You have a reason.

Happy Birthday

*For Thou didst form my inward parts; Thou didst weave me
in my mother's womb. I will give thanks to Thee, for I am
fearfully and wonderfully made; Wonderful are Thy works,
And my soul knows it very well. My frame was not hidden
from Thee, When I was made in secret, And skillfully wrought
in the depths of the earth. Psalm 139:13-16*

Hurrying toward the hospital nursery, the nurse cradled a
soft pink blanket against her starched white uniform. "Wait,"
cried a dark-haired man in his forties. "I think that's our
baby!" he shouted excitedly. As he viewed a petite head full
of dark curls, all doubt was removed. "Just look at this perfect
parcel," murmured the nurse in response, obviously accustomed to greeting glowing relatives.

I don't know the date of your birthday, but this one
is mine. So celebrate with me today, keeping thoughts of
your own special day in mind. Every year my mother has
recounted this story of how my grandfather found me, soon
after my birth, by recognizing my mop of dark hair. He
assumed the role of "proud parent" for my dad, who was
on active duty during World War II.

God rejoiced at your birth. You were fashioned exactly
the way He wanted you. How incredible to comprehend that
when you awake in the morning, God is already thinking
about you! (Psalm 139:17-18)

Prayer — Lord, thank You that I am on Your mind every
single day.

U-Hauls Don't Follow Hearses

Lord, make me to know my end, And what is the extent of my days, Let me know how transient I am. Behold, Thou has made my days as handbreadths, And my lifetime as nothing in Thy sight, Surely every man at his best is a mere breath.
Psalm 39:4-5

From the rich and famous to the poor and hopeless, inestimable numbers of women and men consult astrologers before making major decisions. As Christians we know that no human possesses the ability to access knowledge of future events. The attribute of omniscience, being all-knowing, belongs to God alone.

Our human nature propels us to locate a "celestial video" of our own life, including our ultimate demise. So why didn't God just relate this information?

God wants us to trust Him for our future. To know our lifespan would affect us every day of our life. So, God has guarded this secret as a great favor to us.

In a church we used to attend, the pastor was famous for his story about the man who wanted to have a "U-haul following the hearse" to his funeral. The point of his sermon, of course, was that none of us will take the fruits of our labor with us to our eternal destination. Instead we should concern ourselves with where that final stop will be.

To worry about the future is to be uncertain of your eternity.

Prayer — Lord, it's so easy to get caught up in the glitter of gold. Give me a daily glimpse of heaven, my real home.

The Wise of Heart

*The wise of heart will receive commands, But a babbling fool
will be thrown down. He who walks in integrity walks
securely, But he who perverts his ways will be found out.*
Proverbs 10:8-9

For years James Dobson, president of *Focus on the Family*, has
warned parents about the pitfalls ahead for their strong-
willed children. Personally, we raised our three kids with one
hand on the radio and the other on the Bible. Dr. Dobson's
radio ministry has given us hope and kept us sane.

My repeated prayer for all our children was this: "Lord,
protect them and surround them with Your angels. And if
they're disobedient, let them be found out."

Years into their teens, our kids were convinced that I
had spies stationed all over the city. No matter what they
did, I knew about it within hours. And I can assure you, it
was a direct result of this prayer.

God provided such excellent guidance for us, He
entrusted eight other children into our care who were not
our own. These young people were just kids who needed
special care along the way. We tended to their physical needs
as well as their spiritual ones. We stressed honesty and
obedience and showered them with unconditional love. And
each of them grew to a more secure emotional place.

Is there a young person in your life who needs your
prayers today?

Prayer — Lord, help us to stress honesty, obedience, the
truth of Your Word and shower our kids with unconditional
love so that our children can grow to maturity in a secure
emotional place.

Jesus Drives Out a Demon

Jesus left that place and went to the vicinity of Tyre. He entered a house and did not want anyone to know it; yet he could not keep His presence secret. In fact, as soon as she heard about him, a woman whose little daughter was possessed by an evil spirit came and fell at his feet.
Mark 7:24-25, NIV

Shocking headlines assault us almost daily, relating the horrors children have inflicted upon other children. We ask, "What in the world is going on?" Yet even during the time of Christ, diabolic forces knew no age barriers.

A Gentile woman of Syrophoenician heritage sought out Jesus. A desperate woman, she recognized that her little daughter was demon possessed.

She not only displayed faith in His ability to heal, but she believed that she had the right to ask Him for assistance. Further into the passage note the veiled dialogue between Christ and the woman, which goes something like this. First, she tells Him of her daughter's predicament. He says, " 'Let the children be satisfied first, for it is not good to take the children's bread and throw it to the dogs' " (Mark 7:27). Then she answers Him, " 'Yes, Lord, but even the dogs under the table feed on the children's crumbs' " (Mark 7:28).

Jesus came to bring the Good News to the Jews first. But this woman, a Gentile, says she needs Jesus' touch too. And He responds to her faith. Ask Jesus to touch your life this day.

———————

Prayer — Lord, You are Messiah to all, Jews and Gentiles, and I know You will never turn me away. In this I rejoice!

Commandments or Suggestions?

"You shall consecrate yourselves therefore and be holy, for I am the Lord your God. And you shall keep My statutes and practice them; I am the Lord who sanctifies you. . .You are therefore to keep all My statutes and all My ordinances and do them, so that the land to which I am bringing you to live will not spew you out." Leviticus 20:7–8, 22

When God gave the Laws to Moses, writing them with His own hand upon the tablets of stone, He expected them to be observed. From His perspective they were commandments, not "suggestions."

But how could sinful men ever comply consistantly with these laws? Therefore, throughout Old Testament history humanity was to look forward in time and trust God for the coming Messiah. And His death would finally cleanse them from their sin. Abraham believed this and passed the "promise" on to his descendants. Isaac then brought this seed of expectation to Jacob. And on and on the word of the Lord progressed.

However, so did man's sin. Because God had endowed each person with a free will. Our hope lies in the fact that Jesus Christ has paid the penalty for all our sin, on Calvary's cross, no matter how heinous it might be. And if we confess our sins to Him, then He is faithful and just to forgive us (1 John 1:9).

Prayer — Lord, having a relationship with You is the only way we can keep Your commands. Help us to relinquish our wills to You.

Jesus Is Transfigured

Jesus took with Him Peter and James and John. . .And He was transfigured before them; and His garments became radiant and exceedingly white, as no launderer on earth can whiten them. And Elijah appeared to them along with Moses; and they were talking with Jesus. Mark 9:2-4

We can't even imagine what glory these disciples beheld. Their human eyes were allowed to view Jesus virtually transformed into a supernatural form.

Moses and Elijah also appeared with Christ. Moses represented the Law and Elijah the prophets, both of which find their fulfillment in Christ. We know from the Scriptures that when Satan wanted to take Moses' body God took him away instead. And no one knows where Moses is buried (Deuteronomy 34:6). Similarly, Elijah was taken up to heaven by a whirlwind and never died (2 Kings 2:1-11). Furthermore, it was prophesied that Elijah would come back before the end of time (Malachi 4:5). In fact, John the Baptist preached in the "spirit and power of Elijah" (Luke 1:16-17).

The Greek word for this phenomenon of transfiguration is *metamorphoo,* from which we derive our word, *metamorphosis.* Christ performs the miracle of metamorphosis in us when we come to believe in Him as Lord and Savior. He transforms us, quickening our spirits, so that we are destined to spend eternity with God in heaven. It's a change on the inside which is displayed on the outside—for the unbelieving world to see.

Prayer — Lord, transform me today, by Your Almighty power, into a bold witness of Your Gospel message.

Is It Lawful to Divorce?

And some Pharisees. . .began to question Him whether it was lawful for a man to divorce a wife. And He answered and said to them, "What did Moses command you?" And they said, "Moses permitted a man to write a certificate of divorce and send her away." But Jesus said to them, "Because of your hardness of heart he wrote you this commandment. But from the beginning of creation, God made them male and female. For this cause a man shall leave his father and mother, and the two shall become one flesh; consequently they are no longer two, but one flesh. What therefore God has joined together, let no man separate." Mark 10:2-9

Jesus never allowed the religious leaders to destroy the Word of God. Therefore, instead of debating the issue of whether divorce was lawful, He took them back in time for a glimpse of God's heart and intention.

I remember sitting in a Bible study lecture on the issue of divorce. The leader said, "Divorce is like trying to pull apart two pieces of paper which have been glued together for years and years. It's impossible to do this without tearing them both apart."

That's what Christ states here. Remember, through Moses God permitted divorce so that the women of that time were not abandoned on the whim of their husbands. This bill of divorcement became a legal protection for them.

God wants to bless your marriage.

Prayer — Lord, only You know the physical and mental abuse some married women have endured. Heal their pain and show them how to make wise choices. And forgive me when I miss Your best for me.

The Year of Jubilee

" 'You shall thus consecrate the fiftieth year and proclaim a release through the land to all its inhabitants. It shall be a jubilee for you, and each of you shall return to his own property, and each of you shall return to his family. You shall have the fiftieth year as a jubilee; you shall not sow, nor reap its aftergrowth, nor gather in from its untrimmed vines.' "
Leviticus 25:9-11

Are you scratching your head, wondering why on earth this passage is here? Every fiftieth year God arranged a wonderful, year-long celebration—a jubilee—for His chosen people, the Israelites.

But if everyone were "partying hearty," what did they eat? Watch what God did. " 'But if you say, "What are we going to eat on the seventh year if we do not sow or gather in our crops?" then I will so order My blessing for you in the sixth year that it will bring forth the crop for three years. When you are sowing the eighth year, you can still eat old things from the crop, eating the old until the ninth year when its crop comes in' " (Leviticus 25:20-22). Isn't that incredible?

But it gets even better. " 'The land, moreover, shall not be sold permanently, for the land is Mine. . .Thus for every piece of your property, you are to provide for the redemption of the land. If a fellow-countryman of yours becomes so poor he has to sell part of his property, then his nearest kinsman is to come and buy back what his relative has sold.' " (Leviticus 25:23-25). God's ways are filled with wisdom. If only the world would realize His majesty!

Prayer — Lord, on that day that You create a new heaven and earth, I will know what it really means to celebrate!

In Memory of the Righteous

*The memory of the righteous is blessed, But the name
of the wicked will rot. Proverbs 10:7*

Not long ago I attended the funeral of the mother of one of
my husband's coworkers. Although I'd never met this man
or his mother, knowing that his family had come from the
Philippines drew me to the service. With their homeland
so far away, perhaps there wouldn't be many in attendance.

Warmth, love, and appreciation greeted my husband and
me from the moment we set foot in the chapel, which
overflowed with guests. Somehow this large family had
assembled to provide a magnificent send-off for their precious
"Nanay." Amid the battles of World War II, she was widowed
at twenty-seven and left with three small children. Yet those
difficult days of grief and hardship became her stepping-
stones to faith in Christ. Later she remarried and was blessed
with five more children.

Her parting admonition to the children who gathered
around her deathbed was "be good and love each other."
And then her Lord peacefully escorted her to the mansion
He'd prepared.

This woman had lost so much. And yet, blessed with
true wisdom, she turned to the Lord for solace and found
in Him the foundation on which to build her life. To leave
a rich legacy of love one must be dearly acquainted with the
Author of Love, our Heavenly Father.

Prayer — Lord, I am blessed by the memory of righteous
women. Help me to live in such a worthy manner, that I
might be remembered as following after You all my days.

Jesus Prophesies His Death

*They were amazed, and those who followed were fearful. And
again He took the twelve aside and began to tell them what
was going to happen to Him, saying, "Behold, we are going up
to Jerusalem, and the Son of Man will be delivered to the chief
priests and the scribes; and they will condemn Him to death,
and will deliver Him to the Gentiles. And they will mock
Him and spit upon Him, and scourge Him, and kill Him, and
three days later He will rise again." Mark 10:32-34*

When our family received the ominous news that my father-in-law was terminally ill, I struggled to prepare myself for the grief. Instead, I ended up making myself physically ill. I soon reached the conclusion that I just needed to enjoy my father-in-law's presence for as long as God kept him here on earth. And when our inevitable time of mourning did descend upon our hearts, the Lord would pour out His magnanimous grace towards us.

Christ's disciples couldn't cope with the thought of His leaving and therefore became fearful. Jesus gently encouraged them with the hope of His resurrection.

And when He had risen from the dead, "He opened their minds to understand the Scriptures, and He said to them, 'Thus it is written, that the Christ should suffer and rise again from the dead the third day; and that repentence for the forgiveness of sins should be proclaimed in His name to all the nations, beginning from Jerusalem. You are witnesses of these things' " (Luke 24:45-47).

Prayer — Lord when grief overwhelms us let us remember Your death on Calvary's cross provides our hope of eternal life in heaven.

God Orders a Census

"Take a census of all the congregation of the sons of Israel, by their families, by their fathers' households, according to the number of names, every male, head by head from twenty years old and upward, whoever is able to go out to war in Israel, you and Aaron shall number them by their armies. With you, moreover, there shall be a man of each tribe, each one head of his father's household." Numbers 1:2-4

Have you ever watched small children begin to play? Some just observe toys, randomly tossing them about until they find one that really grabs their attention. Others begin with an overall plan. Now we can chalk up this inborn sense of order to personality, parental patterning, and so on. But I believe all ages participate in creational emulation, in response to the perfect established order of God.

The Israelites, who were constantly at odds with the Gentile nations surrounding them, needed to know the strength of their army. So God showed Moses a systematic way to determine this number.

Notice that men were conscripted to serve Israel's army from the time they were twenty years old until they were no longer able to serve. In doing so, they would be preserving their nation clear into the time in history when Messiah would finally be born.

Prayer — Lord, with You everything has a plan. In a world that is filled with nebulous thinking I can rely on Your consistency.

By Whose Authority Did Jesus Act?

The chief priests, and scribes, and elders came to Him, and begin saying to Him, "By what authority are You doing these things, or who gave You this authority to do these things?" And Jesus said to them, "I will ask you one question, and you answer Me, and then I will tell you by what authority I do these things. Was the baptism of John from heaven, or from men? Answer Me." Mark 11:27-30

One of the mental exercises I wrestled with in a basic psychology course in college concerned unanswerable questions. You've probably seen them on employment tests: For example, "What would you say is your least desirable personality trait?" Now who is going to answer this without trying to put a positive spin on it?

This is the kind of squeeze play the Pharisees and Scribes tried constantly to force Jesus into. No matter what Jesus said, He'd be wrong. And yet this tactic always backfired on them.

The Pharisees, the Jewish religious leaders, made sure the Mosaic laws were adhered to. They read the laws day and night, probably looking for ones which had been broken. The scribes were given the task of recording every "jot and tittle" of the Word of God. Both groups not only knew the law but also understood what the Messiah would do when He came.

Jesus Christ cannot be fooled. He knew the hearts of the Pharisees and scribes and He knows your heart too.

Prayer — Jesus, You spoke plainly about who You are. Help me hear.

Never Take a Drink?

Again the Lord spoke to Moses, saying, "Speak to the sons of Israel, and say to them, 'When a man or woman makes a special vow, the vow of a Nazarite, to dedicate himself to the Lord, he shall abstain from wine and strong drink; he shall drink no vinegar, whether made from wine or strong drink, neither shall he drink any grape juice, nor eat fresh or dried grapes. All the days of his separation he shall not eat anything that is produced by the grape vine, from the seeds even to the skin. All the days of his vow of separation no razor shall pass over his head. He shall be holy until the days are fulfilled for which he separated himself to the Lord, he shall let the locks of hair on his head grow long.' " Numbers 6:1-5

My few experiences drinking liquor as a young woman convinced me it tasted awful and it had an extremely negative effect on my emotions.

When I became a Christian, at age twenty-nine, drinking was the first thing to go out of my life. Along with all the warnings against strong drink that I read in the Bible, there was family history. My father had been an alcoholic.

After making a decision to follow Christ, I recognized the risk of potentially harming the young children my husband and I were raising. Like a Nazarite submitting to his vow, I refused to provide a breeding ground in which this substance might interfere with the plans God desired for my life and future. And the Lord has remained faithful to provide all the inspiration I need.

Prayer — Whatever is preventing me from seeing only You, Lord, provide the strength I require to set it aside.

David Called Him Lord

*And Jesus answering began to say, as He taught in the temple,
"How is it that the scribes say that the Christ is the son of
David? David himself said in the Holy Spirit, 'The Lord said
to my Lord, "Sit at My right hand, Until I put thine enemies
beneath Thy feet." ' " David himself calls Him 'Lord'; and so
in what sense is He his son?" And the great crowd enjoyed
listening to Him. And in His teaching He was saying:
"Beware of the scribes. . .who devour widows' houses, and for
appearance's sake offer long prayers; these will receive greater
condemnation." Mark 12:35-38, 40*

In this age where all of us are overly conscious of being politically correct, it's difficult to understand how extremely direct Christ was being here. The Pharisees, after all, enjoyed a position in which their motives and actions were seldom questioned.

Christ had just explained to the Pharisees that the reason they couldn't comprehend what would take place in the Resurrection was because they understood neither the Scriptures nor the power of God (Mark 12:24).

All of us are responsible not only to read the Word of God with understanding but also to have discernment concerning the clergy who minister to us. Is their primary goal to make sure their flock is ultimately led to God's glory?

Prayer — Am I like those in the crowd who simply "enjoyed listening" to Christ? Help me take time to know You, Lord.

Walking in the Light of God's Goodness

The fear of the Lord prolongs life, But the years of the wicked will be shortened. The hope of the righteous is gladness, But the expectation of the wicked perishes. The way of the Lord is a stronghold to the upright, But ruin to the workers of iniquity. The righteous will never be shaken, but the wicked will not dwell in the land. Proverbs 10:27-30

Instead of being a cause of terror in our hearts, that phrase, "fear of the Lord" means to reverence and honor Him as God. For He alone is God, righteous, and wise enough to intervene and effect positive changes in our lives. Instilling this truth in our children enables them to know the ways of the Lord.

Knowing that everything which emanates from God is good enables us to trust Him in every crisis and walk in His ways. Because in each situation there are two alternative reactions. On the one hand exists the opportunity to act honorably, and on the other freedom to disobey. The choice is entirely ours.

God's very nature is goodness. Therefore, everything which stems from Him reflects His character. This knowledge should cause hope to flood our lives. Unshaken by the winds of change, then we can stand firm in the face of any kind of adversity, like a boat anchored to its strong moorings.

Obedience always brings inner peace, contentment, and happiness, while stepping out from underneath God's umbrella of protection only gets us soaked and saturated with sin.

_____

Prayer — Lord, show us how to raise children who reflect the goodness of Your character!

Sinners from Birth

Behold I was brought forth in iniquity, And in sin my mother conceived me. Psalm 51:5

When Kay Arthur of Precept Ministries had just become a grandmother, she stated in one of her ministry updates, "Well, another little sinner was just born into the world!"

This might seem a strange thing to say about one's precious, be it ever so wrinkled, grandbaby. And yet it's the absolute truth. David knew this thousands of years ago as he was inspired to write this psalm.

You need to get straight in this passage what God's Word is not saying. The union of man and woman, within the bounds of marriage, is absolutely God's design and purpose. These verses are not alluding to the act of love which produces a child. Rather, David is stating that each of us is born with the same sin nature as Adam.

David spoke from the depths of his guilty, broken heart. He had viewed the lovely Bathsheba as she prepared to bathe on her rooftop. Hypnotized by her beauty he "took her to bed." And when she became pregnant, he plotted a murderous solution that would send her husband, Uriah, to the front lines of battle.

Admitting our own sinful state is the first step toward a more sincere Christian walk. And acknowledging the sin in our children makes us more effective Christian parents.

Prayer — David didn't acknowledge his sin until You sent Nathan the prophet to convict his soul. What will it take for me, Lord?

Sibling Rivalry

Then the Lord called Aaron and Miriam. . .He said, "Hear now My words: If there is a prophet among you, I the Lord, shall make Myself known to him in a vision. I shall speak with him in a dream. Not so, with My servant Moses, He is faithful in all My household; With him I speak mouth to mouth, Even openly, And not in dark sayings, and he beholds the form of the Lord. Why then were you not afraid To speak against My servant, against Moses?" Numbers 12:5-8

Sibling rivalry has once again reared its ugly head. God speaks face-to-face with Moses, and Aaron and Miriam become jealous. So God comes down in a pillar of cloud to announce to them that this is His show and He writes the script. When the cloud is withdrawn from over the Tent of Meeting, Miriam's skin has become leprous.

Like a good parent, God leaves Miriam to mull over her rebellious and questioning spirit for seven days. And then the Lord graciously heals her, at the request of Moses.

How could she even think of asking God to explain Himself? But don't we all do the same thing when the going gets rough? How about, "If there's a God then why is there so much suffering?" Well, guess what? Men and women are harming one another. God is not responsible for our sinful nature.

The power to make a choice between good and evil is a gift from God. What we do with the gift is up to us.

Prayer — Lord, although it's human to question things beyond my control, please help me understand that Your actions are always in my best interest.

When Fear Paralyzes

And a certain young man was following Him, wearing nothing but a linen sheet over his naked body; and they seized him. But he left the linen sheet behind, and escaped naked. And they led Jesus away to the high priest; and all the chief priests and the elders and the scribes gathered together. And Peter had followed Him at a distance, right into the courtyard of the high priest; and he was sitting with the officers, and warming himself at the fire. Now the chief priests and the whole Council kept trying to obtain testimony against Jesus to put Him to death; and they were finding none.
Mark 14:51-55

Suddenly you awake at one in the morning to the sound of the doorknob being turned, followed by the sound of creaking boards. Your heart leaps into your throat. What do you do?

When John Mark, the writer of this Gospel, learned that Jesus had been captured by the Roman guards and a trial was pending, he grabbed the sheet off his bed and ran to observe the events himself.

We know John Mark escaped the threatening situation. Yet Jesus Christ remained in the eye of the storm, well aware of the situation yet in perfect sync with the Father. When fear paralyzes, help is only a prayer away.

Prayer — Lord, I believe in all that You are, both God and Man.

The Challenge of Korah

Now Korah the son of Izhar, the son of Kohath, the son of Levi, with Dathan and Abiram, the sons of Eliab, and On the son of Peleth, sons of Reuben, took action, and they rose up before Moses, together with some of the sons of Israel, two hundred and fifty leaders of the congregation. . .And they assembled together against Moses and Aaron, and said to them, "You have gone far enough, for all the congregation are holy, every one of them, and the Lord is in their midst; so why do you exalt yourselves above the assembly of the Lord?"
Numbers 16:1-3

As cult leader David Koresh and his followers were swallowed up by a fiery holocaust of their own making outside Waco, Texas, I wondered if this misguided man had studied Korah in the Bible. The two had much in common.

God had spoken to Moses, telling him that the people were now to begin wearing a blue cord tassel " 'on the corners of their garments throughout their generations' " (Numbers 15:38). This was to be a visible reminder that God wanted them to keep His commandments and remain holy.

Korah didn't want to be called a sinner. Surely he must have known that only God knew the true condition of man's depravity. Yet he opted to pretend this fight for control existed between him and Moses instead of between him and God.

Do you fight for control of your life? Surrender the ultimate control to God and realize the freedom of His perfect plan.

Prayer — Lord, please open my eyes to my own sin and prevent me from leading others astray.

Barabbas Is Released

And Pilate answered them, saying, "Do you want me to release for you the King of the Jews?" But the chief priests stirred up the multitude to ask him to release Barabbas for them instead. And answering again, Pilate was saying to them, "Then what shall I do with Him whom you call the King of the Jews?" And they shouted back, "Crucify Him!" Mark 15:9, 11, 13

During the Feast of the Passover, Pilate had a habit of releasing one prisoner back to the people. The people cried out for the release of a known murderer, Barabbas.

Why did the chief priests incite the people to choose Barabbas? So many had chosen willingly to follow Christ that the "status quo" of the times had been upset.

After all, the chief priests had a nice cushy job making up laws to enforce so that the people were kept in a constant state of guilt. The priests' coffers were kept full from the constant flow of guilt offerings. If Jesus were allowed to gain a foothold in the temple, their positions would surely be in jeopardy.

The priests were but players in the great drama prophesied hundreds of years earlier in the Old Testament. Jesus Christ would be sentenced to death by Pilate, even though Pilate found Him without guilt. Jesus Christ must die for the sins of humankind.

Today we know the truth. And we can share, without fear, without guilt, the kingship of Jesus Christ.

Prayer — What would I have shouted if I had been part of that crowd? And what affirmation do I give You today, Lord?

Joseph of Arimathea

Joseph of Arimathea came, a prominent member of the Council, who himself was waiting for the kingdom of God; and he gathered up courage and went in before Pilate, and asked for the body of Jesus. Mark 15:43

Today's Scripture reading, along with parallel passages from the other three Gospels, discloses that Joseph of Arimathea had become "a secret disciple of Christ." Yet now, accompanied by Nicodemus, another member of the ruling Council of religious leaders, Joseph of Arimathea displayed an incredible boldness of character. For Joseph requested Christ's body for burial, then he and Nicodemus lovingly prepared their Lord for his burial.

Christ nurtured the faith of both these men, safely reserving them for His divine purpose within the realm of authority in which He had placed them. They were needed for just such a time, because down through the ages to come the faith of other believers would hinge on the fact that Christ really died and really was resurrected. Fulfilling Scripture, Christ was placed in the borrowed tomb of a rich man (Isaiah 53:9).

Joseph, present during the sessions in which the Council members solidified decisions concerning Christ, never consented to their plan of action. For Joseph was "a good and righteous man" (Luke 23:50-51). Nicodemus also stood his ground despite the growing tide of voices which called for Christ's arrest and crucifixion (John 7:45-53). These men had been born again through their faith in Christ. And knowing the Scriptures concerning the death of their Savior, they prepared for it.

Prayer — Lord, the tomb is empty and the grave clothes left behind signify for all time that You have risen from the dead. And because You live, we can face whatever tomorrow brings!

The Red Heifer

*" 'Speak to the sons of Israel that they bring you an
unblemished red heifer in which is no defect, and on which a
yoke has never been placed. And you shall give it to Eleazar
the priest, and it shall be brought outside the camp and be
slaughtered in his presence. Next Eleazar the priest shall take
some of its blood with his finger, and sprinkle some of its blood
toward the front of the tent of meeting seven times. Then the
heifer shall be burned in his sight; its hide and its flesh and its
blood, with its refuse, shall be burned.' " Numbers 19:2-5*

So, what in the world is so exciting about a red heifer?
Everything! After the sacrifice had been made to God, the
heifer was burned and its ashes were deposited "outside the
camp in a clean place, and the congregation of the sons of
Israel shall keep it as water to remove impurity; it is purification from sin" (Numbers 19:9).

The heifer was not only sacrificed on the altar for the
sins of the people, but its ashes were preserved and used to
cleanse people of their sins.

The purpose of everything God told the Israelites to
do was to point the way to Christ.

Animal sacrifices will begin again when the antichrist
comes on the scene. He will use such sacrifices to mimic
God Almighty and demand worship for himself.

Are you remaining in the Word? The days ahead
demand that we be knowledgeable women, filled with the
understanding of Jesus Christ.

_____

Prayer — Help me, Lord, to see the Old Testament in light
of the New Testament. For Christ is the fulfillment of all
I seek.

Where Do You Take Refuge?

Be gracious, O God, for man has trampled upon me; Fighting all day long he oppresses me. My foes have trampled upon me all day long, For they are many who fight proudly against me. When I am afraid, I will put my trust in Thee. In God, whose word I praise, In God I have put my trust; I shall not be afraid. What can mere man do to me? Psalm 56:1-4

When my father was away during World War II, my mom, sister, and I lived with my grandparents. At the time I was only three years old or so. Frequently, I'd hide under their long, wooden porch, making my world a little smaller, I suppose. Looking out through the latticed covering, somehow I felt safe.

David wrote this psalm when the Philistines had seized him in Gath. These Philistines had been enemies of the Israelites for a long time. At one point they'd even stolen the ark of the covenant. They'd probably never forgiven David for killing their giant, Goliath. I wonder if David reflected during his present predicament, remembering the time in his youth when he'd faced that giant with only five smooth stones and a sling. He had called upon his God to deliver him, and the Lord had prevailed (1 Samuel 17:37-50).

Where do you go for refuge? I run to the arms of my loving Father, just as David did in his own crisis. And He always comes through.

Prayer — O Lord, You alone are my refuge and strength. Help me to come to You first in a crisis.

John the Baptist Is Born

*In the days of Herod, king of Judea, there was a certain priest
named Zacharias, of the division of Abijah; and he had a wife
from the daughters of Aaron, and her name was Elizabeth.
And they were both righteous in the sight of God, walking
blamelessly in all the commandments and requirements of the
Lord. And they had no child, because Elizabeth was barren,
and they were both advanced in years. Luke 1:5-7*

What the world would have lost if Zacharias had become
bitter over his circumstances! He and Elizabeth were now
old and their dream of sons and daughters had become but
a vapor.

Zacharias could be found day after day in the temple,
obediently "performing his priestly service before God"
(Luke 1:8).

One day, as he offered incense before the altar, an angel
of the Lord appeared and said, " 'Do not be afraid, Zacharias,
for your petition has been heard, and your wife Elizabeth
will bear you a son, and you will give him the name John' "
(Luke 1:13).

Now Zacharias asks, " 'How shall I know this for certain?' " (Luke 1:18) Fulfillment of that promise still looked
impossible to him.

So, poor Zacharias was struck "dumb." Elizabeth did
become pregnant, just as the angel had said. And during her
sixth month, her cousin, Mary, came to tell her that she too
was carrying a child. One day their sons would meet by the
Jordan River. This was God's perfect plan, the fulfillment of
His promises.

———————————

Prayer — Lord, restore my hope in You today.

God's Deterrent to Sin

So Israel joined themselves to Baal of Peor, and the Lord was angry against Israel. And the Lord said to Moses, "Take all the leaders of the people and execute them in broad daylight before the Lord, so that the fierce anger of the Lord may turn away from Israel." Numbers 25:3-4

The Lord had blessed Israel with precious children, remaining true to His promise to Abraham to make the nation of Israel " 'as numerous as the stars' " (Genesis 15: 5). But when the Israelites began to intermarry with the Moabites they also began to worship their pagan gods. And one of the requirements of this idolatrous form of worship was human sacrifices to the insatiable god Baal. The Israelites thus offered up their children—the gifts of God—to this man-made statue.

God had watched over Israel in war and in peace. He had delivered them safely to a land flowing with milk and honey; He had promised them a Messiah. But if the Israelites continued to kill their children, the line to Christ would be wiped out before He ever arrived on the scene.

God was forced to purge from Israel those who chose to lead others astray.

If you're a parent, you probably devote much time and energy keeping your children from getting involved in things that would harm them. In the same way, God, our loving Parent, must pull in the reins when people drift too far from His truth.

Prayer — Lord, shine Your beacon of truth on those who are in leadership, that they may never lead others astray.

Anna, the Prophetess

And there was a prophetess, Anna the daughter of Phanuel, of the tribe of Asher. . . .And she never left the temple, serving night and day with fastings and prayer. And at that very moment she came up and began giving thanks to God, and continued to speak of Him to all those who were looking for the redemption of Jerusalem. Luke 2:36-38

This year, as the National Day of Prayer approached, one woman in my church did her best to evoke an enthusiastic response from members of a daytime Bible study. I watched as many offered her incredulous stares that silently stated, "What planet are you on? What do you mean, meet for prayer?"

Call a prayer meeting at your own church and you'll know what I mean. Only a handful of people bother to attend and it's always the same group. However, if we fail to pray consistently, it is little wonder we are without guidance for our leadership.

Anna had faithfully served in the temple her entire life. And despite her advanced age, she remained there even after others had gone home for the evening. She was a prophetess; she foretold the truths of God to the people. No wonder He used her life.

God had promised Anna that she would see the Messiah before she died. She waited eighty-four years, biding her time in service to the Lord. And He kept His Word. Let us strive to follow Anna's prayerful example, and we too will be blessed by God.

Prayer — Lord, call my heart to faithfulness and prayer. May I serve as an example to encourage others.

God Gave Israel the Land

Then the Lord spoke to Moses, saying, "Among these the land shall be divided for an inheritance according to the number of names. . .each shall be given their inheritance according to those who were numbered of them. But the land shall be divided by lot. They shall receive their inheritance according to the names of the tribes of their fathers." Numbers 26:52, 54, 56

God picked for Himself a people, the Jews. And He blessed them with this land as an inheritance. It's not too late for Israel's enemies to repent. Yet with each new wave of terrorism and attack against Israel, we know that nothing short of divine intervention will free the Jews from annihilation.

One day Christ Himself will return to claim the Holy Land for His people. " 'But immediately after the tribulation of those days The sun will be darkened, and the moon will not give its light, and the stars will fall from the sky, and the powers of the heavens will be shaken, and then the sign of the Son of Man will appear in the sky, and then all the tribes of the earth will mourn, and they will see the Son of Man coming on the clouds of the sky with power and great glory' " (Matthew 24:29-30).

Christ is coming back as the ultimate Judge and Rescuer of Israel. The time is now to be sure of our commitment to Jesus Christ and that of our loved ones.

Prayer — Lord, I pray that men and women repent while there is yet time. I look forward to the establishment of Your perfect kingdom.

One Calling in the Desert

The word of God came to John, the son of Zacharias, in the wilderness. And he came into all the district around the Jordan, preaching a baptism of repentance for forgiveness of sins; as it is written in the book of the words of Isaiah the prophet, "The voice of one crying in the wilderness, 'Make ready the way of the Lord, Make his paths straight.'"
Luke 3:2–4

The Word of God is absolutely specific about the timing, the message, and the messenger, John the Baptist, who paved the way for the Lord Jesus Christ.

As John came into the district around the Jordan River, the religious leaders appeared on the scene to check him out. They used their influence to attempt to dissuade the people from the truth about the Messiah. John called them a "'brood of vipers'" (Luke 3:7). And then he added, "'Therefore bring forth fruits in keeping with repentance, and do not begin to say to yourselves, "We have Abraham for our father," for I say to you that God is able from these stones to raise up children to Abraham'" (Luke 3:8).

Counting on their heritage as a means of automatic salvation, the religious leaders called themselves Abraham's children. Yet to be Abraham's children required that they display faith.

John's exhortations were aimed at the "wilderness of men's souls." How many churchgoers do you know who claim the faith yet exist in a wasteland of sin?

Prayer — Lord, You sent John to proclaim Your beloved Son. Help me to proclaim Your Word and love to anyone, anywhere.

A Refuge from Our Despair

Hear my cry, O God; Give heed to my prayer. From the end of the earth I call to Thee, when my heart is faint; Lead me to the rock that is higher than I. For Thou hast been a refuge for me, A tower of strength against the enemy. Let me dwell in Thy tent forever; Let me take refuge in the shelter of Thy wings. Psalm 61:1-4

King David, writer of this psalm, composed it as a song, acknowledging God as his rock. He clung with tenacity to the fact that no matter how desperate his situation appeared, God was as immovable as a huge rock or boulder. Although David's trials may differ from yours, you too can use strong coping mechanisms.

First, David acknowledged God remained all powerful, despite life circumstances. And second, David looked back at God's past rescues. "O my God, my soul is in despair within me; Therefore I remember Thee from the land of the Jordan, And the peaks of Hermon, from Mount Mizar. Deep calls to deep at the sound of Thy waterfalls; All Thy breakers and Thy waves have rolled over me. The Lord will command His lovingkindness in the daytime; And His song will be with me in the night, A prayer to the God of my life" (Psalm 42:6-8).

Prayer — Lord, I search for a way through the torrents of despair. How precious is the knowledge that You hear and care.

The Israelites Leave Egypt

*The sons of Israel. . .journeyed from Rameses in the first
month, on the fifteenth day of the first month; on the next day
after the Passover the sons of Israel started out boldly in the
sight of all the Egyptians, while the Egyptians were burying
all their first-born whom the Lord had struck down
among them. Numbers 33:1, 3-4*

Have you ever gone on a trip where everything that could
go wrong went wrong? My husband and I headed south to
Oceanside, along the California coast. From the moment
we arrived in the RV park it felt as though demonic forces
were at work. First, it took us over an hour to get the trailer
positioned correctly on an undersized lot so that our water
and sewer hoses could reach their connections.

Then, during the middle of the night, a windstorm
came up, threatening to rip off our awning. We raced outside
to roll it up but since we had wedged into the space on an
angle it got caught on the top of a wooden fence. After a
great deal of maneuvering the awning finally released with a
terrible bang.

The next day we went to the beach. When we returned,
we found that someone had stolen my husband's expensive
bicycle.

God inspired Moses to write the accounts of the trials
of the Israelites, where they traveled and the events which
transpired. At times, their hardships made them long to be
back in bondage in Egypt. But much of their pain was
because they refused to obey.

Prayer — Help me to cling ever closer to You. I'm so grateful You're watching out for me.

Why Mary and Joseph Married

"And every daughter who comes into possession of an inheritance of the tribe of the sons of Israel, shall be wife to one of the family of the tribe of her father, so that the sons of Israel each may possess the inheritance of his fathers. Thus no inheritance shall be transferred from one tribe to another tribe, for the tribes of the sons of Israel shall each hold to his own inheritance."
Numbers 36:8-9

From the time my children were still in grade school, I prayed for the person which each of them would choose as a life partner in marriage. We spoke often, during those formative years, concerning the foundational qualities needed to forge a lasting relationship. Now that two of our children are married, I can see how God's hand faithfully guided them.

The Gospels of Matthew and Luke present Christ's genealogy. Although Joseph was not Christ's father, he belonged to the tribe of Judah, just as Mary did. Both came from a godly line.

Mary had led a life of purity, revering God's Word and looking forward to the Savior whom God had promised. When God sent an angel to announce His plan, Mary responded in obedience.

Mary and Joseph married because they loved each other but more importantly, both of them loved God and desired to be a part of His purpose for man. And within this environment of submission, Israel's inheritance, the Savior, remained secure.

Prayer — Lord, we know that Joseph loved Mary and both were chosen by You. Yet they also obeyed You in their choice of a life partner.

Jesus Is Tempted by Satan

And the devil said to Him, "If You are the Son of God, tell this stone to become bread." And Jesus answered him, "It is written 'Man shall not live on bread alone.'" Luke 4:3-4

Have you ever found yourself so tempted to sin that you ached all the way to your soul? Christ understands that pull toward evil.

Satan wasn't just present in the wilderness to "bug" the Lord Jesus Christ. This was a full-on, frontal attack. And the stakes were high. For if Christ succumbed to Satan's snare, He would be ineligible to make that perfect sacrifice on the cross as the Lamb of God without blemish.

In this first temptation, Satan intimated that there must be something wrong with the Father's love for the Son since He allowed Him to go hungry. Satan's fiery darts of doubt were aimed directly at the Triune God.

With the second temptation, Satan led Christ upward for a better view of "all the kingdoms of the world." Satan attempted to get Christ to bypass the cross and seize the power.

The third temptation involved a literal leap of faith. For Satan declared that Jesus prove Himself as the Son of God and stand on the pinnacle of the temple and throw Himself down. This time the evil one meant to question the Father's faithfulness toward the Son. After all, the Scriptures did say that God would give His angels charge concerning Him.

Prayer — Lord, I thank You for Your Son's perfect victory over Satan.

Shout for Joy

Shout joyfully to God, all the earth; Sing the glory of His name; Make His praise glorious. Psalm 66:1-2

When I first moved to this town, which is about a half hour south of Disneyland, there were only 60,000 people living here.

However, in the past twenty-two years the population has grown to two and one-half times its original size. Even a simple trip to the post office has become a harrowing experience. My children tease me about having a ten-mile driving radius.

To cope with the negative side effects of a burgeoning civilization—we're talking rudeness on the roads—I'm getting inventive. Tapes of Christian music used to relax me, but having any additional noise in the car now just seems to add tension. So I've begun reciting either the names of God or Scriptures.

If you're not familiar with the biblical names of God, an excellent book to read is *Power in His Name* (Barbour Publishing, Inc., 1995). When pondering Jesus as the Friend of Sinners, the Lion of the Tribe of Judah, or The Alpha and Omega, your mind focuses on Him and daily problems diminish.

David knew even in his day that taking time to praise his awesome God provided strength and renewal for his weary soul. Joyfully he worshiped!

Prayer — Lord, my grateful heart declares Your Name in a world that has all but forgotten You still care and watch over the universe.

Matthew, the Tax Collector

*And after that He went out, and noticed a tax-gatherer
named Levi, sitting in the tax office, and He said to him,
"Follow Me." And he left everything behind, and rose and
began to follow Him. And Levi gave a big reception for Him
in his house; and there was a great crowd of tax-gatherers and
other people who were reclining at the table with them.*
Luke 5:27-29

Oh no, not the dreaded tax man! My husband works in the
tax assessor's office for our county. If we attend a party and
people inquire as to what he does for a living, he skirts the
issue. He gets the same reaction Matthew did.

Yet Levi responded to Christ's invitation to follow Him.
Christ changed his name from *Levi* to *Matthew*, which
means "gift of God." Whatever flaws Matthew possessed
prior to this time no longer mattered.

Because of his record-keeping skills and attention to
detail, Matthew made an excellent and meticulous gospel
writer. He'd been regenerated by Christ and the Lord could
use his talents to further the kingdom.

Christ's presence at the reception provided an opportunity for Him to share the Gospel message. We too can seek
out those whom society shuns and offer the compassion of
Christ.

Prayer — Lord, after all these years, attitudes remain the
same about tax collectors. Please help me to see them as
You saw Matthew, as people who know You or are in need
of their Savior.

Moses Appoints Judges

" 'The Lord your God has multiplied you, and behold, you are
this day as the stars of heaven for multitude. May the Lord,
the God of your fathers, increase you a thousand-fold more
than you are, and bless you, just as He has promised you!
Choose wise and discerning and experienced men from your
tribes, and I will appoint them as your heads.' "
Deuteronomy 1:10-13

The Israelites were two million strong when they left
Egypt, and now in "the fortieth year, on the first day of the
eleventh month" (Deuteronomy. 1:3), Moses proclaimed to
them what the Lord had commanded.

The people had been in this same place forty years
earlier. But, the Israelites disobeyed God by refusing to fight
for the land, and trust God for the victory.

Therefore, God announced that this entire generation
of rebellious people, with two exceptions, Caleb and Joshua,
would not see the promised land. Even Moses, who had
displayed a lack of faith, would not set foot there. God
demands trust from His people and His spiritual leaders.

Now that their wandering days were over, Moses
charged these twelve tribal officials to judge fairly the dis-
putes among the people. They were about to take possession
of the land God had promised them.

Do you trust God for everything?

Prayer — Dear Heavenly Father, let my trust in You never
waver. Give me wisdom and courage for this day.

Before Choosing the Twelve

*He spent the whole night in prayer to God. And when day came,
He called His disciples to Him; and chose twelve of them, whom
He also named as apostles: Simon, whom He also named Peter,
and Andrew his brother; and James and John; Philip and
Bartholomew; Matthew and Thomas; James the son of Alphaeus,
and Simon who was called the Zealot; Judas the son of James, and
Judas Iscariot, who became a traitor. Luke 6:12-16*

Just prior to this time, the Pharisees had chided the Lord
Jesus Christ that His followers walked through a grain field
on the Sabbath, picking the heads of grain. They considered
this working on the Sabbath, claiming that God forbid any
labor.

The Pharisees had established thirty-nine books of
Sabbath rules. Men interpreted what God meant instead of
just obeying what God said.

These religious leaders became "filled with rage, and
discussed together what they might do to Jesus" (Luke 6:11).
What audacity! The God of the Creation, and initiator of the
Sabbath, stood before them. And instead of listening and
responding to Him, they thought to still His voice.

So Christ prayed all night for the men who would
preach, teach, heal the sick, raise the dead, and record His
Words. Christ chose a solitary spot, minimizing His distractions. When it's time to do battle we need to be alone first.
Then, after we know God's will, we can solicit the prayers
and fellowship of others.

Prayer — Lord, Thank You for letting me come to You
with all my burdens, large and small. Only You can give
true and lasting peace.

A Father to the Fatherless

A father of the fatherless and a judge for the widows, Is God in His holy habitation. Psalm 68:5

Between the rising divorce rate and those who have chosen to birth children without benefit of marriage, over half of the households in America have become fatherless. The Christian men's movement, Promise Keepers, has sought to rectify this tragedy by calling men to refocus their priorities, first on God and then on their families.

But how about the moms? What can we do to insure that our children aren't among the fatherless? We can make sure that we are fully committed to the Lord. If you're holding down a full-time job, finding the time for Bible study and devotions is a gigantic challenge. It's up to you to get inventive.

Perhaps you can teach the children how to make their own lunches—and use that extra fifteen minutes to read the Word. This is an investment in their future growth: As you learn, so will your children.

If divorce has touched you personally, all that anger, hurt, and pain must be dealt with so that your children don't feel desolate. It's hard enough for them to lose one parent through absence, let alone the other to hostility or depression.

God has promised to be "a father to the fatherless." Count on Him to keep His Word. And instead of attempting to be both father and mother, you can just be a mom to your kids.

Prayer — Lord, life seems like such a futile uphill climb sometimes. Help me to entrust all my heavy burdens to Your care.

Our Triune God

"Hear, O Israel! The Lord is our God, the Lord is one!"
Deuteronomy 6:4

Shema Yisroel Adonai Elohenu Adonai Echad is Hebrew for
" 'Hear, O Israel! The Lord our God is one Lord.' " That one
verse illustrates why many Jews can't grasp the concept of
the Trinity. The three distinct personalities that comprise the
Trinity are all equal within the Godhead: Father, Son, and
Holy Spirit. But the word "one" here should be interpreted
as in a marriage context when the "two become one."

The Bible begins by letting the Jew know that this is
true. Genesis 1:1 states, "In the beginning God created the
heavens and the earth." The Hebrew word for "God" here is
Elohim, a masculine plural noun. Thus the door to a doctrine
of plurality in the Godhead is kicked wide open. When God
speaks of Himself the plural pronoun is used: "Then God
[Elohim] said, 'Let us make man in Our image, according to
Our likeness' " (Genesis 1:26). All three persons of the
Trinity were present.

Throughout the Scriptures there are references to the
contributions of this Triune God while the Father spoke
from heaven, confirming Christ at His baptism, the Holy
Spirit descended upon Christ as a dove (John 1:31-34;
Matthew 3:14-17).

Only God could have omnisciently conceived of the
Trinity. God has always been, and will forever be.

Prayer — Lord, I rejoice in my wonderful Savior, the Father
who sent Him, and the Holy Spirit who gives me insight to
understand Scripture.

The Original "Me Generation"

And He called the twelve together, and gave them power and authority over all the demons, and to heal diseases. And He sent them out to proclaim the kingdom of God, and to perform healing. And He said to them, "Take nothing for your journey, neither a staff, nor a bag, nor bread, nor money; and do not even have two tunics apiece. And whatever house you enter, stay there, and take your leave from there." Luke 9:1-3

Remember what it was like as a kid to dream about having unlimited powers? Such fantasies have inspired cartoonists to create a variety of superheroes. In our hearts we know that these superheroes aren't real men and women. Human beings, if nothing else, are full of flaws, phobias, and fears.

He instructed His apostles not to take any possessions or provisions with them. Jesus wanted them to learn to rely fully on Him. But their lack of faith rendered them too weak to exercise this authority.

These were the men Christ had trained, empowered, and prepared to bring the Gospel message first to the Jews and then the Gentiles. They had been with Christ on a daily basis, learning from His example how to reach out with compassion to those in need. But instead they displayed both selfishness and a lack of love. How could they be left in charge of disseminating the Gospel? And yet they were God's Plan A.

Prayer — Lord, how grateful I am that Your Holy Spirit worked in the lives of these apostles, molding them into strong men of faith. Help me to become unselfish with my time that many more will hear the Gospel.

A Call to Holiness

*When you enter the land which the Lord your God gives you,
you shall not learn to imitate the detestable things of those
nations. There shall not be found among you. . .one who
practices witchcraft, or one who interprets omens, or a sorcerer,
or one who casts a spell, or a medium, or a spiritist, or one who
calls up the dead. For whoever does these things is detestable to
the Lord. Deuteronomy 18:9-12*

Our two sons easily tire of most board games. But they
became immediately fascinated after one of their friends
introduced them to the role-playing game Dungeons and
Dragons. While our older son got a part-time job, which
severely limited his free time, his younger brother went
deeper and deeper into this seductive game.

About the same time, our church encouraged adults
and high schoolers to sign up for the seminar "Basic Youth
Conflicts." By the time the concluding all-day Saturday
session rolled around, each one of us had been convicted
by the Holy Spirit concerning our own "pet sins." All the
way home that last evening our younger son spoke about
how the game had usurped the time he used to spend with
the Lord. He'd even begun feeling a strange sense of power
come over him.

We watched as he pulled out a metal trash can and
burned every one of the game's expensive books. From that
moment Jeff never looked back.

Is God receiving all the glory in your life?

Prayer — Lord, You know better than I what things will
draw my time and attention away from You. Give me the
courage to obey You.

Moses Is in Glory

*And behold, two men were talking with Him; and they were
Moses and Elijah, who, appearing in glory, were speaking of
His departure which He was about to accomplish at Jerusalem.
Luke 9:30–31*

In case you've been feeling sorry for Moses who never got
to enter the Promised Land, just look at what God had in
store for him. These verses tell us that Moses and Elijah
appeared in glory. But what does that really mean?

We are not now what we will become. For whether we
die or are taken up by what is referred to as the Rapture, the
Lord will someday allow this "earthsuit" of ours to fall away
and issue us our "eternity suit."

"For if we believe that Jesus died and rose again, even so
God will bring with Him those who have fallen asleep in
Jesus...For the Lord Himself will descend from heaven with
a shout, with the voice of the archangel, and with the
trumpet of God; and the dead in Christ shall rise first. Then
we who are alive and remain shall be caught up together with
them in the clouds to meet the Lord in the air, and thus we
shall always be with the Lord"(1 Thessalonians 4:14, 16-17).

That day on top of the mountain, at Jesus' Transfiguration, the apostles witnessed Christ's glory and saw Moses
and Elijah. And God spoke from the cloud which encompassed them saying, " 'This is my Son, whom I have chosen;
listen to Him' " (Luke 9:35).

In spite of your life, are you assured of your salvation?

Prayer — Oh Lord, I am so grateful that my place with You
is already reserved!

A Rock of Refuge

*Be Thou to me a rock of habitation, to which I may
continually come; Thou hast given commandment to save me,
For Thou art my rock and my fortress. Psalm 71:3*

For several months before I attended my first writers'
conference in southern California I worked feverishly com-
piling a manuscript for a book. However, when an editor at
the conference looked it over he told me that it needed work.
Being new to the field of writing, his remarks devastated me.

I sought solace upon a large rock situated beside a small
lake. Tears of disappointment streaked down my cheeks and
as others approached I began walking. I happened to encounter a bronze plaque that stated the well-known evangelist,
Billy Graham, had also found peace in this place.

As the sun warmed that beautiful, tranquil setting, I
considered another psalm about the Rock. "Be Thou to me
a rock of strength, A stronghold to save me. For Thou art
my rock and my fortress; for Thy name's sake Thou wilt
lead me and guide me" (Psalm 31:2-3).

Over fifty times in Scripture the word *rock* is used in
reference to God. When everything else fails, He is steadfast,
immovable, and unchangeable.

_____

Prayer — Lord, You remain that Rock on which my faith
stands firm. How grateful I am that You uplift my spirit,
that You desire to use my talents. To God be the Glory!

Why Do We Have Drought?

But it shall come about, if you will not obey the Lord your God, . . .all these curses shall come upon you and overtake you. Deuteronomy 28:15

One of my little fetishes is collecting a column which appears in my local paper, the *Orange County Register*. Every Monday this column, "Earthweek: A Diary of the Planet," displays on a flat map of all the continents a complete overview of the world's weird weather phenomena.

In Psalm 68:6, God says "only the rebellious dwell in a parched land." Is this still true today? Well, what do you call people who refuse to worship God, murder fellow humans, lie, cheat, steal, and torture? As the police might say, "they fit the profile." Breaking God's laws makes us rebellious in His eyes.

Think of all the tornadoes, hurricanes, earthquakes, and outbreaks of deadly diseases we've seen in recent years. Just as a small tremor becomes the first predictor that more intense seismic activity is about to rock the earth, so these catastrophes are but a precursor of what is to come.

Shortly after the Northridge, California, quake this same newspaper carried a nearly hidden tidbit of information. It seems that the triangle formed by the three cities hardest hit by the January 17, 1994, temblor was also the epicenter for nearly seventy companies which crank out more than 95 percent of the pornographic videos made each year in the United States. God's power cannot be denied.

Prayer — Lord, the people of Noah's day refused to heed his preaching. Help me to be a better witness before time again runs out.

Martha and Mary

A woman named Martha welcomed Him into her home. And she had a sister called Mary, who moreover was listening to the Lord's word, seated at His feet. But Martha was distracted with all her preparations; and she came up to Him, and said, "Lord, do You not care that my sister has left me to do all the serving alone? Then tell her to help me." Luke 10:38-40

Isn't this just how we feel when the men in our household excuse themselves from the table as soon as the first dirty dish appears? Martha, ever the perfect hostess, was left to do all the work. It didn't seem fair.

However, what Martha really desired was a release from her compulsive neatness. And that's when the Lord presented her with a process for "chilling out."

" 'Martha, Martha, you are worried and bothered about so many things; but only a few things are necessary, really only one, for Mary has chosen the good part, which shall not be taken away from her' " (Luke 10:41-42). In other words, all the busyness which now preoccupied Martha didn't really matter. Jesus was here and she was passing up a tremendous opportunity to learn from Him.

After all, who knew better than Christ how to put the pressures of life into perspective? He had only three years in which to establish His ministry, train up His disciples, and present the Gospel. Yet we see no record of Him hurrying others or running at a frantic pace.

Have you taken time to get to know your Lord? Perhaps your life, like Martha's, is missing the best part.

Prayer — Lord, I pray for peace today from my busy schedule so I may learn at Your knee.

Circumcision of the Heart

Moreover the Lord your God will circumcise your heart and the heart of your descendants, to love the Lord your God with all your heart and with all your soul. Deuteronomy 30:6

Just after my first son was born a nurse brought in papers for me to sign so that he could be circumcised. For months I'd eaten all the right foods, taken daily vitamins, rested, and even exercised—all to bring safely into this world my precious child. Now the hospital expected me to sign papers so that they could inflict pain on him?

Three months into this pregnancy, Uncle Sam shipped my husband overseas. But my mom was there to reassure me, echoing the doctor's own words, "It's all perfectly normal, dear. You'll be glad later that it's taken care of." So, I signed the papers.

Today's Scripture recalls the days when God called the Israelites to be circumcised. This physical cutting away of the foreskin symbolized that they were God's own, a chosen people. God would someday perform a circumcision on their hearts as well.

When one of the Pharisees asked Christ, " 'Teacher, which is the great commandment in the Law?' " He said to him, " 'You shall love the Lord your God with all your heart, and with all your soul, and with all your mind. . .You shall love your neighbor as yourself' " (Matthew 22:36-37, 39). Does your heart need a checkup?

_____

Prayer — Father, I know circumcision of my heart is wrought by Your Holy Spirit. Lord, make me willing to undergo transformation that I might truly love You, and others.

The Lord of Parables

Listen, O my people, to my instruction; Incline your ears to the words of my mouth. I will open my mouth in a parable; I will utter dark sayings of old, Which we have heard and known, And our fathers have told us. Psalm 78:1-3

Perhaps every family passes on their wise old sayings. My own was certainly no exception. For instance, "Many are cold but few are frozen," was my Irish father's Midwestern, change of season, winter's-bearing-down-on-us witticism.

Not to be outdone, my mother contributed such gems as, "Feed a cold, starve a fever!" We've handed down these tidbits to our own children, and no doubt they'll continue in some form for generations to come.

Christ did not dabble in nonsense. But sometimes Jesus offered His perfect insight in parables, or through stories with hidden meanings. " 'To you it has been granted to know the mysteries of the kingdom of God, but to the rest it is in parables, in order that seeing they may not see, and hearing they may not understand' " (Luke 8:10).

Jesus had just shared with them the parable about the sower and the seed. He knew that those whose hearts were open and receptive to Him would understand its meaning. On the other hand, those whose hearts held only antagonism, jealousy, and self-righteousness would not understand even if He spoke plainly.

Is your heart ready to listen to Jesus?

Prayer — When you examine the content of my heart, Lord, which type of soil have I prepared for Your Word?

Joshua Is Chosen

*"Be strong and courageous, for you shall go with this people
into the land which the Lord has sworn to their fathers to give
them, and you shall give it to them as an inheritance."*
Deuteronomy 31:7

The family matriarch has died, and in the lawyer's chambers,
where the will is about to be unveiled, her nearest and dearest
huddle uncomfortably. And then the lawyer announces the
names of the recipients. Suddenly those inheriting little turn
to spew indignities on those receiving much. How often
have we seen this scenario played out in old movies?

Yet God did not allow those who taunted Moses to
challenge the authority of his successor. Moses, who is preparing to die, names Joshua as his successor. Right there, in
the presence of all Israel, Moses admonishes Joshua to " 'be
strong and courageous.' " God chose Joshua because he had
faithfully served Moses throughout all their years in the
wilderness.

With his last bit of energy Moses recited the words of
the song God had given to him (Deuteronomy 32:1-27,
NIV). " 'Listen, O heavens, and I will speak; hear, O earth, the
words of my mouth, let my teaching fall like rain and my
words descend like dew, like showers on new grass, like
abundant rain on tender plants. . .' " and then it continues for
forty-one more verses. Please take time to read it all.

Prayer — Lord, I forget sometimes that those in leadership are chosen by You. And with responsibility comes
accountability.

The Unforgivable Sin

"And I say to you, everyone who confesses Me before men, the Son of Man shall confess him also before the angels of God; but he who denies Me before men shall be denied before the angels of God." Luke 12:8-9

When I was growing up, life seemed simple. For instance, as a child I learned there were mortal and venial sins. Venial sins could be forgiven; mortal sins guaranteed that your one-way ticket to heaven would never get punched.

However, God says that if we're guilty of breaking one part of the law, then we're guilty of breaking the entire law. So, what hope do any of us have?

Well, God built in a failsafe. As the disciples celebrated the Feast of Pentecost, God fulfilled His promise to send the Holy Spirit (Acts 2:1-4). God's Spirit filled the apostles, compelling them to preach the Gospel in every language of that day, that all might hear the truth (Acts 2:11).

All men are in need of a Savior. And the Bible states clearly that only one person fills this job description. "And there is salvation in no one else; for there is no other name under heaven that has been given among men, by which we must be saved" (Acts 4:12). Jesus Christ is that Savior.

The only sin that has the power to place you on the wrong side of heaven is one of ignorance. If you refuse to be "born again" of God's Spirit, you will not be received in heaven (John 3:5-7).

Prayer — Lord, Your Spirit has shown me the truth about Jesus. Thank You for this inestimable gift of salvation!

Spare the Rod

He who spares his rod hates his son, But he who loves him disciplines him diligently. Proverbs 13:24

As new parents, my husband and I couldn't imagine ever needing to discipline our little son. We anticipated that stating a pleasant "no" would result in immediate compliance. Wrong! Our little progeny had a mind of his own and nothing would dissuade or cut short his determined purpose.

Our second son arrived with that compliant personality we'd joyfully anticipated the first time around. However, when the third one, a daughter, entered the world, we just threw up our arms in surrender!

The day I broke a worn-out wooden spoon while spanking our son was the day I invested in what later became "affectionately" known as "the lion paddle." About one-inch thick, it covered their whole southern exposure when applied properly, and for the time being, resulted in better behavior. Until, that is, the lion paddle conveniently—and divinely—disappeared.

I believe nothing happens by chance. During this time I had become a born-again Christian. And not coincidentally, I had discovered that the fastest way to "redirect" my children's beastly actions was to require an immediate "kindness" as retribution to the injured party. At last I understood that "discipline" is meant to teach the correct behavior. "Punishment" only makes a child bitter.

Prayer — Lord, help me to remember what Ann Ortland teaches, that children are like wet cement. Assist me in making good impressions in their lives.

A Willing Heart

"O Jerusalem, Jerusalem, you who kill the prophets and stone those sent to you, how often I have longed to gather your children together, as a hen gathers her chicks under her wings, but you were not willing!" Luke 13:34, NIV

I hate to bore you by rattling on about diets, so please "indulge" me for a few moments. I struggled for several months, attempting to obtain "abstinence." Yet it remained as illusive as grasping a cloud. My problem? I wasn't willing to let God take control.

Finally, as I obediently worked the first three steps of the Overeaters Anonymous program, peace followed. I admitted to being powerless because the compulsion to eat had made my life unmanageable. And I came to believe that God's power could restore me to sane eating. Then I made a decision to turn my will and life over to the Lord's care. And the "gift" of dietary abstinence became a part of my life.

This was actually the first time I realized that God was truly Almighty. When He made it easy for me to walk through life without being controlled by food, I knew He was real.

How like the Israelites I am! God showed them the path they were to walk in. He even defined the boundaries for them. And yet time after time they leaped beyond the lines of safety and tried to live without Him.

Is it time for you to let God steer the course?

Prayer — Lord Almighty, whatever I desperately need release from today, please show me that You're able to heal as long as my heart is willing.

A Smooth Transition

*Now Joshua the son of Nun was filled with the spirit of
wisdom, for Moses had laid his hands on him; and the sons of
Israel listened to him and did as the Lord had commanded
Moses. Deuteronomy 34:9*

Our God has a perfect sense of order. Therefore, this important "changing of the guard" was a smooth transition. God
had spoken face-to-face with Moses, and now Moses
instructed the people to follow Joshua faithfully.

Each time God's chosen spokesperson on earth changed,
the Lord reiterated the same Abrahamic promises to the new
leader. "The Lord spoke to Joshua the son of Nun, Moses'
servant, saying, 'Moses My servant is dead; now therefore
arise, cross this Jordan, you and all this people, to the land
which I am giving to them, to the sons of Israel. Every place
on which the sole of your foot treads, I have given it to you,
just as I spoke to Moses'" (Joshua 1:1-3).

"Then Joshua commanded the officers of the people,
saying, 'Pass through the midst of the camp and command
the people, saying, "Prepare provisions for yourselves, for
within three days you are to cross this Jordan, to go in to
possess the land which the Lord your God is giving you, to
possess it."'"

Has God been trying to lead you somewhere, and you
haven't followed? _____

Prayer — Father, lead me to new heights in my walk with
You.

The God of Our Salvation

*Help us, O God of our salvation, for the glory of Thy name;
And deliver us, and forgive our sins, for Thy name's sake. Why
should the nations say, "Where is their God?" Let there be
known among the nations in our sight, Vengeance for the blood
of Thy servants, which has been shed. Psalm 79:9-10*

God swore to Israel that He loved them. Now David calls upon the Lord to forgive the people, knowing full well that their present troubles directly correspond to their disobedience.

Have you ever cried out to God for deliverance, recognizing that your own circumstances are a direct result of leaving the Lord out of the decision making? We've all been there at one time or another. But God's not surprised. He's not only aware of what we've done, He watched us make this awful choice and then witnessed the harm we did to ourselves and others.

However, David recognized that if He didn't "own his sin" and ask forgiveness from His Lord, there was absolutely no hope of new beginnings.

In the New Testament, when Jesus asked the Pharisees whose Son they thought Christ was, they answered, " 'The Son of David.' " In Matthew 22:43-45: "Jesus said to them, 'Then how does David in the Spirit call Him "Lord," saying, "The Lord said to my Lord, 'Sit at My right hand, until I put Thine enemies beneath Thy feet' "? If David then calls Him 'Lord,' how is He his son?' " Jesus quoted Psalm 110:1, helping them understand that as God, Messiah is David's Lord. And as man, He is David's son.

Prayer — We thank You that we can come to You as Lord and Messiah. You are truly a God of forgiveness.

The Holocaust Revisited

With cunning they conspire against your people; they plot against those you cherish. "Come," they say, "let us destroy them as a nation, that the name of Israel be remembered no more."
Psalm 83:1-4, NIV

Schindler's List provided a fresh reminder not only of what the Jews suffered during World War II, but that only a remnant survived these atrocities. As I viewed the movie, two age-old questions haunted me. First, how can men and women be so inhumane to others? And then I turned on the news and watched the nightly accounts of the war in Bosnia.

Second, where was God? He painfully watches from heaven waiting until the Scriptures are fulfilled, waiting until the final, demon-inspired, battle against Israel. In this battle, commonly referred to as "Armageddon," every nation gathers against Israel. Again God will spare a remnant: 144,000 Jews will be preserved by God when they choose to believe in Yeshua, their Messiah.

Even in King David's time the survival of the Jews appeared precarious at best. God spared and preserved David from invading armies, despite all odds, and used him to raise up a nation. By David's actions he demonstrated that the God Israel worshiped was worthy of this honor.

In this psalm, David reveals the sinister and evil plot in the hearts of men, which is to "wipe out those whom the Lord cherishes." For this reason, the Lord has placed the archangel Michael in charge of Israel's protection squad (Daniel 10:21).

Prayer — Lord, Your power sustains the Jews. Give them true faith!

God Uses Rahab

Then Joshua the son of Nun sent two men as spies secretly from Shittim, saying, "Go, view the land, especially Jericho." So they went and came into the house of a harlot whose name was Rahab, and lodged there. Joshua 2:1

When the king of Jericho found out that two Israelites had snuck into town, he correctly assessed their intentions. These Israelite spies were investigating the land so they could occupy it. Once Israel left Egypt the surrounding nations feared what would eventually happen. So the king of Jericho sent word to Rahab, a local prostitute, saying, " 'Bring out the men who have come to you, who have entered your house, for they have come to search out all the land' " (Joshua 2:3).

Instead, Rahab hid Joshua's men on her roof, while telling the king's soldiers they had already left the city. Then she explained to Joshua's men: " 'I know that the Lord has given you the land, and that the terror of you has fallen on us, and that all the inhabitants of the land have melted away before you. . .for the Lord your God, He is God in heaven above and on earth beneath' " (Joshua 2:9-11).

Rahab then requested that when Joshua's men conquered the city they would spare her life and also that her family would be delivered from death. A red cord dangling from the window of her house, the one from which these men had escaped, would identify her house as the one to be spared.

Prayer — Lord, how can You use me?

Taxes Must Be Paid

Let every person be in subjection to the governing authorities.
For there is no authority except from God, and those which
exist are established by God. . .For because of this you also pay
taxes, for rulers are servants of God, devoting themselves to
this very thing. Romans 13:1, 6

Knowing the urgent business on your minds today—taxes must be paid!—let's move ahead to Romans. How well I remember all those times my husband and I have searched for a post office that stayed open until midnight on April 15. This past year the post office actually hired people to accept our "contributions" right from our car windows. We called it the "tax parade."

As a tax assessor for our county, my husband claims today's Scripture as his "life verse."

All governments are established by God. And that includes those ungodly dictators who wield their power to control and ravage their constituents. Know that they too are accountable to God for the way they exercised the authority which He placed in their trust.

Have you finished filling out your IRS forms? If we meet at midnight tonight, let's reassure each other that our hard-earned money isn't being thrown away. We're following Scripture. . .we're supporting a government that God has truly blessed.

Prayer — Lord, let me give to the government not grudgingly but out of obedience to You. And please assist those in authority over me to direct wisely the use of these funds.

When Everyone in Heaven Rejoices

"Or what woman, if she has ten silver coins and loses one coin, does not light a lamp and sweep the house and search carefully until she finds it? And when she has found it, she calls together her friends and neighbors, saying, " 'Rejoice with me, for I have found the coin which I had lost!' " In the same way, I tell you, there is joy in the presence of the angels of God over one sinner who repents." Luke 15:8-10

This Scripture brings back a certain trip to the beach. As my husband and I were about to relax in our travel trailer at a California beach, I realized I had misplaced my expensive sunglasses. Frantically retracing my steps, I hunted through both the trailer and the car. We even called the AAA office where we had made a quick stop to secure a few maps. However, the sunglasses never materialized.

How ecstatic this woman was to find this missing coin she'd considered lost forever. When a young girl in Israel married she began wearing a headband containing ten silver coins. This band carried the same significance as our modern wedding rings. To lose one would have been nothing short of a catastrophe.

Jesus compared the woman's deep joy to the celebration that goes on in heaven when a sinner repents and "Sonbeams" of peace finally flood into the soul. It's the feeling of "wholeness" a person hungers for all her life.

Prayer — Lord, I am grateful that Your Word has penetrated the core of my own heart. Hallelujah!

Heaven or Hell?

*"Now there was a certain rich man, . . .gaily living in
splendor every day. And a certain poor man named Lazarus
was laid at his gate, covered with sores, and longing to be fed
with the crumbs which were falling from the rich man's
table; . . .Now it came about that the poor man died and he
was carried away by the angels to Abraham's bosom; and the
rich man also died and was buried. And in Hades he lifted up
his eyes, being in torment, and saw Abraham far away, and
Lazarus in his bosom." Luke 16:19-23*

Jesus tells us what happened when two men died. During his
lifetime, the rich man lavished in all the luxury this world had
to offer. We know the love of God did not dwell in this man
for he possessed no compassion for his fellow man. Instead of
helping poor Lazarus, the rich man literally stepped over his
dying body, on his way out of the house. Certainly our all-
knowing God correctly assessed the ugly selfishness of this
wealthy man's heart.

In life each man chose the final direction his eternal
soul would take. After death both are totally aware not only
of their surroundings, but also of the great chasm that exists
between them. For although Lazarus (not the same man
whom Christ resurrected) could see and recognize the rich
man, he was unable to go to him. Once life has ceased we
no longer have the power to change our eternal destination.
And although he suffered in life, the poor man now resided
in paradise.

Prayer — Father, I thank You that my deeds will not be
assessed, but rather the state of my heart. For I know Your
beloved Son!

Twelve Stones

*"You shall, moreover, command the priests who are carrying
the ark of the covenant, saying, 'When you come to the edge of
the waters of the Jordan, you shall stand still in the Jordan.'"*
Joshua 3:8

Joshua had gathered the people together, revealing the Lord's
words. Then the people left their tents and followed the
priests who carried the ark of the covenant. When they
reached the banks of the Jordan the water stopped flowing
. . .and the nation of Israel crossed over!

Standing on the other side of the Jordan River the
men of Israel now followed God's command, " 'Take up for
yourselves twelve stones from here out of the middle of the
Jordan, from the place where the priests' feet are standing
firm, and carry them over with you, and lay them down in
the lodging place where you will lodge tonight' " (Joshua
4:3). These stones represented each of the tribes of Israel.
Piled up high, they produced a visible monument as to the
miracle God performed.

The 40,000-man liberation force, fully equipped for
battle, then proceeded to cross the desert plains of Jericho.

As the news spread of God's miracle so had the level
of terror. Jericho was "locked down and secured" behind its
gates. But God instructed Israel's warriors to march around
the city for six days. No obstacle can prevent God's plan
from being realized!

Prayer — Lord, please pave my way with stones from You,
stones of dedication, perseverance, and compassion.

A Blast of Terror

And they began bringing children to Him, so that He might touch them; and the disciples rebuked them. But when Jesus saw this, He was indignant and said to them, "Permit the children to come to Me; do not hinder them; for the kingdom of God belongs to such as these. Truly I say to you, whoever does not receive the kingdom of God like a child shall not enter it at all." Mark 10:13-15

She'd just celebrated her first birthday and experienced the freedom and joy of learning to walk. From photographs we know she beamed with her own special kind of spontaneous happiness. But as we watched the firefighter carry the now lifeless body of little Baylee Almon away from the ashes of the Oklahoma City bomb site, each of us probably sighed, "Oh, not that precious baby, Lord!"

How we ached to reach out to all those whose hearts were wrenched with pain, fresh grief, and shock.

When Christ was born there was another "madman" on the loose, wreaking havoc with the lives of innocent people. King Herod sought to kill Christ because He knew this baby had been prophesied to become the King of the Jews. And if this child grew up He would surely usurp the throne from Herod. Therefore, this evil king became enraged and ordered that all male children in Bethlehem and the surrounding towns be slaughtered.

Was their grief less than the suffering of the mothers, fathers, sons, brothers, sisters, spouses, grandparents, and friends of those in Oklahoma City? I think not.

Prayer — Father, only You can offer true comfort to those who have lost little ones.

Circle of Fear

And the Lord said to Joshua, "See, I have given Jericho into your hand, with its king and the valiant warriors. And you shall march around the city, all the men of war circling the city once. You shall do so for six days." Joshua 6:2-5

God gave the Israelites an elaborate battle plan (Joshua 6:2-5). And you won't believe who led them all in battle!

"Now it came about when Joshua was by Jericho, that he lifted up his eyes and looked, and behold, a man was standing opposite him with his sword drawn in his hand, and Joshua went to him and said to him, 'Are you for us or for our adversaries?' And he said, 'No, rather I indeed come now as captain of the host of the Lord.' And Joshua fell on his face to the earth, and bowed down, and said to him, 'What has my Lord to say to his servant?' And the captain of the Lord's host said to Joshua, 'Remove your sandals from your feet, for the place where you are standing is holy.' And Joshua did so" (Joshua 5:13-15).

This is the same Lord who appeared to Abraham at the Oaks of Mamre and announced that Abraham's descendants would become a great and mighty nation (Genesis 18:1-33).

And this is the same Lord who is waiting for you to come to Him each and every day. He's waiting to lift you higher than you ever thought possible.

Prayer — Lord, I need to remember that You are the Lord who not only guarantees victory in the battle, but draws up the winning strategy. Thank You for that assurance.

Rebuke the Sinner

"Be on your guard! If your brother sins, rebuke him; and if he repents, forgive him." Luke 17:3

Back in the 1950s, neighborhood accountability was a fact of life. Families took pride in raising their children properly. And on the rare occasion when someone's kid did act up, it was guaranteed that by suppertime the parents would already have heard about it through the neighborhood grapevine. Punishment was swift and commensurate with the crime.

Since my husband and I had both benefited from the same kind of environment, we agreed completely on how we'd raise our children. However, in the early 1970s, we realized that a whole new breed of parents had evolved. They lacked the faith and fortitude to be disciplined or to discipline their own children.

Their children grew up for the most part without spiritual guidance, morality, or goals.

It still takes the knowledge of Jesus Christ to redeem our world. Here Jesus admonished his disciples to "rebuke" their brothers if they've sinned. Why? Because sin is a progressive fall. And "real love" means intervening that we might get back on track.

Have you shared your love of Jesus with a neighbor? Pray today that God might open a door or window to your witness.

Prayer — Lord, give me the courage to be honest so that children can experience the safety and security of proper boundaries.

Living with a View of Heaven

How lovely are Thy dwelling places, O Lord of Hosts! My soul longed and even yearned for the courts of the Lord; My heart and my flesh sing for joy to the living God. Psalm 84:1-2

My husband and I recently met a man who was instrumental in negotiating the freedom of some of the U.S. troops listed as MIAs in Laos and Vietnam. As he related the horrors of war and the intricacies of bargaining with foreign governments, I realized this man possessed an inner strength and peace which had elevated him above the level of the despairing situations he described. Finally, I acknowledged, "You have a view of heaven which keeps you moving forward, don't you?"

"Yes," he answered emphatically. "And that faith in what lies ahead provides the stability I need despite the sandy soil on which I've stood. For man's promises are nothing, but God's are real."

King David also had an eternal perspective. Israel constantly battled their enemies. How he must have longed for a lasting peace. But he had to settle for that little niche of peace he carved out for himself while pondering what heaven was like, anticipating the day he'd dwell with God. For the God of perfection created for Himself a place of eternal security.

What knowledge we have that God desires to share this incredible place with His imperfect creatures! Despite our sinful nature, God truly loves us with an eternal affection.

Prayer — David accepted Your love for him, Lord. Help me to live in Your will so that my life is a blessing to You.

Jesus Prepares His Disciples

*And He took the twelve aside and said to them, "Behold we
are going up to Jerusalem, and all things which are written
through the prophets about the Son of Man will be
accomplished. For He will be delivered up to the Gentiles, and
will be mocked and mistreated and spit upon, and after they
have scourged Him, they will kill Him; and the third day He
will rise again." Luke 18:31-33*

As you read today's Scripture you've probably either just celebrated Easter or are anticipating this solemn season of remembrance of Christ's sacrifice on Calvary's cross.

Jesus had traveled with the Twelve, eaten meals with them, spoken of what it meant to truly abide in God, and lived out a sinless life before them. Now His time on earth drew to its inevitable close. Jesus began preparing His disciples for the time He'd be gone from them. He needed to help them accept His death, understand the reason for it, and strengthen them for all this would mean once they could no longer be with Him face-to-face.

In these last days, did they ponder the precious words He spoke at their last supper together? " 'I glorified Thee on earth, having accomplished the work which Thou hast given Me to do. I manifested Thy name to the men whom Thou gavest Me out of the world; Thine they were, and thou gavest them to Me, and they have kept Thy word' " (John 17:4, 6). What is Jesus saying to you?
_____

Prayer — Father, I know the days ahead may be difficult. Help me realize, like the disciples, that You are always with me, to the end.

The Sun Stood Still

Then Joshua spoke to the Lord. . .in the sight of Israel, "O sun, stand still at Gibeon, and O moon in the valley of Aljalon." So the sun stood still, And the moon stopped, Until the nation avenged themselves of their enemies.
Joshua 10:12-14

Shortly after Israel's last victory in battle, the Gibeonites donned old worn-out clothes and sandals, pretending to have journeyed from a far distance. Without consulting the Lord, Joshua signed a treaty with them. But within three days the truth was made known. Unable to break the oath of safety he'd extended to them, Joshua made them " 'wood-cutters and water carriers for the house of my God' " (Joshua 9:23, NIV).

Five kings banded together, aligning themselves against not only the Israelites but also the Gibeonites, but God gave Joshua and the people victory over the Amorites by causing huge hailstones to rain down from heaven. Meanwhile the five kings sought refuge in a cave.

Joshua and his men placed a large boulder at the mouth of the cave, sealing the kings inside. And then Joshua uttered the same words that the Lord had said to him: " 'Do not fear or be dismayed!' " (Joshua 10:25) Joshua struck the kings dead and then placed their bodies back into the cave.

If God is able to stop the solar system, He is able to deal with every crisis in your life.

Prayer — Lord, it's hard to read about all this bloodshed. But I know You were rescuing Your people from their enemies.

True and Lasting Justice

"There was in a certain city a judge who did not fear God, and did not respect man. And there was a widow in that city, and she kept coming to him, saying, 'Give me legal protection from my opponent.' And for a while he was unwilling; but afterward he said to himself, 'Even though I do not fear God nor respect man, yet because this widow bothers me, I will give her legal protection, lest by continually coming she wear me out.'" Luke 18:2-5

A few years ago, my brother, a hospital janitor who worked the night shift, was stabbed while emptying the trash behind the main building. The men who attempted to murder him, just to steal his wallet, were never caught.

But God has been good to my brother. Bitterness isn't in his vocabulary. He forgave his attackers even before he was discharged from the hospital. He knows that someday "the just judge" will rule on these men's lives.

Back in New Testament times judges held court in a traveling tent. Whether cases were considered or not depended upon the plaintiffs' ability to "gain the attention of the judges' attendants." This widow in today's Scripture already had three strikes against her. First, as a woman she had no priority standing in the court. Secondly, as a widow she didn't have a husband to fight for her in these legal proceedings. And finally, without the funds to pay for assistance she was without hope.

If you've been denied justice here on earth, you have a God who sees all and knows all. Justice will be served!

Prayer — Lord, You alone judge rightly. You alone will administer to the guilty the punishment they truly deserve.

Carefully Choosing Our Words

*A wise son accepts his father's discipline, But a scoffer does not
listen to rebuke. From the fruit of a man's mouth he enjoys
good, But the desire of the treacherous is violence. The one who
guards his mouth preserves his life; The one who opens wide
his lips comes to ruin. Proverbs 13:1-3*

At the last viewing of a dearly departed friend, my husband
and I appreciated the extraordinarily devoted staff at the
funeral home. Only a year and a half ago this same group had
ministered to us at the death of another family member.
Once again I was inspired by their carefully chosen words.

When that sharp letter opener called grief has ravaged
our hearts, we naturally cling to each word spoken to us,
hoping that it will somehow alleviate our agony. These
people have mastered the craft of tenderness and diplomacy.

As this proverb points out, the very words we speak
denote the depth of our character. "Scoffers" begin as high
school smart alecks and end up as ruthless business tycoons.
However, their reflection in the mirror each morning confirms their compromises.

Each day presents an opportunity to extend to others
words that reach in to soothe and heal souls—or deepen
wounds.

Prayer — Lord, You created women to be more sensitive to
the effects of words. Please give me the wisdom to accept
Your advice and also liberally sprinkle the flavor of graciousness into my speech.

Idols of Their Own Making

Among the gods there is none like you, O Lord; no deeds can compare with yours. . .For you are great and do marvelous deeds; you alone are God. Psalm 86:8, 10

Although my husband hadn't been enthusiastic about taking our travel trailer to Mexico, he didn't want to disappoint our close friends. (Perhaps he figured out that the real reason for this trip was so my girlfriend and I could shop for unusual gift items.)

Pottery-lined aisles drew our interest to the back of one small, cluttered store. And then we saw the "idols." Demonic-looking figures, half-man, half-beast, were intricately carved in wood and stone. With a cold shiver running down our spines, my friend and I exited that store so quickly we probably left a trail of dust.

When men and women refuse to worship the true God they invariably end up trying to fashion one on their own. The reason is natural: We were all created with a "God-shaped void" inside our souls. The purpose of this void is to draw us to the Lord in commitment.

Satan applies every subversive tactic in his arsenal in order to dim our understanding of God's attributes. Therefore, it's up to us to find the truth to combat the evil one's lies. On the other hand, God is constantly guiding us in our search for knowledge and understanding.

Prayer — Lord, You've given me an entire Bible to read so that I might learn of Your love, concern, and compassion. Develop in me that sensitivity to "hear the prompting of Your Spirit" while You guide me toward the truth.

God Instructs Joshua

*Now these are the territories which the sons of Israel inherited
in the land of Canaan, which Eleazar the priest, and Joshua
the son of Nun, and the heads of the households of the tribes of
the sons of Israel apportioned to them for an inheritance, by the
lot of their inheritance, as the Lord commanded through
Moses, for the nine tribes and the half-tribe. For Moses had
given the inheritance of the two tribes and the half-tribe
beyond the Jordan; but he did not give an inheritance to the
Levites among them. For the sons of Joseph were two tribes,
Manasseh and Ephraim, and they did not give a portion to
the Levites in the land, except cities to live in, with their
pasture lands for their livestock and for their property.*
Joshua 14:1-4

At the time of this land distribution to the sons of Israel,
Caleb, who had fought valiantly with Moses, admitted, " 'I
am still as strong today as I was in the day Moses sent me' "
(Joshua 14:11). So when he requested the hill country which
had been promised to him, Joshua blessed Caleb and granted
him Hebron.

Caleb did go into battle, driving out the sons of Anak.
Then Caleb promised his daughter, Achsah, as a wife to
whoever captured the city of Kiriath-sepher.

Joseph's sons' inheritance went from the Jordan at Jericho,
into the wilderness, and ended at the sea (Joshua 16:1-10).
But they failed to drive out the Canaanites. And because
Israel failed to drive out their enemies completely, there has
been conflict in the Middle East ever since.

Prayer — Lord, I know that all things will work to bring
about Your plan. Please continue to protect Your chosen
people.

Riding on a Donkey

*"Go into the village opposite you, in which as you enter you
will find a colt tied, on which no one yet has ever sat; untie it,
and bring it here. And if anyone asks you, 'Why are you
untying it?' thus shall you speak, 'The Lord has need of it.'"*
Luke 19:30-31

Jesus came to them, riding on a donkey, just as it had been
prophesied. "Rejoice greatly, O daughter of Zion! Shout in
triumph, O daughter of Jerusalem! Behold, your king is
coming to you; He is just and endowed with salvation,
Humble, and mounted on a donkey, Even on a colt, the foal
of a donkey" (Zechariah 9:9).

But why a donkey? The reason is that He might present
Himself to them as their humble servant and King. If He
had ridden into Jerusalem on a horse, He would have presented Himself as a warrior, ready for battle. That horse is
already prophesied for the end times.

"And I saw heaven opened; and behold, a white horse,
and he who sat upon it is called Faithful and True; and in
righteousness He judges and wages war" (Revelation 19:11).

Now don't confuse the rider of this second white horse
with the white horse and rider of what is known as the "four
horsemen of the apocalypse." He is not Christ. Later in the
year, when we study the Book of Revelation in more depth,
this will become clear.

Prayer — Lord, thank You for all the "absolutes" of Scripture.
I believe You are exactly who You claim to be, God Incarnate.

Here Comes the Judge

Now it came about after the death of Joshua that the sons of Israel inquired of the Lord, saying, "Who shall go up first for us against the Canaanites, to fight against them?" And the Lord said, "Judah shall go up; behold, I have given the land into his hand." Judges 1:1-2

Back in the days of my early adulthood, I used to enjoy the outrageous hit TV show, "Laugh-In." While the scripts did evoke spontaneous laughter, sexual themes were becoming more dominant, reflecting the sliding morals of that time. Our nation's standards have dropped rapidly since then. Israel suffered a similar decline. Israel was freed from bondage in Egypt, wandered through the desert, and finally took possession of the Promised Land. All the days of Joshua's life Israel had served the Lord.

Unfortunately, the next generation had no direct dealings with God and therefore walked away from Him, plunging Israel into over 300 years of spiritual darkness. These are the days of the judges.

Israel thought they could peacefully coexist with idol worshipers, but little by little they allowed this sea of sin to seep under the undergirding of their own society. When you move away from God's will, all manner of sin can somehow be justified.

_____

Prayer — Lord, as I begin reading about Israel's judges, please show me what things wear away at my own personal spiritual stability.

In the Beginning, Christ

*In the beginning was the Word, and the Word was with God,
and the Word was God. He was in the beginning with God.
John 1:1-2*

An elderly woman once lived next door to us whom everyone came to call "Aunt Esther." At ninety-one, Esther's spunky, conquer-any-obstacle attitude drew people to her.

But the church she attended was nothing more than a cult of false teachers. These teachers presented a new spin on an old lie, saying Jesus Christ did not exist in the flesh but was instead spirit.

As true believers we know differently: "By this you know the Spirit of God: every spirit that confesses that Jesus Christ has come in the flesh is from God; and every spirit that does not confess Jesus is not from God" (1 John 4:2-3).

The apostle John was an eyewitness to the events he was inspired by God's Spirit to record for us. "What was from the beginning, what we have heard, what we have seen with our eyes, what we beheld and our hands handled, concerning the Word of Life—and the life was manifested, and we have seen and bear witness and proclaim to you the eternal life, which was with the Father and was manifested to us" (1 John 1:1-2).

Aunt Esther would sit and take a dose of the Bible, but she followed the Truth with a soul-poisoning gulp from her cult's own book. Over and over I recited the first three verses of John's Gospel to her. At the age of ninety-three she suffered a stroke. Knowing her death was imminent, I lay on the floor next to her bed, praying all through the night. When she died a day later she knew Christ as her Savior.

Prayer — Lord, I am so grateful to You for taking all those who profess Your name to be with You!

Music in the Morning

It is good to give thanks to the Lord, And to sing praises to Thy name, O Most High; To declare Thy lovingkindness in the morning, And Thy faithfulness by night, With the ten-stringed lute, and with the harp; With resounding music upon the lyre. For Thou, O Lord, hast made me glad by what Thou hast done, I will sing for joy at the works of Thy hands.
Psalm 92:1–4

It's spring! Pollen is in the air and, thanks to the regeneration of life, multiplying rapidly! When I'm stuck working inside, glued to my computer chair, I hunger for some melodious tunes to bolster my sagging spirit.

This particular psalm was actually written for a Sabbath celebration. If you ever attend a Messianic service, you'll discover that believers in Yeshua (Jesus' Hebrew name) definitely have the market cornered on celebrating. They sing, dance, and rejoice in finding their Savior. It's the kind of merriment God designed for us to enjoy with Him. And it's probably the closest reenactment of heavenly worship you'll find on this earth.

Interspersed among all those "begats" that bog us down in the book of Genesis there's a "who's who of professions." "Adah gave birth to Jabal; he was the father of those who dwell in tents and have livestock. And his brother's name was Jubal; he was the father of those who play the lyre and pipe" (Genesis 4:20-21). It seems the human family has found joy in music since almost the beginning of time.

Prayer — Lord, thank You for music and the way it uplifts my spirits. No matter what time of day or season, I rejoice in worshiping You.

The Wise Woman Builds Her House

The wise woman builds her house, But the foolish tears it down with her own hands. He who walks in his uprightness fears the Lord, But he who is crooked in his ways despises Him. Proverbs 14:1-2

Among the construction management graduates in our son's class from Cal Poly in San Luis Obispo was one young woman. Striving to succeed in this tough and competitive major, she adapted exceedingly well both academically and socially. Indeed, like the wise woman of Scripture, she learned all the intricacies of proper building techniques.

Every woman must understand God's "building codes" in order to strengthen her own household. The blueprints must be followed. From these a concrete foundation is laid. Likewise, how can a woman provide guidance within her home unless she first seeks wisdom from the Lord?

Next comes the framing. This skeletal structure furnishes the undergirding and strength to support the home. Prayer is just such a sustenance to the family.

Now the insulation is added within the walls. This corresponds to godly friends and church members who provide a cushion to bolster us during the storms of life.

Finally, color-coated stucco and trim put the finishing touches on the exterior of the house. Our family portrays a unique image within our neighborhood. And the love we have for each other reflects the love and worship given to God.

Prayer — Lord, You are the Master Builder. To stay upright I must follow Your blueprints.

He Dwelt Among Us

*And the Word became flesh, and dwelt among us, and we
beheld His glory, glory as of the only begotten from the Father,
full of grace and truth. . .No man has seen God at any time;
the only begotten God, who is in the bosom of the Father, He
has explained Him. John 1:14, 18*

That phrase, "dwelt among us," means God took on the
form of a human body, leaving the peace, security, and hope
of heaven, and came to earth to become a model for men
and women.

How do you teach children not to lie, cheat, or steal? By
being an example before them of proper behavior. Jesus
showed us by example what it means to lead a perfect life,
despite the evil surrounding Him. "For we do not have a high
priest who cannot sympathize with our weaknesses, but one
who has been tempted in all things as we are, yet without sin"
(Hebrews 4:15).

When Satan bombarded Christ during an intense time
of temptation in the wilderness, Christ showed us how to
repel such attacks successfully: through liberal use of the
Word of God, prayer, and obedience.

Blaming Adam for initiating humans into the vicious
cycle of sin doesn't get any of us off the hook. It's our nature
to sin. And that's why we need a new nature.

This is exactly what Christ purchased for us on Calvary's
cross, the right to be indwelt with the very Spirit of God. A
fresh start, isn't that what all of us are seeking?

Prayer — Lord, strengthen my faith today. Help me to
overcome the evil one's daily temptations.

Israel Breaks the Covenant

*"I brought you up out of Egypt and led you into the land which I
have sworn to your fathers; and I said, 'I will never break My
covenant with you, and as for you, you shall make no covenant
with the inhabitants of this land; you shall tear down their
altars.' But you have not obeyed Me." Judges 2:1-2*

No sooner had the Israelites taken possession of their land
than they forgot all the Lord's admonitions.

"Then the sons of Israel did evil in the sight of the Lord,
and served the Baals, and they forsook the Lord, the God of
their fathers, who had brought them out of the land of Egypt,
and followed other gods from among the gods of the peoples
who were around them" (Judges 2:11-12).

God's hand was now against them for choosing to worship idols instead of honoring Him. Discipline was required to
bring them back. But God never stopped loving these people
He'd chosen. "And when the Lord raised up judges for them,
the Lord was with the judge and delivered them from the
hand of their enemies all the days of the judge; for the Lord
was moved to pity by their groaning because of those who
oppressed and afflicted them" (Judges 2:18).

For a while the people followed the judges, but as soon
as one of these leaders died, the Israelites sought out their
idols again.

So God left five enemy nations as strongholds within
the region to test Israel's obedience to His command-
ments: "the five lords of the Philistines and all the
Canaanites and the Sidonians and the Hivites who lived in
Mount Lebanon, from Mount Baal-hermon as far as
Lebo-hamath" (Judges 3:3).

Prayer — Lord, cleanse my soul and fill me with Your strength
that I might not backslide into the pit of disobedience again.

A Discerning Woman

Wisdom reposes in the heart of the discerning and even among fools she lets herself be known. Proverbs 14:33, NIV

Dorothy, a precious older woman, faithfully attended my Bible study group each week despite the fact that she suffered from congestive heart failure. She was the kind of person one treasured as a gift, knowing the time with her would be all too brief. She shared the contents of her heart freely, no longer restricted behind the confining walls of decorum. From her perspective, the word *cherish* didn't exist in her husband's vocabulary.

We would pray and cry together over the grief her marriage had caused her soul. And then she'd sit and play a beautiful hymn on the piano. This is the way the Lord ministered to her pain. Confident of her eternal destination, she exuded serenity, wisdom, peace, and love. And the Lord called her home that year because He valued her tremendously. She's buried in a cemetery near my house and I smile when I pass by, knowing she's found a refuge where the music never stops and people never cry.

Today's proverb says that, "wisdom reposes in the heart of the discerning." How well Dorothy understood this. And although she couldn't change her husband's heart, her own was filled with wisdom. She'd learned the art of holding life like a kite, giving it enough room to float freely and then watching as it returned to her.

Prayer — Lord, everyone has a cross to bear. But because you bore Calvary's cross for me, I have the hope of eternal life.

Israel Enslaved Again

The Lord strengthened Eglon the king of Moab against Israel, because they had done evil in the sight of the Lord. And he gathered to himself the sons of Ammon and Amalek; and he went and defeated Israel, and they possessed the city of the palm trees. And the sons of Israel served Eglon the king of Moab eighteen years. Judges 3:12-14

Israel's first judge was Othniel, son of Kenaz. The land knew peace for forty years. However, when Othniel died, the Israelites again fell into of idol worship.

Therefore, Eglon, king of Moab, joined forces with the Ammonites and Amalekites, overpowered Israel, and took possession of the city of palms. They were now forced to serve the king of one of their enemies for eighteen years.

Finally, they cried out for deliverance and the Lord sent Ehud. "The Israelites sent him with tribute to Eglon king of Moab" (Judges 3:15, NIV). Now along with this tribute, Ehud also fashioned a double-edged sword. Promising to tell the king a secret message from God, Ehud retired to the king's private quarters where he plunged the knife deep into the king's massive body and escaped. The Israelites killed about 10,000 Moabites and took possession of the land. Peace reigned for eighty years.

"After Ehud died, the Israelites once again did evil in the eyes of the Lord. So the Lord sold them into the hands of Jabin, a king of Canaan, who reigned in Hazor" (Judges 4:1-2). And the next judge was a woman named Deborah.

Prayer — Lord, please instill in me a hunger for daily study and worship, that I might not sin.

The Gift of Manna

They asked, and He brought quail, And satisfied them with the bread of heaven. Psalm 105:40

Who wouldn't welcome the delivery of free bread on their doorstep each morning? Well, the Israelites had it made and they still complained. "Same old, same old" they'd have cried out in today's vernacular. A one-day supply of this sticky, white, honey-flavored nourishment, called manna, covered the ground each morning. After gathering it, the Israelites ground it between two millstones or beat it with a mortar, boiled it in the pot, and made cakes with it. The taste was similar to cakes baked with oil (Numbers 11:8).

However, after forty years, the thought of waking up to this substance didn't exactly entice one to crawl out of their tent in anticipation.

After repeated complaints, God gave the Israelites some quail to eat (Numbers 11:31). No matter how God cared for them, the Israelites found something to criticize.

Another life-giving bread is symbolically offered to us under the new covenant. Jesus said, " 'I am the living bread that came down out of heaven; if anyone eats of this bread, he shall live forever; and the bread also which I shall give for the life of the world is My flesh' " (John 6:51). Christ Himself compared the two breads: " 'This is the bread which came down out of heaven; not as the fathers ate, and died, he who eats this bread shall live forever' " (John 6:58).

Prayer — Lord, I long to live forever in Your glorious presence.

Elijah Will Come

And they asked him, "What then? Are you Elijah?"
And he said, "I am not." John 1:21

Around 433 B.C. God spoke through the prophet Malachi, whose name means "My messenger." In the first part of his prophecy Malachi writes, " 'Behold, I am going to send My messenger, and he will clear the way before Me. And the Lord, whom you seek, will suddenly come to His temple; and the messenger of the covenant, in whom you delight, behold, He is coming,' says the Lord of hosts" (Malachi 3:1).

The second part of Malachi's prophecy reveals this: " 'Behold, I am going to send you Elijah the prophet before the coming of the great and terrible day of the Lord. And he will restore the hearts of the fathers to their children, and the hearts of the children to their fathers, lest I come and smite the land with a curse' " (Malachi 4:5-6). For over 400 years after these words God was silent. No wonder the Israelites were anxious to find out if John the Baptist were the promised Elijah.

Clearly, John answers the Jews, saying that he is not Elijah. However, he did come in the spirit and power of Elijah and even dressed as Elijah had. John preached a message of judgment for the religious leaders of Israel who should have both known and understood the Word of God but refused to listen.

———————————

Prayer — Father, Jesus and John the Baptist delivered the truth of Your Word but people refused to heed their messages. Lord, help me to listen and respond.

Motives of the Heart

The plans of the heart belong to man, But the answer of the tongue is from the Lord. All the ways of a man are clean in his own sight, But the Lord weighs the motives. Commit your works to the Lord, And your plans will be established. The Lord has made everything for its own purpose, Even the wicked for the day of evil. Proverbs 16:1-4

Horoscopes in newspapers and psychic telephone hotlines exist because people have a natural curiosity to know the future. Despite the phenomenal success of recent Hollywood blockbusters, I can assure you an attack by aliens is not on the horizon. No, our real threat will come from within the very real but unseen spiritual realm, not the extraterrestrial.

You've heard the expression, "Men are from Mars and women are from Venus." But the Bible does not distinguish between the hearts of men and women: "The heart is more deceitful than all else And is desperately sick; Who can understand it?" (Jeremiah 17:9)

Surrounding us are beings from another world, but they belong to Satan. And their sole purpose is to seduce us into wavering from the truth. They dangle and then entangle us from the scaffolding of unbelief. Did God mean what He said? Doesn't He want us to have any fun? Do we really need Him telling us what to do? Absolutely! Only God can give us a secure, peaceful, and perfect future. An eternal future in heaven with Him.

Prayer — Lord, there have been times when I compromised the Truth of Your Word. Please help me get back on track. Place my feet firmly on the pavement of Your Word.

Deborah, Judge and Prophetess

Now Deborah used to sit under the palm tree of Deborah
between Ramah and Bethel in the hill country of Ephraim;
and the sons of Israel came up to her for judgment.
Judges 4:4-5

Deborah is best known for her mediating role in one of Israel's greatest battles, against King Jabin of Canaan.

The commander of Jabin's army was Sisera. With his 900 iron chariots he oppressed the sons of Israel for twenty years. The time had come for Israel's liberation.

So Deborah sent for Barak, and said, " 'Behold, the Lord, the God of Israel, has commanded, "Go and march to Mount Tabor, and take with you ten thousand men from the sons of Naphtali and from the sons of Zebulun. And I will draw out to you Sisera, the commander of Jabin's army, with his chariots and his many troops to the river Kishon; and I will give him into your hand" ' " (Judges 4:6-7).

Barak's response was tepid: " 'If you will go with me, then I will go; but if you will not go with me, I will not go' " (Judges 4:8). Now how could Deborah pass up an opportunity like this? She answered, " 'I will surely go with you; nevertheless. . .the Lord will sell Sisera into the hands of a woman' " (Judges 4:9).

High above the river Kishon, atop Mount Tabor, a spectacular vantage point, Barak observed for himself those 900 chariots gathering for battle below (to be continued in tomorrow's devotional!). Is the Lord on your side too?

Prayer — Lord, thank You for using a woman to save Israel!

Deborah Trusts God

"Arise! For this is the day in which the Lord has given Sisera into your hands; behold, the Lord has gone out before you."
Judges 4:14

At the look of terror on Barak's face, Deborah sprung into action. Barak knew that he'd either have to take God at His Word or live as a broken and defeated man before all of Israel.

God began to display His awesome power. A great storm arose, and the rain and hail pelted the faces of Sisera's troops rendering vision impossible. Israel, with their backs to the storm, began the attack. Forceful winds blew as the ground beneath gave way, causing the chariots to turn with reckless abandon into the mud and slosh. Many drivers were thrown from their iron steeds and trampled by the horses who had pulled them. Those among Sisera's troops who weren't killed by Israel's swords were thrown into the raging waters of the river Kishon where they drowned. Meanwhile Sisera fled on foot.

Barak and his troops chased the enemy, killing them all. Then Barak backtracked to search for Sisera, their retreating general.

A woman named Jael, the wife of Heber, waited outside her tent for Barak. " 'Come, and I will show you the man whom you are seeking.' And he entered with her into the tent, and there was Sisera lying dead with the tent peg in his temple" (Judges 4:22). Jael had given him warm milk and then killed him as he slept. Deborah's prophecy had come true.

Prayer — Lord, Your Word can still convict me. Help me listen.

Adonai, My Lord

The Lord says to my Lord: "Sit at My right hand; Until I make Thine enemies a footstool for Thy feet," The Lord will stretch forth Thy strong scepter from Zion, saying, "Rule in the midst of Thine enemies." Psalm 110:1-2

Unless you know that the Hebrew word *Adonai* refers to God alone, it's easy to misinterpret this passage. Who's having this conversation?

We know that God represented Himself by the use of the plural pronouns "us" and "our." " 'Let Us make man in Our image, according to Our likeness' " (Genesis 1:26).

It's obvious that David understands the mystery of the Trinity and calls his Messiah God, Adonai, recognizing his Savior's equality with God the Father. This one passage represents two of the personalities within the Godhead.

David's Messiah was Jesus Christ, the son of David, his Savior from eternity past. And the answer as to who was speaking in Psalm 110 is provided as we read the cross-reference in the Gospel of Matthew. Jesus asked the Pharisees, " 'What do you think about the Christ, whose son is He?' They said to Him, 'The son of David.' He said to them, 'Then how does David in the Spirit call Him "Lord," saying, "The Lord said to my Lord, 'Sit at my right hand, Until I put thine enemies beneath Thy feet' "? If David then calls Him "Lord," how is He his son?' And no one was able to answer Him a word, nor did anyone dare from that day on to ask Him another question" (Matthew 22:41-46).

Prayer — Father, I thank You that I can call You many names, and all of them are beautiful and holy.

Finding the Messiah

*He found first his own brother, Simon, and said to him, "We
have found the Messiah" (which translated means Christ).
John 1:41*

I'll never forget the day that I accepted Jesus Christ as my
Savior. I'd been drawn to church twice that day, aware that
my soul ached for peace. So many Christians had told me
that all I needed to do was "pray and ask Christ into my life."
But that seemed overly simplistic. How could this action
change my life?

A short time before, while recovering from a compres-
sion fracture in my back, I began attending a Bible study.
Now those Scriptures I'd heard there began to come back
to me. It wasn't a matter of reciting words. Instead, asking
Christ into my life meant being willing to trade all the emptiness and estrangement within my soul for the completeness
which He alone could provide.

At the age of twenty-nine, on Father's Day, I prayed to
receive Christ, relinquishing control of my life to the Lord.

Andrew, speaking in today's Scripture, also found the
Messiah and couldn't wait to tell his brother, Peter. That's
how we all feel when God's light is at last turned on inside
the dungeon of our souls.

How blessed for Andrew that his brother responded
and they shared the love of the Lord together. In many
families this never happens. Perhaps in reading this you
understand what it means to be ridiculed because of your
faith in Christ.

Prayer — Lord, I pray for strength to share Your love with
unbelieving family members.

The Stone the Builders Rejected

The stone which the builders rejected Has become the chief corner stone. Psalm 118:22

When a building is started, a cornerstone must be placed precisely, because the rest of the structure is lined up with it. Likewise, Jesus Christ is the cornerstone of the Church. And His church is comprised of both Jews and Gentiles, united as the Body of Christ and dependent upon Him for guidance.

Before the world began, God envisioned His Church. Jesus Christ, the Son, would come and die for its members, that they would be cleansed from sin. And Christ would be the very foundation upon which this Church would stand. " 'Where were you when I laid the foundation of the earth? Tell Me, if you have understanding, who set its measurements, since you know? Or who laid its cornerstone, when the morning stars sang together, and all the sons of God shouted for joy?' " (Job 38:4-7)

But long before Christ came on the scene in recorded history, God prepared the Jews to accept their Messiah as the "cornerstone." Each year, as they celebrated the Feast of Passover they sang this psalm. And when Jesus, the chief cornerstone of God's mighty edifice, His kingdom, was in their very midst these melodious tones were sung by Him.

Is Jesus Christ the true cornerstone of your church? If you're looking for a church home, make sure you check the "foundation" first.

Prayer — Lord Jesus Christ, You alone are to be the cornerstone of my life. Please help me to discard those concerns that block my view of You.

God's Protection for Widows

The Lord will tear down the house of the proud, But He will establish the boundary of the widow. Proverbs 15:25

Christmas shopping preoccupied my father's thoughts as he picked out one special gift for each child, something he or she had wanted all year. But just after the last gift had been purchased, a severe heart attack overtook my dad. Although he was rushed to the hospital adjacent to the shopping center, he died almost immediately.

My mother's first concern was how she might continue caring for her children, all ten of whom lived at home.

Although she hadn't worked outside the home in years, Mom donned a beret and smock, and began selling pastel portraits at the local swap meet.

Eventually Mom also filled artists' chairs at Knotts Berry Farm and the Movieland Wax Museum. Her beautiful pastel portraits still hang in homes throughout our area. And the friendships she made with other artists endure to this day.

No matter what her hardships, Mom has honored God, in whom she placed her faith and the care of her life. She's now been widowed far longer than the years she was married. She's raised her children, paid off her mortgage, and passed down her love of art to all her grandchildren.

Prayer — Father, let me share Your Word with those women who now find themselves alone — "Now she who is a widow, indeed, and who has been left alone has fixed her hope on God, and continues in entreaties and prayers night and day" (1 Timothy 5:5).

An Angel Visits Ophrah

Then the angel of the Lord came and sat under the oak that was in Ophrah. . .Gideon was beating out wheat in the wine press in order to save it from the Midianites. And the angel of the Lord appeared to him and said to him, "The Lord is with you, O valiant warrior." Judges 6:11-12

The Lord was about to sell a very surprised man named Gideon on the idea of becoming Israel's next judge. God knew Gideon longed for deliverance for Israel. Once again Israel had turned to their age-old sin of idolatry.

Gideon said to the Lord, " 'O my lord, if the Lord is with us, why then has all this happened to us? And where are all His miracles which our fathers told us about, saying, "Did not the Lord bring us up from Egypt?" But now the Lord has abandoned us and given us into the hand of Midian' " (Judges 6:13). For once again the Israelites were enslaved as a result of disobedience.

"And the Lord looked at him and said, 'Go in this your strength and deliver Israel from the hand of Midian. Have I not sent you?' " (Judges 6:14)

Have you ever felt that the weight of the world rested on your shoulders? Well, that's Gideon for you. " 'O Lord, how shall I deliver Israel? Behold, my family is the least in Manasseh, and I am the youngest in my father's house' " (Judges 6:15). The Lord answered Gideon with the same resounding message of assurance which He always gives to His servants: " 'Surely I will be with you' " (Judges 6:16). God is with us in the fight and that's enough!

Prayer — Father, hold my hand today and every day.

Mary Requests Christ's Help

And when the wine gave out, the mother of Jesus said to Him, "They have no wine." John 2:3

Jesus and His earthly mother Mary are guests at a wedding celebration in Cana, a celebration that suddenly becomes dimmed by a crisis. To run out of wine at such an event would have brought great shame on the host family, as in those days a wedding feast went on for an entire week. Mary's tender heart couldn't allow her friends to suffer such humiliation. At no time did she attempt to tell Christ what to do. She simply appealed to His inborn kindness and resourcefulness.

Christ's response is a statement of fact. " 'Woman, what do I have to do with you? My hour has not yet come' " (John 2:4). Jesus was not yet ready to declare publicly to Israel His true identity. And performing an astonishing miracle would undoubtedly draw unwanted attention to Him, as well as detract from the bride and groom.

But Mary had risked her very life for Him. When she was betrothed to Joseph, God sent an angel to ask her to bear the Messiah. She responded in obedience, and the Holy Spirit placed this child in the virgin's womb (Luke 1:26-35). An angel also appeared to Joseph, telling him that the child Mary had conceived was the Messiah (Matthew 1:18-25). But the scandal persisted. Jews were referred to as the son of their father. In Christ's case, people called Him "the son of Mary." Yet she'd accepted this indignity for Him. How could Christ possibly deny her the favor she asked? Confident of His intervention, Mary admonishes the servants, " 'Whatever He says to you, do it' " (John 2:5).

Prayer — Father, You are still the God of miracles. I thank You that You know my needs.

Knowing God's Precepts

Teach me Thy statutes. Make me understand the way of Thy precepts, So I will meditate on Thy wonders. My soul weeps because of grief; Strengthen me according to Thy word. Remove the false way from me, And graciously grant me Thy law. Psalm 119:26-29

Have you ever felt as if you've reached the end of the road and the only choice ahead of you is a brick wall? When you reach that point the only remedy is to look up! God is waiting for you to come to your senses.

In these verses we learn the principles that can set things right. The first, revival, occurs when we truly "seek the Lord with all our hearts." Martin Luther, an Augustinian monk, recognized that the precepts he learned from studying the Scriptures didn't mesh with the teachings of the Roman Catholic Church. Therefore, in 1517, he openly stated his objections to the Catholic Church by nailing his Ninety-five "Theses" to the door of the church at Wittenberg. This began the revival which led to the formation of the Protestant church.

Confession of sin is the beginning of true hope. For when we acknowledge that we've failed, God can use our broken and contrite heart, through the Holy Spirit, to mold us anew.

Understand and walk in the way of the precepts by meditating on God's Word. If you're not participating in an in-depth Bible study, consider finding or starting one.

Prayer — Lord, teach me Your ways, that I might live out Your precepts before my family and loved ones.

Seek Wisdom, Not Self

When a wicked man comes, contempt also comes, And with dishonor comes reproach. Proverbs 18:3

The delightful movie *Doctor Doolittle* presented a magical animal called the "Push me, pull you." Such is the woman who has a divided heart! She can never truly go forward in life.

One young woman whom I counseled certainly fit this description. She'd fallen in love with a worthless wretch of a man and become convinced that she somehow possessed the power to change him. Not only could she not change him, she was also unable to raise her children properly. Because this mother was emotionally paralyzed, her children never received godly examples of faith, integrity, and stability.

Women become vulnerable the instant truth is replaced with desire. It's like when the tip of an arrow finds the one small point of vulnerability and penetrates a suit of armor.

So how can we teach our daughters to be wise? By acquiring knowledge ourselves. As we study and store God's Word in times of peace, our first thoughts during periods of stress or crisis will be Scripture. People falter because they fail to plan. If we just do what God expects of us, despite the magnetic pull of sin, we gain strength of character. Negotiating with evil nets us a zero every time.

Prayer — Lord, sometimes I want so badly to be loved that I trust the wrong people. Please guide me to those who are trustworthy.

A Great Teacher

"Truly, truly, I say to you, unless one is born again, he cannot see the kingdom of God." John 3:3

Nicodemus came to Christ under cover, by night. Although the Pharisees, the group of religious leaders to which he belonged, had reached the conclusion that Christ was sent from God, they hadn't bridged the gap to full understanding. Instead, they stood on the shore of uncertainty. They not only read the Scriptures, they taught them. And yet they bypassed the obvious and miraculous fulfillment to all the prophecies.

Note the timing of this visit by Nicodemus. The celebration of Passover was going on, and Jesus had just cleansed the temple of those who were, in His words, " 'making My Father's house a house of merchandise' " (John 2:16).

Nicodemus obviously heard what Christ said and couldn't shake it loose from his thoughts. He sought the truth, so Christ made it as clear as a starlit night.

Later in the Scriptures we see Nicodemus as the one who boldly risks his life to help Joseph of Arimathea take Christ's body from the cross. And Nicodemus brought an expensive "mixture of myrrh and aloes, about a hundred pounds weight" (John 19:39). "And so they took the body of Jesus, and bound it in linen wrappings with the spices, as is the burial custom of the Jews" (John 19:40).

Prayer — Lord, You told Nicodemus he must be born again. I praise You that You are the God of second chances, the God of truth!

Strength Is Not in Numbers

*And the Lord said to Gideon, "The people who are with you
are too many for Me to give Midian into their hands, lest
Israel become boastful, saying, 'My own power has delivered
me.' Now therefore come, proclaim in the hearing of the people,
saying, 'Whoever is afraid and trembling, let him return and
depart from Mount Gilead.'" Judges 7:2-3*

Why can't we get it through our heads that if God is on our
side, we don't need anyone else? Perhaps because we can't
see Him.

Gideon had the same challenge. His own "battle strategy" included amassing a multitude which would obliterate
the Midianites. And God told him no. God did not desire to
perform a miracle that might be misconstrued as an act
accomplished by human hands.

Instead, God had Gideon keep whittling down that
number of troops. Finally, with a mere 300 men Gideon
crossed the Jordan and won the battle. But the people who
followed him still hadn't understood.

These men said to Gideon, " 'Rule over us, both you and
your son, also your son's son, for you have delivered us from
the hand of Midian' " (Judges 8:22). Gideon answered them,
" 'I will not rule over you, nor shall my son rule over you; the
Lord shall rule over you' " (Judges 8:23).

Gideon served as Israel's judge for forty years and the
land was undisturbed during that time. "Then it came about,
as soon as Gideon was dead, that the sons of Israel again
played the harlot with the Baals, and made Baal-berith their
god" (Judges 8:33).

Prayer — Lord, have I watched Your hand of deliverance in
my own life only to become complacent? Help me repent!

Fearfully and Wonderfully Made

*For Thou didst form my inward parts; Thou didst weave me
in my mother's womb. I will give thanks to Thee, for I am
fearfully and wonderfully made; Wonderful are Thy works,
and my soul knows it very well. My frame was not hidden
from Thee, When I was made in secret, And skillfully wrought
in the depths of the earth. Thine eyes have seen my unformed
substance; And in Thy book they were all written,
The days that were ordained for me, when as yet
there was not one of them. Psalm 139:13-16*

Are you one of those people who picks up a new book and
reads the last page first? Well, if your life could be compared
to a book, only God knows the "ending" as well as the beginning. Despite the "pages" in the middle which might prove
disappointing at times, God has a definite purpose for your
life. And if you are in His will, the last page will have a very
happy ending!

As we survey this "sea of humanity," we can feel as insig-
nificant as a grain of sand. And yet one granule piled on top
of another makes for a gorgeous beach.

Each of us has not only an inborn sense that there is a
God, but also an understanding that we possess a designed
intent. Your parents aren't responsible for your creation, God
is. Had He not willed your very existence, you would not have
happened. God wants to use your life to further His kingdom.

Prayer — Lord, please renew my understanding that You
created me in Your own image and likeness with a body,
mind, and spirit.

The Virtuous Woman

An excellent wife, who can find? For her worth is far above jewels. The heart of her husband trusts in her, And he will have no lack of gain. She does him good and not evil All the days of her life. Proverbs 31:10-12

When my husband was discharged from active duty with the army, we returned to California from Okinawa. We'd received a regular paycheck and housing allowance. Now we were thrust into an uncertain economy with a glut of civil engineers out of work. Consequently, my husband had to choose another major.

Dreams of evenings at home together spent with our growing family never materialized as my husband was either at his night school classes or in the library. The burden fell on my shoulders to keep our children occupied each night. We read books or worked on crafts together. At times, my days with the kids seemed endless, especially since none of them was yet in school.

After the little ones were finally tucked into bed, there were still a couple of hours before my bedraggled husband would reappear. I filled them with my own crafts, letter writing, reading, and Bible study.

The virtuous woman in today's Scripture did good to her husband and not evil. All her activities were geared toward building up her home. Through all those lonely hours, this is the example I followed. Years later, when my husband finally graduated with a degree in a new field, his family remained intact.

———————

Prayer — Lord, disregard my selfish tendencies and show me the path to virtue.

Absolute Assurance of Eternal Life

"He who believes in the Son has eternal life; but he who does not obey the Son shall not see life, but the wrath of God abides on him." John 3:36

Rigo Lopez sought assurance one evening, alone in a motel room, as he surveyed the shattered pieces of his life. He'd just left his second wife and his children. Tears rolled down his cheeks and he had no answers.

He turned on the TV, and by the grace of God, Billy Graham's voice carried to him a message of hope. "You can have absolute assurance today of your salvation," Graham preached. Those words became like a heat-seeking missile, going directly to the source of pain in Rigo's heart. Rigo then prayed, "God, give me that assurance. Help me to know that You can forgive me, make me whole, and salvage the ruins of my life."

Armed with this knowledge, Rigo returned home to his family and began again. He read, studied, and eventually taught the Bible to others. This is the point at which I came to know him, as a member of my church. For years he and his wife Nancy taught Sunday school. Yet even when Rigo was diagnosed with incurable cancer, these two faithfully continued at their post. He was only in his forties when God called him home. The large church contained so many mourners that many had to stand in the vestibule.

The Word of God says that we can have absolute assurance of eternal life today. Rigo grasped onto God's truth and his life was transformed.

Prayer — Lord, I am assured of my salvation. Help me share this absolute truth with those in despair.

An Arrogant King

And Abimelech the son of Jerubbaal went to Shechem to his
mother's relatives, saying, "Speak now, in the hearing of all the
leaders of Shechem, 'Which is better for you, that seventy men,
all the sons of Jerubbaal, rule over you, or that one man rule
over you?' Also, remember that I am your bone and your flesh."
Judges 9:1-2

After the death of Jerubbaal (Gideon), one of his own sons
devised a plot to fill the power gap and become king.

"Then he went to his father's house at Ophrah, and
killed his brothers the sons of Jerubbaal, seventy men, on
one stone. But Jotham the youngest son of Jerubbaal was
left, for he hid himself" (Judges 9:5).

Even knowing this man to be a murderer, the men of
Shechem and the surrounding area gathered together and
crowned Abimelech king.

Jotham called these people of Shechem to accountability, reminding them of how fairly they'd been treated by
Gideon. When they refused to listen, he called for a curse
from God upon them and escaped to Beer. The people chose
to follow Abimelech for three years.

"Then God sent an evil spirit between Abimelech and
the men of Shechem; and the men of Shechem dealt treach-
erously with Abimelech, in order that the violence done to
the seventy sons of Jerubbaal might come" (Judges 9:23-24).
The God of justice always intervenes to bring the course of
history in line with His own design.

Prayer — Lord, Your eyes see everything. You are a God of
unswerving justice.

Praise and Dance

Praise the Lord! Praise God in His sanctuary; Praise Him in His mighty expanse. Praise Him for His mighty deeds; Praise Him according to His excellent greatness. Praise Him with timbrel and dancing. . . Let everything that has breath praise the Lord. Praise the Lord! Psalm 150:1-2, 6

In other words, "Praise Him with all you've got to make noise with!" Isn't that what true worship is, using our entire beings to give Him the glory He deserves?

I know people who believe that dancing is a sin. But God said He wanted His people dancing and praising Him. This worshipful motion accompanied the psalms as they were sung.

In just this one psalm we are given a formula for worship.

Whom are we to praise? The Lord! Where are we to praise? Wherever His congregation gathers. For what are we praising? For who He is, what He's done, and the way He's done it. How are we to praise? With our voices, our instruments, and our bodies as we dance in worship.

You've heard people say, "I don't need church, I can worship God anywhere." They usually mean that formal church service usurps precious moments spent in personal pursuits. They are denying any accountability to God.

The church is God's provision for all the spiritual and physical needs of His people. In a society that has become so mobile as to practically abandon the idea of closeness with extended family, the church picks up the slack.

Prayer — Lord, help me to yield my spirit up to You in true worship.

Encounter at the Well

So He came to a city of Samaria, called Sychar. Jesus therefore, being wearied from His journey, was sitting thus by the well. It was about the sixth hour. There came a woman of Samaria to draw water. Jesus said to her, "Give Me a drink." John 4:5-7

Here lived a woman of ill repute. Gathering water was a task customarily performed by the village women early in the day. Her presence at the well late in the afternoon was an acknowledgment that she didn't fit in. She was shunned by those who led wholesome lives. After all, she had had five husbands and now lived with a man.

Although men didn't speak to women in public, Jesus asked this woman for a drink of water. Shocked, the woman responded, " 'How is it that You, being a Jew, ask me for a drink since I am a Samaritan woman?' " (John 4:9) No self-respecting Jew would stoop to address pagans.

Jesus Christ goes right to the heart of her problem. " 'If you knew the gift of God, and who it is who says to you, 'Give Me a drink,' you would have asked Him, and He would have given you living water' " (John 4:10). And when she asked where to get this living water, He explained the process of eternal life to her.

Transformed, she ran back to town relating her amazing news: " 'Come, see a man who told me all the things that I have done; this is not the Christ, is it?' " (John 4:29)

Prayer — Father, help me to seek out those who for whatever reason are shunned and despised. They need You so much.

A Hasty Vow

*Now Jephthah the Gileadite was a valiant warrior, but he
was the son of a harlot. And Gilead was the father of
Jephthah. And Gilead's wife bore him sons; and when his
wife's sons grew up, they drove Jephthah out and said to him,
"You shall not have an inheritance in our father's house, for
you are the son of another woman." Judges 11:1-2*

Two more judges led Israel following the death of Abimelech.
Not surprisingly, the feckless Israelites once again began to
serve the pagan Baals and Ashteroth.

Finally, the Israelites acknowledged their sin and cried
out again for God's intervention. He chose Jephthah as their
judge and his brothers came to him for deliverance. Victorious over many enemies, Jephthah made a vow to the Lord
that if He would give them deliverance from the sons of
Ammon, Jephthah would sacrifice a burnt offering to God of
whatever came out of his house first, upon his return from
battle.

Tragically, Jephthah's only child, a daughter, bounded
out the front door to meet him "with tambourines and with
dancing" (Judges 11:34). After her father explained the
vow he'd just made, she said to him, " 'My father, you have
given your word to the Lord; do to me as you have said' "
(Judges 11:36).

She was sacrificed, just as Jephthah had promised.
"Thus the daughters of Israel went yearly to commemorate
the daughter of Jephthah the Gileadite four days in the year"
(Judges 11:39-40).

Prayer — Lord, help me turn to You for my deliverance and
not make hasty, costly vows.

All Is Vanity!

The words of the Preacher, the son of David, king in Jerusalem. "Vanity of vanities," says the Preacher, "Vanity of vanities! All is vanity." Ecclesiastes 1:1-2

At the end of his life, King Solomon, who is thought to be the writer of Ecclesiastes, concludes that the things of earth are but fleeting. Perhaps you too are prone to reflect on the tasks which occupy your days, concluding that nothing gets accomplished.

From the very beginning my husband and I decided that I would stay home with the kids and he'd work to support us. We have always managed to own a home in a nice neighborhood, send our kids to good schools, and afford at least a summer "camping vacation."

At times I'd lust after the sumptuous decor of a neighbor's home or envy those who lived in the two-story homes in the adjacent tract. But we stayed put. Years later, I finally appreciated that "low mortgage" when we were able to refinance and send three kids to college.

As we go through Ecclesiastes, Solomon repeatedly uses two key word pictures, "meaningless" and "under the sun." As king over Israel he had seen "all the works which have been done under the sun, and behold, all is vanity and striving after wind. . .Because in much wisdom there is much grief, and increasing knowledge results in increasing pain" (Ecclesiastes 1:14, 18). Solomon had experienced the best the world has to offer. . .and it wasn't enough.

Prayer — Lord, as I begin to learn the truths contained in this book, please help me view my priorities from Your perspective.

Healed Miraculously

*Now there is in Jerusalem by the sheep gate a pool. . .having
five porticoes. In these lay a multitude of those who were sick,
blind, lame, and withered, (waiting for the moving of the
waters; for an angel of the Lord went down at certain seasons
into the pool, and stirred up the water; whoever then first,
after the stirring up of the water, stepped in was made well
from whatever disease with which he was afflicted.)*
John 5:2–4

So many times when we cry out to the Lord for healing, He
seems to be asking us the same question He posed to the
man who had been sitting at this gate for thirty-eight years
waiting for healing: " 'Do you wish to get well?' " (John 5:6)

In other words, do you honestly desire to rid yourself
of the things which debilitate? For true healing of our souls
requires a change of direction.

Evidently, this man had never asked for assistance in
reaching the restorative waters. Instead, he just lay there day
after day, on the fringe of what "could have been." A few
verses later Jesus zeroes in on the core of the man's problem.
" 'Do not sin anymore' " (John 5:14).

Now everyone who is sick is not necessarily guilty of
sin. Later, Christ is asked by the disciples whether or not a
man sinned. Jesus answered, " 'It was neither that this man
sinned, nor his parents; but it was in order that the works
of God might be displayed in him' " (John 9:3). Only God
knows the content of one's heart.

Prayer — Lord, if sin is at the root of my infirmity, then bring
me to swift repentance. But if my suffering is to point others
toward Your glory, quench my thirst with Your living water.

Unremarkable Lives

Then Jephthah the Gileadite died and was buried in one of the
cities of Gilead. Now Ibzan of Bethlehem judged Israel after
him. And he had thirty sons, and thirty daughters whom he
gave in marriage outside the family, and he brought in thirty
daughters from outside for his sons. And he judged Israel seven
years. Then Ibzan died and was buried in Bethlehem.
Judges 12:7-10

What do you want etched into your own tombstone? Personally, I'd like to be remembered this way: "Studied the Word
of God diligently and cared about bringing it to others."

But no such accolades are recorded for the four judges
Jephthah, Ibzan, Elon, and Abdon. Jephthah is known
mainly for his "rash vow," while Ibzan's claim to fame is a
large family, whom he married off to the pagans dwelling in
that area. That's the route which led to unbelief and pagan
idolatry over and over during the time in which the judges
ruled Israel. Nothing is learned about Abdon except that "he
had forty sons and thirty grandsons who rode on seventy
donkeys" (Judges 12:14). What other tangible effects of his
presence on earth did he leave behind?

How can we discern the will of God for our lives? Daily
prayer is definitely the main source. And this involves not
only relating our needs to God, but also listening for His
directions. For He never meant for us to traverse through
this maze called life without the road maps He would supply.

Prayer — Lord, remind me to linger in prayer, listening for
Your voice.

Search for Happiness

I said to myself, "Come now, I will test you with pleasure. So enjoy yourself." And behold, it too was futility. I explored with my mind how to stimulate my body with wine while my mind was guiding me wisely, and how to take hold of folly, until I could see what good there is for the sons of men to do under heaven the few years of their lives. Ecclesiastes 2:1–3

Ah, the endless search for happiness. Remember when you thought that new dress or outfit would bring you happiness? And it did until you wore it again and again. Then you moved on to bigger and better things, like a brand-new car or a twenty-five-hundred-square-foot house or a summer home. . . .

Solomon explored with his mind how to stimulate his body. Then he enlarged his empire, built houses, planted vineyards, made gardens and parks, engineered ponds of water to irrigate a forest, bought male and female slaves, flocks, and herds, and collected silver and gold. All that his eyes desired he achieved. But did any of this bring him true happiness?

"Thus I considered all my activities which my hands had done and the labor which I had exerted, and behold all was vanity and striving after wind and there was no profit under the sun" (Ecclesiastes 2:11). It finally occurred to Solomon that in the end he would die and leave it all to others who followed him.

Prayer — Lord, help me not to be drawn away from You by the endless pursuit of things. Instead, I desire Your presence, guidance, and wisdom.

Jesus, Bread of Life

*"As the living Father sent Me, and I live because of the Father,
so he who eats Me, he also shall live because of Me. This is the
bread which came down out of heaven; not as the fathers ate,
and died, he who eats this bread shall live forever."*
John 6:57-58

Have you ever sat in a large lecture hall, listening to an intellectual speaker who extended your mind past the breaking point? Well, this is how the Jews of this day reacted to Christ as He spoke these words to them. They hadn't the vaguest notion as to how they might apply this information. If their minds had been file drawers, they'd have been in a quandary as to which file category to place it all under.

These listeners knew what the Scriptures said and yet they had no real comprehension that these God-breathed words were being fulfilled before their very eyes. So, they applied human understanding to Christ's words.

Some said that Jesus' teachings were too difficult to even bother with, while others stated that Christ was speaking about cannibalism. But the majority just walked away, refusing to follow Christ anymore. To continue following Him required faith and commitment.

To truly partake of Christ is to accept Him as He is, fully God and fully man, sent from God, recognizing our need for Him. He came first to the Jews, but they refused the message. What is your response? _____

Prayer — Lord, when I don't understand the Scriptures, Your Holy Spirit will provide me with comprehension.

Samson Is Conceived

Then the angel of the Lord appeared to the woman, and said to her "Behold now, you are barren and have born no children, but you shall conceive and give birth to a son." Judges 13:3

Once again, God was about to raise up a deliverer for Israel. And the woman joyfully brought the news to her husband. " 'A man of God came to me and his appearance was like the appearance of the angel of God, very awesome. . .He said to me, "Behold, you shall conceive and give birth to a son, and now you shall not drink wine or strong drink nor eat any unclean thing, for the boy shall be a Nazarite to God from the womb to the day of his death" ' " (Judges 13:6-7).

From the moment of conception, Samson's mother was to abstain from alcohol. God didn't want Samson to be born with a dependence on alcohol: Samson's mind needed to be clear so that he could receive the Lord's direction and guidance to lead Israel.

Also, God made it clear to her that "from the moment of conception" this was in fact a son. No confusion here either. But abortion advocates tell us otherwise, despite the Lord's pronouncement that following the union of the sperm and egg, a unique human has been created. Truly the wisdom of the Lord defies time, technology, and human arrogance.

Prayer — Lord, as I read Your Word, open my eyes to Your infinite wisdom and understanding.

A Case against Abortion

*Just as you do not know the path of the wind and how bones
are formed in the womb of the pregnant woman, so you do not
know the activity of God who makes all things.*
Ecclesiastes 11:5

In yesterday's Scripture, we saw clearly that God created
Samson. To reinforce that "all Scripture is inspired by God"
(2 Timothy 3:16), look what's presented for today: It is
God who creates life.

In an earlier devotional, we focused on this passage from
Psalm 139:13-14: "For Thou didst form my inward parts;
Thou didst weave me in my mother's womb. I will give
thanks to Thee, for I am fearfully and wonderfully made."

As women, it's up to us to uphold the sanctity of life.
Each life comes into this world with a purpose. Therefore,
when that life is abruptly ended so are all the accomplishments that were intended for this unique person.

To claim ignorance about conception is to lie. And
who instigates this lie? None other than Satan.

Abortion is wrong, no matter what the circumstances.
When the world attempts to tell us there's no way out of a
pregnancy dilemma, as Christians we should cry out in
response. We can always turn to God for His infinite wisdom
and insight. Exercising our option to go against His commandments is never the right choice.

Prayer — Lord, give me insight to offer Christian counsel
to a woman weighing the future of her unborn child. Give
me words to describe Your greatest gift—life.

Not Even His Brothers Believed

Now the feast of the Jews, the Feast of Tabernacles, was at
hand. His brothers therefore said to Him, "Depart from here,
and go into Judea, that Your disciples also may behold
Your works which You are doing. For no one does anything
in secret, when he himself seeks to be known publicly.
If You do these things, show Yourself to the world."
For not even His brothers were believing in Him. John 7:2-5

One of the most difficult challenges any believer faces is reaching her family with Christ's message. Although Jesus' own brothers had daily viewed His sinless life, they were as blind as the Pharisees to who He really was.

Surely these siblings, Christ's earthly half-brothers (Matthew 13:55-56, Mark 6:1-6), knew that the Jews were seeking to kill Him (John 7:1). But they were headed for Jerusalem to attend the Feast of Booths, as required by God. Jesus' brothers were embarking on a journey to a religious feast and yet rejecting their own Messiah.

Their unbelief had been prophesied in Psalm 69:8: "I have become estranged from my brothers, And an alien to my mother's sons."

Christ's half-brothers were completely in tune with the world, and not with God. Jesus tells them, " 'My time is not yet at hand, but your time is always opportune. . .Go up to the feast yourselves; I do not go up to this feast because My time has not yet fully come'" (John 7:6-8). After his brothers left, Christ went secretly to the feast.

Prayer — Thank You, Jesus, for reminding me to wait for God's timing in my life, especially when the pressure applied by others would have me rush on ahead.

Samson Grows Older, Not Wiser

Then the woman gave birth to a son and named him Samson;
and the child grew up and the Lord blessed him.
Judges 13:24

As Samson struck out on his own, the first thing he did was fall in love with a Philistine woman. Although his parents cautioned him against marrying a pagan, he was bound and determined to have her. On the way to ask for her hand, "the Spirit of the Lord came upon him," and Samson tore a lion to shreds with his own hands (Judges 14:6).

Later, when he returned for his bride he passed by the carcass of the lion which contained a swarm of bees and honey. During the marriage feast he would taunt the party-goers with a riddle: " 'Out of the eater came something to eat, And out of the strong came something sweet' " (Judges 14: 12-14).

When none of the guests could solve his riddle, his intended bride had a crying jag, to get Samson to divulge the secret. After she related the answer to her relatives, Samson went down to Ashkelon and killed thirty men. Then he stomped off back to his father's house.

When Samson returned, his bride's father had given her in marriage to one of Samson's closest companions. Enraged, Samson set torches between pairs of 300 foxes, and turned them loose to burn the Philistines' grain supply. Samson's misuse of power caused the Philistines to kill his bride and her father (Judges 15:3-7). Samson clearly was not in the Lord's will.

Prayer — Lord, I pray for discernment in my own life that I may prosper and not selfishly hurt others.

A Time to Mourn

*There is an appointed time for everything. And there is a time
for every event under heaven. . .A time to weep, and a time to
laugh; A time to mourn, and a time to dance.*
Ecclesiastes 3:1, 4

Once we've finally accepted that God truly loves us, it's
hard to face the first discouraging episode or tragedy that
follows. One young family had received a strong call from
the Lord to the mission field. At the beginning of a fund-
raising trip they were involved in an accident that totaled
their van. What would they do? They transferred their
focus away from the problem and to their faithful Lord
who never disappoints.

Somehow we reach the faulty conclusion that if God
loves us all negative incidents are nixed. Do we doubt that
the Father loved the Son and yet allowed the Son to suffer
a cruel death on the cross? The penalty for sin was death, a
penalty that had to be paid by someone absolutely sinless
in order for us to be forgiven. Only Jesus Christ could fill
that role.

If Christ Himself suffered, then why should we be
immune from all maladies?

Occasionally a time of mourning enters our lives, sometimes stealing in almost silently, sometimes brashly breaking
down the door to our well-constructed sense of security.
Neither path reflects nor distorts the fact that God loves us.
But tragedy and mourning are both part of the ebb and flow
or "rhythm of life."

Prayer — Lord, through my veil of tears help me to view Your
rescuing hand, that I might reach out to grasp You more
firmly.

An Adulterous Woman

And the scribes and the Pharisees brought a woman caught in adultery, and having set her in the midst, they said to Him, "Teacher, this woman has been caught in adultery, in the very act. Now in the Law Moses commanded us to stone such women; what then do You say?" John 8:3-5

What a scene! The Jewish religious leaders had dragged this woman right out of bed. But where is her partner in crime? Since Jewish law required that both parties involved in this sin be stoned, it's a sham from the beginning. It was staged by the Pharisees as a trap for Jesus.

The Pharisees meant to pit Christ's ruling against what Moses had commanded. However, their plot backfired! "But Jesus stooped down, and with His finger wrote on the ground" (John 8:6). At first they blindly persisted in asking His opinion on this matter.

Then, "He straightened up, and said to them, 'He who is without sin among you, let him be the first to throw a stone at her.'" Had he etched out their sins for all to read? We don't know for sure, but when He stooped down to continue writing again, "they began to go out one by one, beginning with the older ones, and He was left alone, and the woman, where she had been, in the midst" (John 8:7, 9).

"And straightening up, Jesus said to her, 'Woman, where are they? Did no one condemn you?' And she said, 'No one, Lord.' And Jesus said, 'Neither do I condemn you; go your way, from now on sin no more'" (John 8:10-11).

Prayer — Lord, forgive me, no matter what my sin, that I might turn from it and faithfully serve You.

Samson Uses Brawn, Not Brains

*Now Samson went to Gaza and saw a harlot there, and went
in to her. . .Now Samson lay until midnight, and at midnight
he arose and took hold of the doors of the city gate and the two
posts and pulled them up along with the bars; then he put
them on his shoulders and carried them up to the top of the
mountain which is opposite Hebron. After this it came about
that he loved a woman in the valley of Sorek, whose name was
Delilah. Judges 16:1, 3-4*

The Gazites had lain in wait for Samson all night, planning
to kill him in the morning. What a sight awaited them when
they discovered the gates to their city were now situated
on top of a mountain.

The rest of the story is the stuff of legend as the
Philistines use Delilah, a beautiful temptress, to bring down
the gullible Samson. After repeated nagging Samson finally
confesses to Delilah that the secret of his strength lies in his
long hair. "And she made him sleep on her knees, and called
for a man and had him shave off the seven locks of his hair.
Then she began to afflict him, and his strength left him"
(Judges 16:19).

"Then the Philistines seized him and gouged out his
eyes; and they brought him down to Gaza and bound him
with bronze chains, and he was a grinder in the prison"
(Judges 16:21). But Samson's hair grew back. In the assembly
hall where the Philistines gathered to offer a sacrifice to their
god, Dagon, Samson literally brought down the house, killing
himself and 3,000 Philistines.

Prayer — Lord, give me the gift of discernment that my life
may be a consistent testimony of my love for You.

The Days of Your Youth

Remember also your Creator in the days of your youth, before the evil days come and the years draw near when you will say, "I have no delight in them." Fear God and keep His commandments, because this applies to every person. God will bring every act to judgment, everything which is hidden, whether it is good or evil. Ecclesiastes 12:1, 13–14

Most of us have encountered women who freely share biblical truths "handed down to them" from their grandmothers or mothers. Is the faith being displayed in their lives?

The Book of Ecclesiastes concludes with the admonition not only to remember our Creator when we are young, but to continue following His precepts throughout our time on earth. For nothing is sadder than to see those who began the race of life with so much vigor and potential now sitting on the sidelines watching the parade pass by.

High school reunions are great places to witness such scenes. Those girls whose faces glowed with extraordinary promise at eighteen may now display ones that appear more like a map of New York City. They've been betrayed, besieged, and bewildered by people promising much and delivering little.

Have you forgotten the God of your youth? Have His principles been compromised away by the pressures of a world that teaches the Ten Commandments are optional? With the Lord's help, it's not too late to turn it all around.

Prayer — Lord, if I look back and see a trail of regret, please give me the courage to change the view.

Jesus, Light of the World

*And as He passed by, He saw a man blind from birth. And
His disciples asked Him, saying, "Rabbi, who sinned, this man
or his parents, that he should be born blind?" Jesus answered,
"It was neither that this man sinned, nor his parents;
but it was in order that the works of God might
be displayed in him." John 9:1-5*

When you walk into a darkened room, you reach for the light
switch. Back in Christ's time, you might have waited for the
first rays of sunlight to break through the morning sky.
However, for the man in today's Scripture that first glimmer
of daily hope had never arrived. He'd been born blind.

But Jesus intervened. "He spat on the ground, and made
clay of the spittle, and applied the clay to his eyes, and said
to him, 'Go, wash in the pool of Siloam.' And so he went
away and washed, and came back seeing" (John 9:6-7).

Some of the neighbors who had known the man as a
beggar were astonished, while others doubted that he was
even the same man.

Then the Pharisees brought in the man's parents, questioning them. And even when they heard the truth they
refused to believe, becoming divided as to whether a mere
man had performed a miracle. "Don't confuse us with the
facts," they seemed to say.

Rather than believe that the man had actually been
healed, the Pharisees once again donned their mask of
spiritual blindness, threatening to excommunicate the man
from temple worship. No miracle of God was about to shake
up their world!

Prayer — Lord, open my eyes to Your miracles.

Ruth, Faithful Daughter-in-law

Then Elimelech, Naomi's husband, died; and she was left with her two sons. And they took for themselves Moabite women as wives; the name of the one was Orpah and the name of the other Ruth. And they lived there about ten years. Ruth 1:3-4

Ruth was a young woman when her husband died. In one of the greatest testaments of love in the Bible, she chose to remain with her widowed mother-in-law, Naomi, even choosing to believe in her God.

Naomi's encouragement that Ruth return to her homeland only deepened Ruth's commitment to follow. " 'Do not urge me to leave you or turn back from following you; for where you go, I will go, and where you lodge, I will lodge. Your people shall be my people, and your God, my God. Where you die, I will die, and there I will be buried. Thus may the Lord do to me, and worse, if anything but death parts you and me' " (Ruth 1:16-17).

Few daughters-in-law would have persisted in devotion to a woman whose life held such abysmal tragedy and so little prospect for positive change. However, God had a glorious plan. "Now Naomi had a kinsman of her husband, a man of great wealth, of the family of Elimelech, whose name was Boaz" (Ruth 2:1).

Ruth gathered leftover grain from Boaz's fields so that she and Naomi might have food. And Boaz showed her favor. In time, Ruth would become Boaz's bride and mother to his son, a son whose lineage would include David and the Messiah, Jesus Christ.

Prayer — Lord, may I learn from Ruth's example of abiding love.

Hannah's Prayer Is Observed

And she, greatly distressed, prayed to the Lord and wept bitterly. And she made a vow and said, "O Lord of hosts, if Thou wilt give Thy maidservant a son, then I will give him to the Lord all the days of his life, and a razor shall never come on his head." 1 Samuel 1:10-11

Hannah has gone to the temple year after year and pleaded with God for a son. Her husband says, " 'Hannah, why do you weep and why do you not eat and why is your heart sad? Am I not better to you than ten sons?' " (1 Samuel 1:8)

Eli the priest happened upon the scene. He had missed Hannah's heartfelt prayer. All he saw was her mouth moving. Eli concludes that Hannah is drunk and says, " 'How long will you make yourself drunk? Put away your wine from you' " (1 Samuel 1:14).

But Hannah answered and said, " 'No, my lord, I am a woman oppressed in spirit; I have drunk neither wine nor strong drink but I have poured out my soul before the Lord. Do not consider your maidservant as a worthless woman; for I have spoken until now out of my great concern and provocation' " (1 Samuel 1:15-16).

Finally, Eli did rally, giving Hannah a blessing, " 'Go in peace; and may the God of Israel grant your petition that you have asked of Him' " (1 Samuel 1:17). The persistent prayers of a Christian woman should never be underestimated!

Prayer — Lord, help me to realize that "our help is in the name of the Lord!" (Psalm 124:8)

The Song of Solomon

"My beloved responded and said to me, 'Arise, my darling, my beautiful one, And come along. For behold, the winter is past, The rain is over and gone. The flowers have already appeared in the land; The time has arrived for pruning the vines, And the voice of the turtledove has been heard in our land. The fig tree has ripened its figs, And the vines in blossom have given forth their fragrance. Arise, my darling, my beautiful one, And come along!'" Song of Solomon 2:10-13

Crucial to understanding the Scriptures is analyzing the composition or type of literature within each book of the Bible.

The Song of Solomon is a book of poetry. During the eighth day of Passover the Jews would sing portions of this book which they compared to the most holy place in the temple.

Approaching this unique little book with the understanding that it's a love story enables the reader to appreciate its lyrical quality. Yet the Song of Solomon also addresses issues of pertinence to women. Understanding ourselves and our mates, the importance of intimacy and purity, and the concept of fidelity within the marital union are all discussed.

Most importantly, the Song of Solomon explores the spiritual relationship we have with God. In his letter to the church at Corinth (2 Corinthians 11:2), the apostle Paul also speaks to this issue. "For I am jealous for you with a godly jealousy; for I betrothed you to one husband, that to Christ I might present you as a pure virgin. Have you forsaken your first love?"

Prayer — Lord, make me a woman who is faithfully devoted to You.

Jesus, the Good Shepherd

*"He who enters by the door is a shepherd of the sheep. To him
the doorkeeper opens, and the sheep hear his voice, and he calls
his own sheep by name, and leads them out." John 10:2-3*

Sheep just aren't very bright. They need constant overseeing,
tender treatment, and strict boundaries. The shepherd took
them to the best pastures, found safe lodging for them during the night, and then led them out again in the morning.
He was the ultimate caregiver!

In fact, the shepherd would stretch his own body out
across the opening to the sheep pen. What a graphic picture
of protection this provides as we consider that Christ considers Himself our Shepherd.

As the world screams out for us to follow every wind of
doctrine, Christ's voice calls us back to obedience: " 'When
he puts forth all his own, he goes before them, and the sheep
follow him because they know his voice' " (John 10:4). His
voice will never call us to rebellion, sinful pleasures, or departure from His Word.

In our day we hear those who defend heinous acts by
saying, "Voices told me to do it." Certainly the one they
chose to listen to was not the voice of Jesus Christ, for He
cannot contradict Himself. True sheep listen only for the
voice of their Shepherd.

God calls us by name, just as the shepherd has pet names
for his sheep. Someday, when the King of Kings, our Good
Shepherd, calls us home to heaven, we'll hear the name He
calls us.

Prayer — Lord, guide me to safe pastures today. Never
leave me.

Samuel Is Born

*And it came about in due time, after Hannah had conceived,
that she gave birth to a son; and she named him Samuel,
saying, "Because I have asked him of the Lord." 1 Samuel 1:20*

Hannah, a woman of real faith, wanted to keep her promise to God. After Samuel was born and she had weaned him, she took him promptly to the temple. There she said to Eli, " 'Oh, my lord! As your soul lives, my lord, I am the woman who stood here beside you, praying to the Lord. For this boy I prayed, and the Lord has given me my petition which I asked of Him. So I have dedicated him to the Lord; as long as he lives he is dedicated to the Lord' " (1 Samuel 1:26-28).

Every year Hannah and Elkanah returned for their sacrifice at the temple, and every year Hannah brought Samuel a new robe to wear. For her faithfulness, God blessed Hannah with three more sons and two daughters (1 Samuel 2:21).

God was now training Samuel to take over as judge of Israel, as Eli's own sons had no regard for the Lord. As Samuel continued to grow "in favor with the Lord" (1 Samuel 2:26), the Lord declared, " 'Those who honor me I will honor, but those who despise me will be disdained' " (1 Samuel 2:30, NIV).

Prayer — Lord, If You should give me a child, guide me as You guided Hannah— to sincere faithfulness.

Isaiah, a Major Prophet

The vision of Isaiah the son of Amoz, concerning Judah and Jerusalem which he saw during the reigns of Uzziah, Jotham, Ahaz, and Hezekiah, kings of Judah. Listen, O heavens, and hear, O earth; for the Lord speaks, "Sons I have reared and brought up, But they have revolted against Me. My people do not understand." Isaiah 1:1-3

Had the word "clueless" been coined during Isaiah's lifetime, he would probably have used it to describe the people of Israel who foolishly continued to abandon the Lord. However, through the prophet Isaiah, God provides extraordinary clues to His character. This prophet was surely named appropriately, for *Isaiah* means "Jehovah saves" or "salvation of Jehovah."

Isaiah's very lifeblood would be poured out as he brought this message of hope to Israel, for it is written that he was sawed in two by Manasseh, the king of Judah who reigned after Hezekiah (2 Kings 21:16).

Reading Isaiah provides a necessary heart check. Like Israel, if we fail to turn from our defiant ways, we must ask, "Where will you be stricken again, As you continue in your rebellion? The whole head is sick, And the whole heart is faint. From the sole of the foot even to the head there is nothing sound in it, Only bruises, welts, and raw wounds, Not pressed out or bandaged, Nor softened with oil" (Isaiah 1:5-6).

Prayer — Lord, this book of prophecy displays Your promises and prophecies. Open my mind to receive Your truth. And keep me from confusion, that I might know You as both Messiah and Lord.

Jesus Raises Lazarus

Now a certain man was sick, Lazarus of Bethany. . .The sisters therefore sent to Him, saying, "Lord, behold, he whom You love is sick." John 11:1, 3

When we hear that a good friend is critically ill we run to his side. Why then does Jesus tarry? "But when Jesus heard it, He said, 'This sickness is not unto death, but for the glory of God, that the Son of God may be glorified by it'" (John 1:4).

Obviously, this remark puzzled His disciples. They had honestly laid out the situation for Him. Lazarus was about to breathe his last. And yet Christ seemed to be denying the gravity of the situation. We can almost picture Mary and Martha wringing their hands and consoling each other that soon Jesus would be there and everything would be all right again.

Instead, Jesus took His time getting there, four days as a matter of fact. And when He did arrive, Lazarus had been buried! Now Christ was only a few miles away from Bethany. It took all the human restraint He possessed not to run to Lazarus's aid. But Jesus has, as always, a greater purpose.

At the tomb of His friend Jesus called: "'Lazarus, come forth'" (John 11:43). And Lazarus arose from the tomb and walked out, his grave clothes dangling from his body. Have you allowed Christ to exercise His authority to bring you forth to new life?

———————————

Prayer — Lord, strengthen my faith so that when tragedy strikes, I know that You are the Resurrection and the Life.

Hannah Acknowledges Her Savior

*Then Hannah prayed and said, "My heart exults in the Lord;
My horn is exalted in the Lord, My mouth speaks boldly
against my enemies, Because I rejoice in Thy salvation. There
is no one holy like the Lord, Indeed, there is no one besides
Thee, Nor is there any rock like our God. Boast no more so very
proudly, do not let arrogance come out of your mouth; for the
Lord is a God of knowledge, And with Him actions are
weighed." 1 Samuel 2:1-3*

Recently my husband and I toured William Randolph Hearst's
castle in San Simeon, California. Surrounded by opulence and
indulgence, embodied by his fabled art collection, Hearst had
missed what was truly valuable—the reality of Christ's
powerful light invading the darkness of one's sin-ridden soul.

Hannah, on the other hand, is very aware of the one
truth of her life and she expresses it eloquently: " 'I rejoice in
Thy salvation.' "

Hannah spent her time in the temple, praying and
serving others. And God granted the deepest longing of her
heart, despite the fact that she was just a sinner who could
offer God nothing but her brokenness and yielded spirit.

Hannah refers to her Savior as a " 'God of knowledge' "
for she revered or honored His Word. She took to heart all
that God had done for her people in the past and accepted
that He alone could change her circumstances. To whom do
you turn for solutions?

Prayer — Lord, You alone can lift me from the depths of
despair and set me on high places.

Listen, My Children

Your land is desolate, your cities are burned with fire, Your fields—strangers are devouring them in your presence; It is desolation, as overthrown by strangers. . .Unless the Lord of hosts Had left us a few survivors, We would be like Sodom, we would be like Gomorrah. Hear the word of the Lord, You rulers of Sodom; Give ear to the instruction of our God, You people of Gomorrah. Isaiah 1:7, 9-10

"Listen, my children, and you shall hear of the midnight ride of Paul Revere. . ." So begins the poem "Paul Revere's Ride" by Henry Wadsworth Longfellow, required reading for many during our school days. But Paul Revere was only one of three messengers who were sent to warn the people that the British were coming.

The prophet Isaiah was also sent to warn the people of impending disaster. Here he uses an example from the past, that of Sodom and Gomorrah, to point to their own imminent doom if they fail to listen. "Hear the word of the Lord," he reminds them. These were the cities which God destroyed because Abraham couldn't even find ten men there who remained obedient to God. Therefore, He rained down fire and brimstone upon them (Genesis 19:24). Before this annihilation took place, God sent His angel to warn the people. But they refused to obey.

Israel's besetting sin was idolatry, and no matter how many prophets God sent, "everyone did what was right in his own eyes" (Judges 21:25).

Prayer — Lord, Thank You for sending Your messengers to minister to my heart. Through them the light of Your truth finally dawned in my heart. Thank You for Your peace.

Mary's Expensive Gift

*Mary therefore took a pound of very costly perfume of pure
nard, and anointed the feet of Jesus, and wiped His feet with
her hair; and the house was filled with the fragrance
of the perfume. John 12:3*

While our three children were growing up, another young
man came to live with us for nearly a year. He turned to the
Lord in total obedience. We remained part of his extended
family.

While he and his bride were on their honeymoon I
went over to clean and prepare the house he'd been sharing
with several male roommates. His wife has never forgotten
my wedding "gift."

The gift of pure nard which Mary used to anoint Jesus'
feet was extremely extravagant, costing about a year's wages.
But then, Jesus had raised her brother Lazarus from the dead.
Mary's lavish use of this burial perfume represented her deep
gratitude to Christ.

On another visit in Bethany when Jesus had been
invited to the home of Simon the leper, a woman of ill repute
entered the home. She too had been touched by the Lord
and poured the contents of an alabaster vial of perfume on
His head as He reclined at the table (Matthew 26:6-13).

As both of these incidents took place, the disciples were
indignant, calling the gifts these women gave "a waste"
(Matthew 26:8-9; John 12:4-6). Jesus' followers had somehow missed what He had been relating to them concerning
His own imminent death.

Prayer — Lord, let me never take You for granted.

A Man of God Speaks to Eli

*Then a man of God came to Eli and said to him, "Thus says
the Lord, 'Did I not indeed reveal Myself to the house of your
father when they were in Egypt in bondage to Pharaoh's
house? And did I not choose them from all the tribes of Israel
to be My priest? . . . Why do you kick at My sacrifice and at
My offering which I have commanded in My dwelling,
and honor your sons above Me?'" 1 Samuel 2:27-29*

I can't wait to show you who was actually speaking to Eli.
The Hebrew word for "man of God" is *iysh elohiym*. And He
spoke to Eli in the first person: " 'Did I not indeed reveal
Myself to the house of your father. . .?'" It was the Lord God
Himself.

When God's leaders fail to follow obediently they are
removed from their positions. Eli and his family had been
chosen by the Lord to be priests in the temple. Yet Eli and
his sons had misused their authority. They not only kept all
the best sacrifices for themselves, but Eli refused to discipline
his sons. In 1 Samuel 2:12 Eli's offspring are described as
"sons of Belial." They were sons of destruction or wickedness,
evil and ungodly. And there's no way the Lord could allow
them to be priests in the temple.

" 'I did indeed say that your house and the house of your
father should walk before me forever; but now the Lord
declares, "Far be it from Me—for those who honor Me I will
honor, and those who despise Me will be lightly esteemed.
Behold, the days are coming when I will break your strength
and the strength of your father's house so that there will not
be an old man in your house" ' " (1 Samuel 2:30-32).

Prayer — Lord, instill obedience in me also.

The Work of Their Hands

*Thou has abandoned Thy people, the house of Jacob, Because
they are filled with influences from the east, And they are
soothsayers like the Philistines. Their land has also been filled
with silver and gold, and there is no end to their treasures;
Their land has also been filled with horses, And there is no end
to their chariots. Their land has also been filled with idols;
They worship the work of their hands, that which their fingers
have made. Isaiah 2:6-8*

Let's just take this passage one phrase at a time. Let's compare the things which distracted Israel from worship with our own possible list.

First, they were "filled with influences from the east." Instead of worshiping the living God, the people of Israel had succumbed to the pagan mentality of the nations which surrounded them.

Next, "their land has also been filled with silver and gold." Yet God has plainly told us, " 'Do not lay up for yourselves treasures upon earth, where moth and rust destroy, and where thieves break in and steal. But lay up for yourselves treasures in heaven. . .for where your treasure is, there will your heart be also' " (Matthew 6:19-21).

Their land was also filled with horses and chariots. In other words, they had methods of travel in abundance. And speaking of chariots, you should see our daughter's white Camaro with its T-top!

And last but not least, their land was filled with idols. Is your career more important than raising a family or making a weekly commitment to be at church?

Prayer — Lord, be in charge of my own priority list.

His Light Dispels Darkness

And Jesus cried out and said, "He who believes in Me does not believe in Me, but in Him who sent Me. And he who beholds Me beholds the One who sent me. I have come as light into the world, that everyone who believes in Me may not remain in darkness." John 12:44-46

Several years ago when I worked for a countercult ministry, our group hosted a debate between one of our staff theologians and a cult leader who denied the existence of the Trinity. Although I'd read many of this man's ideas on paper, nothing prepared me for the depth of spiritual darkness he displayed that evening. But the saddest moment was peering into the spiritually dead eyes of his followers who sat only a few feet away from me.

How people can read the Word of God and reach such faulty conclusions mystifies me. If you have a question about one verse of Scripture, first, you need to pray that God's Spirit will provide enlightenment. Then, get a good study Bible that has cross-referencing indexed on each page along with the text.

Next, invest in or borrow from your church library a theological text that deals with the Bible book you are studying. Ask your pastor or minister for his personal recommendations. With such a guide at hand, God's Word becomes clearer and your faith is sure to deepen.

Prayer — Your truth is readily available, Lord. Therefore, I know with certainty that I will one day see You face-to-face. Deepen my faith so that I might penetrate the spiritual darkness around me.

Learning to Hear God's Voice

The Lord called Samuel; and he said, "Here I am."
1 Samuel 3:4

A sleepy and startled young Samuel heard the voice calling him. Thinking it was Eli, Samuel ran to him. But Eli said, " 'I did not call, lie down again.' " Being an obedient lad, Samuel again rested. But the Lord called to him again. And the whole scenario repeated again, as he went to inquire of Eli. Dismissing him, Eli told him to rest.

When this happened for the third time, Eli finally figured out that God had called to Samuel. Eli *tells* Samuel, " 'Go lie down, and it shall be if He calls you, that you shall say, "Speak, Lord, for Thy servant is listening" ' " (1 Samuel 3:9). Sure enough, the Lord did speak again. And this time Samuel responded as Eli had instructed. The Lord proceeded to say to Samuel, " 'Behold, I am about to do a thing in Israel at which both ears of everyone who hears it will tingle. In that day I will carry out against Eli all that I have spoken concerning his house, from beginning to end. For I have told him that I am about to judge his house forever for the iniquity which he knew, because his sons brought a curse on themselves and he did not rebuke them' " (1 Samuel 3:11-13).

Of course this rattled Samuel's sense of well-being. Samuel wanted to keep this information from Eli, but good old Eli had already surmised that if God were ready to talk to Samuel instead of him, then He must be ready to act in judgment. So Eli asked for the truth and Samuel related the message as God presented it.

Prayer — Lord, keep me close to You, that I may always hear You.

The Lord Provides a Sign

But Ahaz said, "I will not ask, nor will I test the Lord!" Then he said, "Listen now, O house of David! Is it too slight a thing for you to try the patience of men, that you will try the patience of my God as well? Therefore the Lord Himself will give you a sign: Behold, a virgin will be with child and bear a son, and she will call His name Immanuel." Isaiah 7:12, 14

In the days of Ahaz, king of Judah, two other kings went up to Jerusalem to wage war but were unable to conquer it. Their foiled efforts did not prevent King Ahaz from feeling apprehension bordering on terror.

At this point, the Lord spoke to Isaiah, saying, "Go out now to meet Ahaz. . .and say to him, 'Take care, and be calm, have no fear and do not be fainthearted. . .on account of the fierce anger of Rezin and Aram, and the son of Remaliah. Because Aram, with Ephraim and the son of Remaliah, has planned evil against you. . .It shall not stand nor shall it come to pass' " (Isaiah 7:3-5, 7).

The Lord then foretold the fact that within sixty-five years Ephraim would be shattered and no longer even a people. However, this word from the Lord wasn't sufficient proof for King Ahaz. Therefore, God said that He would provide a sign. This prediction of Christ's conception was delivered over 700 years before He was actually born (the fulfillment is recorded in Matthew 1:23). In announcing to Joseph that Mary was with child by the power of God's Spirit, the angel used these exact words from Isaiah.

Prayer — Lord, what You have said always comes to pass. While I may entertain thoughts about being "in charge," You're out there making things happen!

Jesus' Last Passover

And during the supper, the devil having already put into the heart of Judas Iscariot, the son of Simon, to betray Him, Jesus, knowing that the Father had given all things into His hands, and that He had come forth from God, and was going back to God, rose from supper, and laid aside His garments; and taking a towel, He girded Himself about. Then He poured water into the basin, and began to wash the disciples' feet, and to wipe them with the towel with which He was girded. John 13:2-5

In this one paragraph we are given reams of information about the last supper Jesus shared with His disciples. How difficult it must have been for Christ to say good-bye to them, knowing they still didn't fully comprehend His impending death! So Jesus set about to love them. By His example, He wanted to show them that they were called likewise to be servants.

Christ removed his outer garment and then placed the garb of a servant, a towel, about his waist. Then He began washing the dust from the disciples' feet. Usually a servant would administer this kindness to those who came in for the banquet supper. But the God who had created them desired that His followers know the depth of His humility. His gesture made them uncomfortable. When Peter balked as the Lord stooped to wash his feet, Jesus said, " 'Do you not know what I have done to you? You call Me Teacher and Lord; and you are right, for so I am. If I then, the Lord and the Teacher, washed your feet, you also ought to wash one another's feet' " (John 13:12-14).

Prayer — Lord, help me to cultivate the heart of a true servant.

The Day of the Lord

The oracle concerning Babylon which Isaiah the son of Amoz saw. Lift up a standard on the bare hill, Raise your voice to them, Wave the hand that they may enter the doors of the nobles. I have commanded My consecrated ones, I have even called My mighty warriors, My proudly exulting ones, To execute My anger. A sound of tumult on the mountains, Like that of many people! A sound of the uproar of kingdoms, Of nations gathered together! The Lord of hosts is mustering the army for battle. . .Wail, for the day of the Lord is near! It will come as destruction from the Almighty. Isaiah 13:1-4, 6

Many in our nation seemed prepared to rally behind General Colin Powell for President of the United States. However, he wasn't ready to answer the call. And nothing could entice him to run. But what instigated the call for a military officer to occupy the Oval Office? Terrorism.

When Isaiah wrote these verses Israel dwelled in the midst of just such a confusing time.

Isaiah's words are filled with prophecy, both imminent and in the far-distant future, concerning the impending destruction of the Babylonian Empire. Therefore, it may be difficult for you to separate which things are happening in Isaiah's day and which are reserved for what he terms the day of the Lord. For there is a specific time in history when the final judgment against the disobedient will take place.

Prayer — Lord, thank You for Your Word which contains not only the promise of salvation, but the promise of judgment.

A Counselor for the Troubled

"In My Father's house are many dwelling places." John 14:2

Jesus Christ has promised to prepare a place for us in heaven. Does it get any better than that? The only problem is that we have to wait down here until He's got our mansion ready for us. There are days when it's so hard to stay tied to earth, especially with the realization that a perfect place exists.

My father-in-law is now in the last stages of emphysema and each breath is excruciating for him. Consequently, we've talked about his true future elsewhere. "What if I don't like it there?" he posed during one of our conversations. I responded, "How can you possibly think you won't?"

Heaven is truly the place where God exists. John, the gospel writer, was given a vision of heaven so that we might know what it looks like. God's Spirit inspired him to record it in the Book of Revelation.

"Behold, a throne was standing in heaven, and One sitting on the throne. And He who was sitting was like a jasper stone and a sardius in appearance; and there was a rainbow around the throne, like an emerald in appearance . . . And from the throne proceed flashes of lightening and sounds and peals of thunder" (Revelation 4:2-3, 5).

Entertainers use special effects to hold the attention of their audiences. But God has the ultimate performance already prepared for us.

Prayer — Lord, thank You for the Holy Spirit, who brings us peace and comfort until we can be united with You in heaven.

The Ark of the Covenant

So the Philistines fought and Israel was defeated, and every man fled to his tent, and the slaughter was very great; for there fell of Israel thirty thousand foot soldiers. And the ark of God was taken; and the two sons of Eli, Hophni and Phinehas, died. 1 Samuel 4:10-11

Remember that prediction of the Lord, the message Samuel didn't want to deliver? Well, not only were the wicked sons of Eli put to death, but the sacred ark of the covenant was captured.

God had commanded the exact specifications for this ark. This was the portable altar which the Israelites took with them as they left Egypt and headed for the Promised Land.

The ark contained the tablets of the Ten Commandments, which God had inscribed with His own hand. Also in the ark were a lampstand of pure gold, the altar of incense, and the bronze altar. These were used for the sacrifices, along with a bronze laver where the priest washed before offering the sacrifice.

As long as the Israelites kept the ark of God with them, they were invincible to the nations which sought to conquer them, for the Lord's presence was among them. However, their defeat had taken place long before the ark had been captured. The Israelites had forsaken the true God, and He was about to teach them what life would be like without Him on their side.

For seven months the ark was gone.

Prayer — Heavenly Father, I know that You taught Israel a powerful lesson. May I never be guilty of such wickedness.

Samuel's Wicked Sons

*And it came about when Samuel was old that he appointed his
sons judges over Israel. . . His sons, however, did not walk in
his ways, but turned aside after dishonest gain and took bribes
and perverted justice. 1 Samuel 8:1, 3*

Remember when Eli's sons were such an abomination that
God not only removed them from being in the line of
judges, but let them die? How could Samuel have made the
same mistakes?

Well, he didn't. For unlike Eli, Samuel had walked in
obedience to God. His children just chose not to follow in
his footsteps of faith. "Then all the elders of Israel gathered
together and came to Samuel at Ramah; and they said to
him, 'Behold, you have grown old, and your sons do not
walk in your ways. Now appoint a king for us to judge us
like all the nations'" (1 Samuel 8:4-5).

These elders could readily see the wickedness of Samuel's
sons, yet they were blinded to their own inadequacies. They
asked for a human king, so they might be " 'like all the
nations.' " But they'd always been the envy of these other
nations, which knew that Israel's king was God Almighty.

Samuel sought the Lord's guidance in this matter.
"And the Lord said to Samuel, 'Listen to the voice of the
people in regard to all that they say to you, for they have not
rejected you, but they have rejected Me from being king
over them'" (1 Samuel 8:7).

Prayer — Lord, by giving Israel what they wanted You taught
them lessons they might never have learned. Give me insight
to make the right choices in my life.

Jesus, the True Vine

*"I am the true vine, and My Father is the vinedresser. Every
branch in Me that does not bear fruit, He takes away; and
every branch that bears fruit, He prunes it, that it may bear
more fruit. You are already clean because of the word which I
have spoken to you. Abide in Me, and I in you. As the branch
cannot bear fruit of itself, unless it abides in the vine, so neither
can you, unless you abide in Me. I am the vine, you are the
branches; he who abides in Me, and I in him, he bears much
fruit; for apart from Me you can do nothing."*
John 15:1-5

Christ used word pictures to clarify concepts to His followers. And this parable about the vine and the branches was
extremely familiar to them.

Consider Isaiah 5:1-4: "Let me sing now for my well-
beloved a song of my beloved concerning His vineyard. My
well-beloved had a vineyard on a fertile hill. And He dug it
all around, removed its stones, and planted it with the
choicest vine. And He built a tower in the middle of it, and
hewed out a wine vat in it; then He expected it to produce
good grapes, but it produced only worthless ones. 'And now,
O inhabitants of Jerusalem and men of Judah, judge
between Me and My vineyard. What more was there to do
for My vineyard that I have not done in it?' " No matter how
faithful God was, Israel was still disobedient.

This same offer to abide in the vine is extended to all
who hear the Gospel message. Have you responded? And
how diligently are you abiding?

Prayer — Lord, help me to abide in You.

Dependence Day

*"Then the glory of the Lord will be revealed, And all flesh will
see it together; For the mouth of the Lord has spoken."*
Isaiah 40:5

No, today's title is not misspelled, and no, I'm not thinking
of Independence Day. Only when we are totally dependent
on our Redeemer are we are truly free!

Carefully woven throughout chapters forty to sixty-six
of Isaiah are specific portraits of Christ, presented by the
names He called Himself throughout His ministry on earth.
"Like a shepherd He will tend His flock, In His arm He will
gather the lambs, And carry them in His bosom; He will
gently lead the nursing ewes" (Isaiah 40:11).

Then we see Him as the Counselor. "Who has directed
the Spirit of the Lord, or as His counselor has informed
Him?" (Isaiah 40:13)

We can know Him as Creator. "Do you not know?
Have you not heard? The Everlasting God, the Lord, the
Creator of the ends of the earth Does not become weary or
tired. His understanding is inscrutable" (Isaiah 40:28).

Jesus is the First and the Last. " 'Who has performed
and accomplished it, Calling forth the generations from the
beginning? I, the Lord, am the first, and with the last. I am
He' " (Isaiah 41:4). Christ clarifies this further in Revelation
1:8: " 'I am the Alpha and Omega,' says the Lord God, 'who
is and who was and who is to come, the Almighty.' "

Prayer — Lord Jesus, I rejoice in the words from Isaiah 53:
4-6, that You came to be my Redeemer. Hallelujah! Amen!

A New Name for Israel

For Zion's sake I will not keep silent, And for Jerusalem's sake I will not keep quiet, Until her righteousness goes forth like brightness, And her salvation like a torch that is burning. And the nations will see your righteousness, And all kings your glory, And you will be called by a new name, which the mouth of the Lord will designate. Isaiah 62:1-2

Whenever God sets about to perform a work of regeneration He also provides a new name. For instance, Abraham was known simply as *Abram* prior to God's promise that he would be the father of a great nation (Genesis 17:1, 5-6).

Similarly, God changed Jacob's name to Israel, and he became the father of the twelve tribes of Israel (Genesis 32:28).

Then there are the passages we've studied concerning the names God picked out for people before they were even born. Zechariah was told to name his son John. Mary and Joseph were told that our Savior's name was to be Jesus Christ.

In today's Scripture the Lord is addressing His people's repeated disobedience which has caused Israel's name to became synonymous with "Forsaken" and "Desolate" (Isaiah 62:4). However, they will one day become the Redeemed of the Lord, God's Holy People. Then they will be called, "Sought out, a city not forsaken" (Isaiah 62:12).

Prayer — Lord, my name remains the same, but my heart is forever changed by Your love.

The Role of the Holy Spirit

"But I tell you the truth, it is to your advantage that I go away;
for if I do not go away, the Helper shall not come to you;
but if I go, I will send Him to you. And He, when He comes,
will convict the world concerning sin, and righteousness,
and judgment." John 16:7–8

Have you ever encountered someone who seems to have no spiritual awareness and seems oblivious to her loss? The Holy Spirit must first awaken a person to commune with God.

At Pentecost, fifty days after the Resurrection, "suddenly there came from heaven a noise like a violent, rushing wind, and it filled the whole house where they were sitting. And there appeared to them tongues as of fire distributing themselves, and they rested on each one of them. And they were all filled with the Holy Spirit and began to speak with other tongues, as the Spirit was giving them utterance" (Acts 2:2-4).

The Holy Spirit was presented to the disciples as a tongue of fire, that they might have visible proof of His appearance. For they had to know that God's Spirit, which in the past had come upon men and women for equipping, now dwelt inside them. The Holy Spirit would be with them every moment to guide, and to convict the world concerning sin, righteousness, and judgment. Are you aware of these things in your own life?

Prayer — Lord, You gave the disciples the ability to speak forth Your powerful Word to others. And the Gospel message went out. I rejoice that I no longer have to live in spiritual blindness.

Saul, Israel's King

Now there was a man of Benjamin whose name was Kish the son of Abiel, the son of Zertor, the son of Becorath, the son of Aphiah, the son of a Benjamite, a mighty man of valor. And he had a son whose name was Saul, a choice and handsome man, and there was not a more handsome person than he among the sons of Israel; from his shoulders and up he was taller than any of the people. 1 Samuel 9:1-2

Isn't that exactly what our society looks for in the way of leaders? One who is tall and handsome and reeks of success! But outward appearance means nothing if that person isn't fully committed to God.

Saul had been on a mission. It seems that his father's donkeys had gotten loose. As Saul and his servant went from place to place attempting to track them down, they reached the land of Zuph and frustrated, decided to return home. But this servant knew that there was a man of God in the town and he encouraged Saul to speak to the man.

Of course, God had already prepared Samuel's heart: " 'About this time tomorrow I will send you a man from the land of Benjamin, and you shall anoint him to be prince over My people Israel, and he shall deliver My people from the hand of the Philistines. For I have regarded My people, because their cry has come to Me' " (1 Samuel 9:16).

God chose Saul to be Israel's king so that this nation might eventually learn their need for spiritual discernment.

Prayer — Lord, when I seek a direction which You have neither sanctioned nor initiated, please reveal the truth to me, that I might not have to learn life's lessons the hard way.

Heaven His Throne, Earth His Footstool

"Heaven is My throne, and the earth is My footstool.
Where then is a house you could build for Me?
And where is a place that I may rest?
For My hand made all these things,
Thus all these things came into being,"
declares the Lord. Isaiah 66:1-2

During their flight from Egypt, the Israelites had known the presence of the Lord in their traveling temple. Hundreds of years later, God instilled in King David's heart the desire to make a permanent temple. Although David gathered most of the treasured items which would comprise the temple, Solomon, his son, saw to the actual building (2 Samuel 7:5, 13).

In the New Testament, we see this concept of God's authority being established both in heaven and on earth. " 'But I say to you, make no oath at all, either by heaven, for it is the throne of God, or by the earth, for it is the footstool of His feet, or by Jerusalem, for it is the city of the great king' " (Matthew 5:34-35).

The temple was the earthly place that God established for worship, so that men and women could fellowship together in praise of their Creator. However, true worship begins in our hearts. To the woman at the well Jesus said, " 'But an hour is coming, and now is, when the true worshipers shall worship the Father in spirit and truth; for such people the Father seeks to be His worshipers. God is spirit; and those who worship Him must worship in spirit and truth' " (John 4:23-24).

Jesus Christ is not only our Creator, but He is head of the Church and the world is His footstool.

Prayer — Lord, You have said, "For in Him all things were created. . .all things have been created through Him and for Him" (Colossians 1:16). I serve the Creator!

An Intimate Conversation

"And this is eternal life, that they may know Thee, the only true God, and Jesus Christ whom Thou has sent. I glorified Thee on earth, having accomplished the work which Thou hast given Me to do. And now, glorify Thou Me together with Thyself, Father, with the glory which I had with Thee before the world was." John 17:3-5

Have you ever unwittingly overheard an intimate conversation? Well, that's exactly what this chapter of John is like. We are privileged to overhear Jesus as He speaks to the Father.

Christ was with the Father before the world was. That makes Him not only eternal but equal with the Father. These are the claims Jesus made to the Pharisees who constantly confronted Him concerning His origin.

Christ's prayer to the Father also includes concern for whom the Father has given to Him. "'I manifested Thy name to the men whom Thou gavest Me out of the world; Thine they were, and Thou gavest them to Me, and they have kept Thy Word'" (John 17:6). Notice that these are the people who respond to God's message and keep His Word.

Then Jesus also asks the Father to keep us in His name. "'Holy Father, keep them in Thy name, the name which Thou has given Me, that they may be one, even as We are'" (John 17:11). Christ prayed that God's power would keep us from being swayed by the world and the evil one (John 17:15).

Prayer — Lord Jesus Christ, I acknowledge You as God and Savior.

Called to Conquer?

"About this time tomorrow I will send you a man from the land of Benjamin, and you shall anoint him to be prince over my people Israel; and he shall deliver My people from the hand of the Philistines." 1 Samuel 9:16

Despite Israel's repeated disobedience, God continued to love Israel and respond to the people's requests. And although the Israelites stubbornly refused to allow Him to rule over them as King, they did desire an earthly king.

When Saul met with Samuel, Samuel, acting as mediator between God and man, related that the donkeys Saul had been seeking were now found. Samuel confirmed that this special leadership call was from the Lord. "Then Samuel took the flask of oil, poured it on his head, kissed him and said, 'Has not the Lord anointed you a ruler over His inheritance?'" (1 Samuel 10:1)

God had already prepared a celebration for Saul, befitting his royal status. And the Lord instructed him to go to the oak of Tabor, a sacred spot where Jacob had built an altar when God had revealed Himself to him (Genesis 35:6, 7; 1 Samuel 10:3).

Notice that Saul's call was to conquer the Philistines. His anointing had been done secretly, but now Samuel assembled all Israel and "the tribe of Benjamin was taken by lot" (1 Samuel 10:20). When Saul failed to appear ". . .they inquired further of the Lord. . .So the Lord said, 'Behold, he is hiding himself by the baggage'" (1 Samuel 10:22).

Prayer — Lord, help me trust in Your strength to instill, infuse, and instruct so that I serve You obediently.

Jeremiah's Revival

Now the word of the Lord came to me saying, "Before I formed you in the womb I knew you, And before you were born I consecrated you; I have appointed you a prophet to the nations."
Jeremiah 1:4-5

Knowing that he was called, chosen, and consecrated should have given Jeremiah a great deal of confidence. However, like any true prophet, he felt consumed because of his own inadequacies. "Then I said, 'Alas, Lord God! Behold, I do not know how to speak, Because I am a youth'" (Jeremiah 1:6).

"But the Lord said to me, 'Do not say, "I am a youth," Because everywhere I send you, you shall go, And all that I command you, you shall speak. Do not be afraid of them, For I am with you to deliver you,' declares the Lord. Then the Lord stretched out His hand and touched my mouth, and the Lord said to me, 'Behold, I have put My words in your mouth'" (Jeremiah 1:7-9). And Jeremiah proceeded forward, fulfilling his mission.

Jeremiah prophesied prior to and during Babylon's three sieges of Judah. Revival came when the Word of the Lord was found in the house of God as Josiah, the last king of Judah, called the people to repentance. However, following this great time of worship, Israel's disobedience once again set in, bringing upon them yet again God's heavy hand of judgment. And Jeremiah the prophet wept.

Prayer — Lord, I pray for answers to the dilemmas which plague our society. Not knowing whom You have called for special service, let me respect and revere each life with hope, anticipation, and gratitude.

Jesus Is Arrested and Tried

Jesus. . .went forth with His disciples over the ravine of the Kidron, where there was a garden. . .Now Judas also, who was betraying Him, knew the place; for Jesus had often met there with His disciples. John 18:1-2

What could possibly be worse than being betrayed? Having the one who is disloyal rise up from among those who called you friend!

Although Judas Iscariot, one of the twelve disciples, had walked in step with the others, pretending to believe all that Jesus taught, secretly he waited for Christ to overthrow the Roman government. But when Jesus began speaking of His death, Judas knew this rebellion would never occur. Therefore he struck a deal with the chief priests.

Judas's scheme was calculated, and well-planned. When the capture was imminent, Judas handed Jesus over to the authorities for thirty pieces of silver (Matthew 26:15). This exact amount of silver had been prophesied in the Old Testament, in Zechariah 11:12-13.

Suddenly the tranquility of the garden was transformed into a scene of treachery as Judas led the Roman soldiers, chief priests, and Pharisees toward Christ where he betrayed Him with a kiss (Luke 22:47-48). Did membership in this treacherous mob impart courage to Judas? We only know that later he would completely despair of his action and commit suicide.

Prayer — Lord, make straight my wavering path! Help me abide in Your truth with confidence.

Saul's Reign Ends in Disgrace

"Fill your horn with oil, and go; I will send you to Jesse the Bethlehemite, for I have selected a king for Myself among his sons." 1 Samuel 16:1

Saul's outward appearance had made him the people's choice. But God knew the content of his heart. When it came time for him to be publicly announced to Israel, Saul was " 'hiding himself by the baggage' " (1 Samuel 10:22). "Saul was forty years old when he began to reign, and he reigned thirty-two years over Israel" (1 Samuel 13:1). Saul had been summoned by the Lord for service in an extremely responsible position. Yet here he is, a forty-year-old man, shirking from his first official presentation. He had relied on his own strength and it had failed him. This character flaw eventually brought him down to complete disgrace.

Poised and ready for battle against the Philistines, Saul grew tired of waiting for Samuel to come and offer a burnt offering to the Lord to ensure the victory. Therefore, Saul offered it himself (1 Samuel 13:11-14). He had usurped the God-given role of Samuel.

"Then the word of the Lord came to Samuel, saying, 'I regret that I have made Saul king, for he has turned back from following Me, and has not carried out My commands'" (1 Samuel 15:10-11). And so in today's Scripture we read that the Lord chose another king.

Prayer — Lord, keep me from misusing the power and authority You give me.

Jeremiah's Vision

"For, behold, I am calling all the families of the kingdoms of the north," declares the Lord; "and they will come, and they will set each one his throne at the entrance of the gates of Jerusalem, and against all its walls round about, and against all the cities of Judah. And I will pronounce My judgments on them concerning all their wickedness, whereby they have forsaken Me and have offered sacrifices to other gods, and worshiped the works of their own hands." Jeremiah 1:15-16

Israel's roller-coaster ride of faithfulness had once again begun its downward plunge. Despite all God's warnings, the people failed to responded to Him unless they were in dire pain. Therefore, the Lord encourages Jeremiah by saying, " 'Now, gird up your loins, and arise, and speak to them all which I command you. Do not be dismayed before them, lest I dismay you before them. . .And they will fight against you, but they will not overcome you, for I am with you to deliver you' " (Jeremiah 1:17, 19).

We humans are resilient, able to withstand almost any hardship as long as we know we're not abandoned. God always provides a way through, for Israel and for us. His instructions to Israel read almost like a love letter: " 'I remember concerning you the devotion of your youth, the love of your betrothals, your following after Me in the wilderness, through a land not sown. Israel was holy to the Lord, the first of His harvest. . .' " (Jeremiah 2:2-3).

Prayer — Lord, if I'm about to head off in the wrong direction, please call me back. I'll never be truly happy apart from You.

Question the Witnesses

The high priest therefore questioned Jesus about His disciples, and about His teaching. Jesus answered him, "I have spoken openly to the world; I always taught in synagogues, and in the temple, where all the Jews come together; and I spoke nothing in secret. Why do you question Me? Question those who have heard what I spoke to them; behold, these know what I said."
John 18:19-21

In our courts of law the jury is instructed to listen carefully and then weigh the testimony in order to make a proper judgment. Christ calls the high priest to do the same.

How do we respond to the truth of Christ's testimony? How we treat His messengers is, in effect, a measure of our acceptance of Him.

Jesus Christ didn't come for a few souls; He presented the Gospel message openly for all to hear. Teaching in the Jewish temple, which was frequented not only by those who sought knowledge but also those in search of an explanation of the truth, Jesus provided both.

As we go out into a world that is hostile to the Gospel message, there are those who listen to our testimony and then draw near to its refreshing waters. Others sit on the river banks, vowing that nothing will force them to make a life change. And then there are those who deny the metamorphosis has even taken place. Their hearts are closed to receive the truth.

Prayer — Lord, break down my walls of stubbornness which prevent me from hearing, seeing, and rallying to Your message.

David Slings a Stone

"Who is this uncircumcised Philistine, that he should taunt the armies of the living God?" 1 Samuel 17:26

David, while still a youth, came up against a giant of a man. "Then a champion came out from the armies of the Philistines named Goliath, from Gath, whose height was six cubits and a span" (1 Samuel 17:4).

This superhuman specimen had the audacity to taunt Israel's God. And David refused to allow this attitude to stand unchallenged.

Then David said to the Philistine, " 'You come to me with a sword, a spear, and a javelin, but I come to you in the name of the Lord of hosts, the God of the armies of Israel, whom you have taunted. This day the Lord will deliver you up into my hands, and I will strike you down and remove your head from you. And I will give the dead bodies of the army of the Philistines this day to the birds of the sky and the wild beasts of the earth, that all the earth may know that there is a God in Israel' " (1 Samuel 17:45-46).

"And David put his hand into his bag and took from it a stone and slung it, and struck the Philistine on his forehead. And the stone sank into his forehead, so that he fell on his face to the ground" (1 Samuel 17:49).

Prayer — David's victory came by the power of the Lord, not by man's might. Lord, remind me of this when I face my own "giants."

A Promise of Unity

"In those days. . . ," declares the Lord, "they shall say no more,
'The ark of the covenant of the Lord.' And it shall not come to
mind, nor shall they remember it, nor shall they miss it, nor shall
it be made again. At that time they shall call Jerusalem 'The
Throne of the Lord,' and all the nations will be gathered to it,
for the name of the Lord in Jerusalem,; nor shall they walk any
more after the stubbornness of their evil heart. In those days the
house of Judah will walk with the house of Israel, and they will
come together from the land of the north to the land that I gave
your fathers as an inheritance." Jeremiah 3:16–18

Jeremiah delivered hope to the people of Israel during Judah's three-stage siege.

This three-pronged prophecy also related God's future plans for Israel. First, the ark of the covenant would be gone, not remembered, and never made again. Next, Jerusalem would be called "The Throne of the Lord," where all nations would be gathered in the name of the Lord. Finally, the houses of Judah and Israel, separated due to the Babylonian captivity, would once again be united.

In the year 586 B.C., Solomon's temple was utterly destroyed. At the same time, the ark of the covenant was lost. God's glory had departed from Israel. For this reason, God's confirmation that Jerusalem would once again become the center for worship became critically important. During King Herod's reign the temple was rebuilt, fulfilling part of this prophecy. And when Jesus Christ came, it had once again become the center of worship.

Prayer — True peace will reign in Israel when Christ returns again to earth (Matthew 24:29-39). Lord, help me wait!

A Sign on the Cross

*And Pilate wrote an inscription also, and put it on the cross.
And it was written, "Jesus the Nazarene, the King of the
Jews." Therefore this inscription many of the Jews read,
for the place where Jesus was crucified was near the city;
and it was written in Hebrew, Latin, and in Greek.
And so the chief priests of the Jews were saying to Pilate,
"Do not write, 'The King of the Jews'; but that He said, 'I am
King of the Jews.' Pilate answered, 'What I have written I
have written.' " John 19:18-22*

The sign of the cross is used by many to bless themselves
before they pray. It is a reminder of Calvary's cross and the
great sacrifice Christ made for us there. But it was the sign
over the cross which caused so much furor in the first
century. Indeed, God overruled the Jews' request when Pilate
refused to change what had been written. Pilate knew Christ
was exactly who He claimed to be, King of the Jews, the
promised Messiah.

But Pilate had to live in this place long after Christ was
gone and he chose not to be the instigator of an uprising. Just
moments before, the people had shouted, " 'If you release this
man, you are no friend of Caesar; every one who makes
himself out to be a king opposes Caesar' " (John 19:12).

Pilate had already stated, " 'Behold, I am bringing Him
out to you, that you may know that I find no guilt in Him' "
(John 19:4). Yet Pilate lacked the gumption to stand by his
strong conviction.

Prayer — Lord, give me the courage to stand firmly in my
convictions.

The Lord's Anointed

"Behold, this day your eyes have seen that the Lord had given you today into my hand in the cave, and some said to kill you, but my eye had pity on you; and I said, 'I will not stretch out my hand against my lord, for he is the Lord's anointed.' Now, my father, see! Indeed, see the edge of your robe in my hand! For in that I cut off the edge of your robe and did not kill you, know and perceive that there is no evil or rebellion in my hands, and I have not sinned against you, though you are lying in wait for my life to take it." 1 Samuel 24:10-11

Saul's rejection by God fueled his anger, causing his vengeful spirit to pursue David relentlessly.

David and his band of men came upon Saul as he slept. And David's followers suggested that he kill Saul. However, David settled for cutting off a small corner of Saul's robe as a gesture of his love and respect for God's anointed (1 Samuel 24:5).

David then relates this incident to Saul. " 'The Lord therefore be judge and decide between you and me; and may He see and plead my cause, and deliver me from your hand' " (1 Samuel 24:15). Despite his circumstances and discomfort, David would allow the Lord charge over this matter.

Saul responded by weeping. Then he said to David, " 'You are more righteous than I; for you have dealt well with me, while I have dealt wickedly with you. . .and now, behold, I know that you shall surely be king, and that the kingdom of Israel shall be established in your hand' " (1 Samuel 24:17, 20).

Prayer — Lord, curb my stubborn, wrongful desires.

Christ as Mediator

"Their Redeemer is strong, the Lord of hosts is His name;
He will vigorously plead their case, so that He may bring rest
to the earth, but turmoil to the inhabitants of Babylon."
Jeremiah 50:34

This Scripture speaks of Judah's Redeemer. Who is this Redeemer? "For there is one God, and one mediator also between God and men the man Christ Jesus, who gave Himself as a ransom for all, the testimony borne at the proper time" (1 Timothy 2:5-6).

How do we know that Christ is the same mediator spoken of in both the Old and New Testaments? Again, we look to Scripture. "Now the promises were spoken to Abraham and to his seed. He does not say, 'And to seeds,' as referring to many, but rather to one, 'And to your seed,' that is, Christ. What I am saying is this: the Law, which came four hundred and thirty years later, does not invalidate a covenant previously ratified by God, so as to nullify the promise. . .Now a mediator is not for one party only; whereas God is only one . . .For you are all sons of God through faith in Christ Jesus" (Galatians 3:16-17, 20, 26).

Abraham looked forward in time to redemption by the Messiah, while we take a view back in time to the cross on which our Redeemer died. Christ then becomes the central focus, for both the Old and New Testaments.

Prayer — Lord, I'm grateful that the cross of Christ has provided a clear path to You, Father.

Crown of Mockery

Then Pilate therefore took Jesus, and scourged Him. And the soldiers wove a crown of thorns and put it on His head, and arrayed Him in a purple robe; and they began to come up to Him, and say, "Hail, King of the Jews!" and to give Him blows in the face. John 19:1-3

They pretended to shower Him with all the outward trappings of royalty. But this homage was one of cruel mockery. The thorns were razor-sharp briars about an inch and a half long. We can only imagine the taunting voices of these men, triumphant glances spreading across their faces as they pressed this crown into Christ's head until blood ran down His face.

Then the men handed Him "a reed in His right hand; and they kneeled down before Him and mocked Him saying, 'Hail, King of the Jews!' And they spat on Him, and took the reed and began to beat Him on the head. And after they had mocked Him, they took His robe off and put His garments on Him, and led Him away to crucify Him" (Matthew 27: 29-31). This action fulfilled the prophetic Psalm 22:18: "They divide my garments among them, and for my clothing they cast lots."

"He was despised and forsaken of men, A man of sorrows, and acquainted with grief; And like one from whom men hide their face, He was despised, and we did not esteem Him" (Isaiah 53:3).

Prayer — Lord, in my behalf You withstood extreme torture. Am I adding new but invisible wounds each time I refuse to crown You King of my own life?

Jonathan, Faithful to the End

Now the Philistines were fighting against Israel, and the men of Israel fled from before the Philistines and fell slain on Mount Gilboa. And the Philistines overtook Saul and his sons; and the Philistines killed Jonathan and Abinadab and Malachi-shua the sons of Saul. 1 Samuel 31:1-2

Who has faithfully stood beside you through life's triumphs and tragedies? For David this person was Jonathan.

Jonathan walked a tightrope, remaining faithful to God, to Saul, his father, and to David. Considering Saul's obsession with killing David, this task took on monstrous proportions.

Their friendship began shortly after David killed the giant Goliath. Jonathan even gave David his "armor, including his sword and bow and belt" (1 Samuel 18:4). And how quickly David would need these weapons! David's accomplishments in battle became the stuff of legend and song, and this, of course, enraged Saul.

From then on Jonathan's time was spent trying to help David keep one step ahead of Saul. "So Jonathan told David saying, 'Saul my father is seeking to put you to death. Now therefore, please be on guard in the morning, and stay in a secret place and hide yourself. And I will go out and stand beside my father in the field where you are, and I will speak with my father about you; if I find out anything, then I shall tell you'" (1 Samuel 19:2-3).

Prayer — Father, help me to be a faithful, loving, and unforgettable friend.

His Glory Has Departed

*The Lord has become like an enemy. He has swallowed up
Israel. . .And He has violently treated His tabernacle like a
garden booth; He has destroyed His appointed meeting place;
The appointed feast and Sabbath in Zion, And he has despised
king and priest In the indignation of His anger. The Lord has
rejected His altar; He has abandoned His sanctuary; He has
delivered into the hand of the enemy The walls of her palaces.*
Lamentations 2:5-7

Carefully carved into the top of the wooden entry doors
of the Precious Moments Chapel in Carthage, Missouri, are
the words of Habakkuk 2:20: " 'But the Lord is in His holy
temple. Let all the earth be silent before Him.' " This is in
direct contrast to the sense of abandonment which Israel
felt in today's Scripture.

Sam Butcher created his first Precious Moments draw-
ing in 1974, the series was introduced to the public in 1975,
and the rest is history. God has honored and blessed Sam's
work because he has revered Him, even to the point of building a chapel where people can come and view the Scriptures
portrayed through his artwork.

The Book of Lamentations was read annually by the
Jews as a reminder of the fall of Jerusalem and the destruction of the temple. The words were meant to remind Israel
of all they'd lost as a result of their refusal to worship the
true God.

Prayer — Lord, instill in my heart a reverence for Your
house. May I worship You in Spirit and in truth.

The First to View the Resurrection

Mary Magdalene came early to the tomb, while it was still dark, and saw the stone already taken away from the tomb. And so she ran and came to Simon Peter, and to the other disciple whom Jesus loved, and said to them, "They have taken away the Lord out of the tomb, and we do not know where they have laid Him." John 20:1-2

If only the disciples had understood the Scriptures concerning Christ's resurrection.

Peter and John ran to the tomb, viewed the linen wrappings, and then left again (John 20:8-10). They left too soon, missing the miracle. "But Mary was standing outside the tomb weeping; and so, as she wept, she stooped and looked into the tomb; and she beheld two angels in white sitting, one at the head, and one at the feet, where the body of Jesus had been lying. And they said to her, 'Woman, why are you weeping?' She said to them, 'Because they have taken away my Lord, and I do not know where they have laid Him.' When she had said this, she turned around, and beheld Jesus standing there, and did not know that it was Jesus" (John 20:11-14).

Mary supposed that Christ was a gardener. Therefore, she said to him, " 'Sir, if you have carried Him away, tell me where you have laid Him, and I will take Him away' " (John 20:15).

But then He said, " 'Mary!' " And the sound of His voice calmed her frantic fears, dried her tears, and warmed her heart.

Prayer — Lord, many times I miss the miracle You have already prepared. Open my eyes!

David Learns of Saul's Death

*"The people have fled from battle, and also many of the people
have fallen and are dead; and Saul and Jonathan his son are
dead also." 2 Samuel 1:4*

A young Amalekite man had related to David that Saul and
Jonathan were dead. Then he confessed that Saul had been
impaled on his own sword and begged him to kill him. After
complying with this request, the Amalekite then removed
the crown from Saul's head and the bracelet which was on
his arm and brought these royal ornaments to David.

First David led Israel in a time of mourning for Saul.
"Then David took hold of his clothes and tore them, and so
also did all the men who were with him. And they mourned
and wept and fasted until evening" (2 Samuel 1:11-12).

Following this expression of sorrow came a time of
retribution. "Then David said to him, 'How is it you were
not afraid to stretch out your hand to destroy the Lord's
anointed?' And David called one of the young men and
said, 'Go, cut him down.' So he struck him and he died"
(2 Samuel 1:14-15).

David poured forth his personal anguish by writing a
song for Saul and Jonathan. One verse reads, " 'Saul and
Jonathan, beloved and pleasant in their life, and in their
death they were not parted; they were swifter than eagles,
they were stronger than lions' " (2 Samuel 1:23).

Prayer — Lord, what an example David was, as he refused to
gloat over Saul's death. David turned to You and requested
guidance, and You gave him a fresh call to leadership. I
rejoice!

Ezekiel's Call

While I was by the river Chebar among the exiles, the heavens were opened and I saw visions of God. (On the fifth of the month in the fifth year of King Jehoiachin's exile, the word of the Lord came expressly to Ezekiel the priest, son of Buzi, in the land of the Chaldeans by the river Chebar; and there the hand of the Lord came upon him.) Ezekiel 1:1-3

Sometimes God's plans are so different from what we expect to be doing with our lives that it's really astonishing.

Although he was only eighteen years old when some of the nobles and princes were captured by King Nebuchadnezzar and taken from Judah to Babylon, Ezekiel had already been groomed for the priesthood.

Ezekiel's life plan became forever altered ten years later, in 597 B.C., when he was among those taken in Nebuchadnezzar's second siege against Jerusalem. Never again would he view the temple where he had hoped to serve God. However, when he was thirty years old the Lord gave him a vision of a new temple and another Jerusalem. His call was to prophesy concerning Judah and Jerusalem, Israel's coming restoration, and the temple.

Ezekiel's visions parallel those of John recorded in the Book of Revelation. These dreams show that no matter how bleak Israel's present situation might be, their future would be bright.

Prayer — Lord, despite my own problems and challenges I can keep going forward as long as You show me a vision of hope. As I read the prophecies of Ezekiel, fill me with expectation!

Jesus Holds a Fish Fry

*But when the day was now breaking, Jesus stood on the beach;
yet the disciples did not know that it was Jesus. Jesus therefore
said to them, "Children, you do not have any fish, do you?"
They answered Him, "No." And He said to them, "Cast the net
on the right-hand side of the boat, and you will find a catch."
They cast therefore, and then they were not able to haul it in
because of the great number of fish. John 21:4-6*

It was shortly after the Resurrection and the third time
Christ had appeared to the disciples in their familiar work
setting. Remember when Jesus first called them, promising
to make them " 'fishers of men' "? He would bolster their
aching souls that they might fulfill this call.

Here Christ renewed His leadership invitation to Peter,
asking him three times if Peter loved Him. Peter's answer in
the affirmative publicly restored their relationship.

Peter would die for Christ. " 'Truly, truly I say to you,
when you were younger, you used to gird yourself, and walk
wherever you wished; but when you grow old, you will
stretch out your hands, and someone else will gird you, and
bring you where you do not wish to go.' Now this He said,
signifying by what kind of death he would glorify God. And
when He had spoken this, He said to him, 'Follow Me!' "
(John 21:18-19)

When Peter requested information concerning the
future of the disciple John, Jesus replied, " 'If I want him to
remain until I come, what is that to you? You follow Me!' "
(John 21:22)

Prayer — Lord, in this special encounter You call me to be
accountable for my own walk with You. Please enable me!

David, King of Judah and Israel

*And David brought up his men who were with him, each with
his household; and they lived in the cities of Hebron. Then the
men of Judah came and there anointed David king over the
house of Judah. 2 Samuel 2:3-4*

We assume that once God makes His choice in a leader that
everyone else then follows that person. Nothing could be
further from the truth. Since Ish-bosheth, one of Saul's sons,
had survived the massacre, Abner, the son of Ner, commander
of Saul's army, made him king over Gilead and even over all
Israel (2 Samuel 2:8-10). Ish-bosheth ruled in Gilead for two
years, while the house of Judah followed David.

As time went on, Saul's son continued to cause division
between Judah and the rest of the tribes known as Israel. But
God was still faithful. "So all the elders of Israel came to the
king of Hebron, and King David made a covenant with them
before the Lord at Hebron; then they anointed David king
over Israel. David was thirty years old when he became king,
and he reigned forty years. At Hebron he reigned over Judah
seven years and six months, and in Jerusalem he reigned
thirty-three years over all Israel and Judah. . .And David
became greater and greater, for the Lord God of hosts was
with him" (2 Samuel 5:3-5, 10).

Prayer — Lord, I know that You appointed David as king of
Israel, uniting Your chosen people. May I submit my own
life to You that You might use me to create unity among
believers.

Ezekiel Speaks to the Lost

Then He said to me, "Son of man, go to the house of Israel and speak with My words to them." Ezekiel 3:4

How did you become a Christian? By hearing the Word of God? That's the way I came to know Him as Savior. We respond to the message of truth which is given to us. The powerful Word of God convicts our hearts of sin and turns us toward the Lord.

Knowing this, the apostle Paul wrote, "For I am not ashamed of the gospel, for it is the power of God for salvation to everyone who believes, to the Jew first and also to the Greek. For in it the righteousness of God is revealed from faith to faith" (Romans 1:16-17). The same power which resurrected Christ can be with us today!

Did you wonder why the Gospel should be given "to the Jew first and also to the Greek"? All through history God has desired to communicate salvation to His chosen people, so that they could then bring this hope to the Gentiles. But when they refused to respond, He brought the message to all the unbelieving nations. And now we who are Gentiles are bringing the message back to the Jews. The Word is coming full circle.

At times we are unwilling to risk presenting the Gospel message because of personal rejection. However, the outcome isn't our problem, it's God's. And He says the same thing to us that He did to Ezekiel: " 'But you shall speak My words to them whether they listen or not, for they are rebellious' " (Ezekiel 2:7).

Prayer — Lord, help me depend on Your Word to accomplish all You intend, by Your powerful Spirit.

Christ Ascends into Heaven

"John baptized with water, but you shall be baptized with the Holy Spirit not many days from now." Acts 1:5

The disciples had learned how to live out the Christian life from observing Jesus Christ during His three years of ministry. Now they would watch Christ ascend to heaven; no longer would they speak to Him face-to-face. However, Jesus sent them His Spirit, that they might have God's power within them as His Church began.

During their last visit with Jesus, the disciples presented a burning question. "And so when they had come together, they were asking Him, saying, 'Lord, is it at this time You are restoring the kingdom to Israel?' He said to them, 'It is not for you to know times or epochs which the Father has fixed by His own authority; but you shall receive power when the Holy Spirit has come upon you; and you shall be My witnesses both in Jerusalem, and in all Judea and Samaria, and even to the remotest parts of the earth.' And after He had said these things, He was lifted up while they were looking on, and a cloud received Him out of their sight. And as they were gazing intently into the sky while He was departing, behold, two men in white clothing stood beside them; and they also said, 'Men of Galilee, why do you stand looking into the sky? This Jesus, who has been taken up from you into heaven, will come in just the same way as you have watched Him go into heaven'" (Acts 1:6-11).

Prayer — Lord, thank You for Luke's eyewitness account of Your ascension.

The Desire of David

The king said to Nathan the prophet, "See now, I dwell in a house of cedar, but the ark of God dwells within tent curtains." And Nathan said to the king, "Go, do all that is in your mind, for the Lord is with you." 2 Samuel 7:2-3

How can we truly discern the will of God in our lives? My own decision-making process is threefold. First, I pray, seeking God's wisdom concerning the issue. Next, I read His Word, making sure that what is in my heart isn't in conflict with His clear messages. And last, I look for confirming circumstances. When all three of these steps fall in line, I can be fairly certain that I am acting in obedience to God's will. And a final check is to ask my husband, who can provide additional insight.

Nathan the prophet supplied David with a quick agreement to his plan to build the temple. However, when Nathan inquired of the Lord he received a different answer. " 'Now therefore, thus you shall say to My servant David, "Thus says the Lord of hosts, 'I took you from the pasture, from following the sheep, that you should be ruler over My people Israel. . . When your days are complete. . .I will raise up your descendant after you, who will come forth from you, and I will establish his kingdom. He shall build a house for My name, and I will establish the throne of his kingdom forever' " ' " (2 Samuel 7:8, 12-13).

God chose Solomon, David's son, to build the temple. Nevertheless, David gathered all the gold, wood, and precious treasures which would comprise God's holy temple.

Prayer — Lord, help me discern Your will.

The Same Vision

Then the Spirit lifted me up, and I heard a great rumbling sound behind me, "Blessed be the glory of the Lord in His place." Ezekiel 2:12

Ezekiel's vision can be compared to one that John, the writer of the Gospel of John and the Book of Revelation, described.

John records, "After these things I looked, and behold, a door standing open in heaven, and the first voice which I had heard, like the sound of a trumpet speaking with me, said, 'Come up here, and I will show you what must take place after these things.' Immediately I was in the Spirit; and behold, a throne was standing in heaven, and One sitting on the throne" (Revelation 4:1-2).

Both saw Jesus sitting on His throne. Again, John says "And He who was sitting was like a jasper stone and a sardius in appearance; and there was a rainbow around the throne, like an emerald in appearance" (Revelation 4:3).

Ezekiel writes, "Now above the expanse that was over their heads was something resembling a throne, like lapis lazuli in appearance; and on that which resembled a throne, high up, was a figure with the appearance of a man. . .and there was a radiance around Him. As the appearance of the rainbow in the clouds on a rainy day, so was the appearance of the surrounding radiance. Such was the appearance of the likeness of the glory of the Lord" (Ezekiel 1:26-28).

Prayer — Lord, I'm so grateful that You have intricately woven Your Word for me. Thank You that Your very Spirit enables me to understand these difficult passages.

The Day of Pentecost

And when the day of Pentecost had come, they were all together in one place. And suddenly there came from heaven a noise like a violent, rushing wind, and it filled the whole house where they were sitting. And there appeared to them tongues as of fire distributing themselves, and they rested on each one of them. And they were all filled with the Holy Spirit and began to speak with other tongues, as the Spirit was giving them utterance. Acts 2:1-4

Pentecost was not new to the Jews, as they had observed this God-ordained feast for thousands of years (Leviticus 23: 16-21). But now Christ poured out His Spirit on those who believed in Him, fulfilling the promise and prophecy of Joel: " 'I will pour out My Spirit on all mankind; And your sons and daughters will prophesy, Your older men will dream dreams, Your young men will see visions. And even on the male and female servants I will pour out My Spirit in those days' " (Joel 2:28-29).

The Spirit of God speaks to and guides the Church. And there are angels who watch over the Church. " 'As for the mystery of the seven stars which you saw in My right hand, and the seven golden lampstands: the seven stars are the angels of the seven churches, and the seven lampstands are the seven churches' " (Revelation 1:20). The seven churches in the Book of Revelation typify the characteristics of the original first-century congregations from God's perspective, with both their strengths and weaknesses listed.

Prayer — I honor Your Holy Spirit, not only for insight into Your Word, but for the power to obey You.

David's Family Tree

Now when evening came David arose from his bed and walked around on the roof of the king's house, and from the roof he saw a woman bathing; and the woman was very beautiful in appearance. So David sent and inquired about the woman. And one said, "Is this not Bathsheba, the daughter of Eliam, the wife of Uriah the Hittite?" And David. . .lay with her; and when she had purified herself from her uncleanness, she returned to her house. And the woman conceived; and she sent and told David, and said, "I am pregnant." 2 Samuel 11:2-5

The Bible presents the true account of man's record on this earth, warts and all! Although David should have accompanied his men into battle against the sons of Ammon, he instead stayed home. And there was beautiful Bathsheba, washing herself on her rooftop in the warmth of the evening. At any rate, David succumbed to temptation, and Bathsheba later realized she was with child.

David knew Bathsheba was Uriah's wife but he seduced her anyway. But an even greater sin occurred as David tried to cover his tracks. He sent for Uriah and told him to go home, hoping that Uriah would then sleep with Bathsheba and all would appear fine. However, Uriah decided instead to deny himself the comforts which his soldiers on the battlefront were also lacking and instead he "slept at the door of the king's house with all the servants of his lord. . ." (2 Samuel 11:9).

David then implemented "plan B" and had Uriah sent to the front lines where he was killed. After a period of mourning David took Bathsheba to be his wife.

Prayer — Lord, help me to be accountable to You.

Always a Remnant

*"So as I live," declares the Lord God, "surely, because you have
defiled My sanctuary with all your detestable idols and with
all your abominations, therefore I will also withdraw,
and My eye shall have no pity and I will not spare."*
Ezekiel 5:11

Only the nation of Israel has managed to survive being scattered all over the globe and then come back to become a world power. How is this possible? God always preserves a remnant of His people. And it will be so until the end of time on this earth. " 'One third of you will die by plague or be consumed by famine among you, one third will fall by the sword around you, and one third I will scatter to every wind, and I will unsheathe a sword behind them' " (Ezekiel 5:12).

God is executing judgment on them because they abandoned their worship of the true God, choosing instead to adopt the ways of the pagan nations which surrounded them.

But how do we know this cycle will continue until the end of time? Four angels stand ready to execute God's judgment on the whole world. And they are restrained from action until "one hundred and forty-four thousand were sealed from every tribe of the sons of Israel" (Revelation 7:4). Twelve thousand from each of the tribes of Israel will be marked by God's own hand.

Many terrible plagues and judgments will take place upon the earth. However, God will bring this remnant of Israel safely through it all.

Prayer — Father, I rejoice in Your Word: " 'And then He will send forth the angels, and will gather together His elect. . .from the farthest end of the earth, to the farthest end of heaven' " (Mark 13:27).

At God's Right Hand

"Therefore having been exalted to the right hand of God, and having received from the Father the promise of the Holy Spirit, He has poured forth this which you both see and hear. For it was not David who ascended into heaven, but he himself says, 'The Lord said to my Lord, "Sit at my right hand, Until I make thine enemies a footstool for thy feet." ' Therefore let all the house of Israel know for certain that God has made Him both Lord and Christ—this Jesus whom you crucified." Acts 2:33-36

A fresh new boldness filled the disciples as they brought the message of salvation to the Jews who had come to Jerusalem for the Feast of Pentecost.

" 'Men of Israel, listen to these words: Jesus the Nazarene, a man attested to you by God with miracles and wonders and signs which God performed through Him in your midst, just as you yourselves know—this Man, delivered up by the predetermined plan and foreknowledge of God, you nailed to a cross by the hands of godless men and put Him to death. And God raised Him up again, putting an end to the agony of death, since it was impossible for Him to be held in its power' " (Acts 2:22-24).

Jesus Christ, the fulfillment of all that had been prophesied concerning their Redeemer, had become the bridge between the Old Testament and New Testament. Everything in their history had pointed to this moment.

Prayer — Lord, strengthen my faith today.

God Takes David's Child

"Because by this deed you have given occasion to the enemies of the Lord to blaspheme, the child also that is born to you shall surely die." 2 Samuel 12:14

The stillborn death of our first child was a devastating blow to my husband and me. I had contracted pneumonia during this pregnancy and, as a result, our child died. As I read this passage of David's suffering, my heart could readily identify with the pain he endured.

Is a child's death a sign that one of the parents has sinned? Of course not. However, in this particular case God took the child which David and Bathsheba had conceived in deliberate sin. David was the visible representation of authority to God's chosen people, the king which God had anointed to rule over them. He disobeyed and then flaunted his rebellious actions before the surrounding unbelieving nations. David had to be held accountable. How could a nation follow him if he failed to obey the God he supposedly served?

For seven days David fasted, wept, and prayed about his great sin, even as he watched his son become increasingly ill. And then the child died. However, he did not become bitter against God. Instead, David accepted God's judgment. "Then David comforted his wife Bathsheba, and went in to her and lay with her; and she gave birth to a son, and he named him Solomon" (2 Samuel 12:24).

Prayer — Lord, help me look to You for my own help, gracious Lord.

A False Peace

"So My hand will be against the prophets who see false visions and utter lying divinations. They will have no place in the council of My people, nor will they be written down in the register of the house of Israel, nor will they enter the land of Israel, that you may know that I am the Lord God. It is definitely because they have misled My people by saying, 'Peace!' when there is no peace." Ezekiel 13:9-10

People today get sick of hearing modern doomsday forecasters who shout, "Turn or burn." Those living in Ezekiel's day reacted the same way. They preferred to listen to those who preached a message of peace rather than the need for repentance.

I'll never forget one Thanksgiving Day prayer. The peace accord between Israel and Egypt had just been signed and so at the dinner table one of our relatives proclaimed that peace now reigned upon the earth. Although I knew he was sincere, I couldn't help but stare in amazement. Didn't he realize there would never be true peace until the Prince of Peace reigned in people's hearts? Of course, true to form, unrest began again.

Just as Ezekiel could not remain complacent in the midst of false peacegivers, those of our own day who know the truth are obligated to bring the message of repentance and salvation to others. How else will they hear and respond?

Prayer — Lord, help me to share Your truth or assist others to do so, even in the midst of an apathetic and, yes, hostile world.

Peter, Empowered and Bold

Then Peter, filled with the Holy Spirit, said to them, "Rulers and elders of the people, let it be known that. . .Jesus Christ the Nazarene, whom you crucified, whom God raised from the dead is the stone which was rejected by you, the builders, but which became the very corner stone. And there is salvation in no one else; for there is no other name under heaven that has been given among men, by which we must be saved."
Acts 4:8-12

Talk about a dynamic change! Remember when Christ was arrested and led off during the middle of the night? Peter had become instantly intimidated by the servant girl who recognized his Galilean accent and accused him of being a follower of Christ. Peter had then denied even knowing the Lord.

Now he demonstrates the powerful change which the Holy Spirit has infused into his being.

"The whole multitude of the disciples began to praise God joyfully with a loud voice for all the miracles which they had seen, saying, 'Blessed is the King who comes in the name of the Lord; Peace in heaven and glory in the highest!' And some of the Pharisees in the multitude said to Him, 'Teacher, rebuke Your disciples.' And He answered and said, 'I tell you, if these become silent, the stones will cry out!' " (Luke 19: 37-40) To know Him as Savior is too great a joy to be contained!

Prayer — Lord, Your Spirit fills me with indescribable hope. How can I possibly be silent about it? Hallelujah!

David's Rock, Fortress, and Deliverer

"The Lord is my rock and my fortress and my deliverer; My God, my rock, in whom I take refuge; My shield and the horn of my salvation, my stronghold and my refuge; My savior, Thou dost save me from violence." 2 Samuel 22:2-3

David's understanding of his Lord, using this concept of refuge, is a picture of the peace, comfort, and security we seek for our lives.

Although David spoke of the Rocks of the Wild Goats (1 Samuel 24:2), where he and his men hid from Saul, this analogy was also used to describe the believer's destination of spiritual serenity in the Rock, who is Christ.

David depended on the Lord as his Rock of faith. "Let the words of my mouth and the meditation of my heart Be acceptable in Thy sight, O Lord, my rock and my Redeemer" (Psalm 19:14).

However, to those who choose not to believe, Christ becomes only a stumbling block. "But Israel, pursuing a law of righteousness, did not arrive at that law. Why? Because they did not pursue it by faith, but as though it were by works. They stumbled over the stumbling stone, just as it is written, 'Behold, I lay in Zion a stone of stumbling and a rock of offense, And he who belives in Him will not be disappointed' " (Romans 9:30-33).

Prayer — I praise You only, Jesus, my Rock of Faith and Redeemer.

Daniel's Diet

But Daniel said to the overseer whom the commander of the officials had appointed over Daniel, Hananiah, Mishael and Azariah, "Please test your servants for ten days, and let us be given some vegetables to eat and water to drink. Then let our appearance be observed in your presence, and the appearance of the youths who are eating the king's choice food; and deal with your servants according to what you see." So he listened to them in this matter and tested them for ten days. And at the end of ten days their appearance seemed better and they were fatter than all the youths who had been eating the king's choice food. Daniel 1:11-14

The prophet Daniel's ministry was spent in Babylon where he'd been taken captive by King Nebuchadnezzar. Given to prayer and fasting, two "staples" of his spiritual diet, Daniel convinced the "commander of the officials" over him to observe the difference between him and those who over-indulged at the table of the king.

"Then at the end of the days which the king had specified for presenting them. . .the king talked with them, and out of them all not one was found like Daniel, Hananiah, Mishael and Azariah; so they entered the king's personal service. And as for every matter of wisdom and understanding about which the king consulted them, he found them ten times better than all the magicians and conjurers who were in all his realm. And Daniel continued until the first year of Cyrus the king" (Daniel 1:18-21).

Prayer — Lord, help me to walk with You that Your will might be accomplished on earth.

Baptism of Repentance

"Repent, and let each of you be baptized in the name of Jesus Christ for the forgiveness of your sins; and you shall receive the gift of the Holy Spirit." Acts 2:38

Many of us were christened or baptized as infants. While this is a beautiful as well as meaningful service, such a rite does not cleanse a person from sin.

Jesus said, " 'The time is fulfilled, and the kingdom of God is at hand; repent and believe in the gospel' " (Mark 1:15). There's no getting around His meaning here. One first has to come face-to-face with her need for salvation before she can receive this great gift. How can an infant make such a choice?

Belief comes in response to presentation of the Word: "Then He opened their minds to understand the Scriptures, and He said to them, 'Thus it is written, that the Christ should suffer and rise again from the dead the third day; and that repentance for forgiveness of sins should be proclaimed in His name to all the nations, beginning from Jerusalem' " (Luke 24:45-47).

Also, it's critical to note that the Holy Spirit is given at the moment of repentance (Acts 2:38). In the Gospel of Mark, quoted above, we know for certain that God's time-table for obtaining salvation has begun.

Prayer — Lord, I thank You that those who lived before Jesus came to earth were given the same gospel message through the prophets. I thank You that You have always provided a way to salvation.

Bathsheba's Influence

*As David's time to die drew near, he charged Solomon his son,
saying, ". . .Keep the charge of the Lord your God, to walk in
His ways, to keep His statutes, His commandments, His
ordinances, and His testimonies, according to what is written
in the law of Moses, that you may succeed in all that you do
and wherever you turn, so that the Lord may carry out His
promise which He spoke concerning me, saying, 'If your sons
are careful of their way, to walk before me in truth with all
their heart and with all their soul, you shall not lack a man on
the throne of Israel.'" 1 Kings 2:1, 3-4*

In almost every family there are those who feel that certain
honors or personal effects should be their rightful inheritance. David's family was no exception. One of his sons
attempted to use Bathsheba's influence for his personal gain.

Adonijah, the son of David's wife, Haggith, came to
Bathsheba requesting that she speak to Solomon. He
desired to have Abishag as his wife. Adonijah didn't simply
want to wed the girl who had served as David's nurse.
Instead, he wanted David's throne (1 Kings 1:5).

David, proud of this son, probably felt that in time
Adonijah would accept the reality that God had called
Solomon to the position. However, he had only become more
insistent. And when he enlisted Bathsheba's intervention, it
showed he planned a full challenge to Solomon's leadership,
even including war. "So King Solomon sent Benaiah the son
of Jehoida; and he fell upon him so he died" (1 Kings 1:25).

Prayer — Lord, Adonijah's failure to accept Your choice cost
him his life. Please help me to graciously accept Your will
and be satisfied.

A Dance in the Fiery Furnace

*Then Nebuchadnezzar the king sent word to assemble the
satraps, the prefects and the governors, the counselors, the
treasurers, the judges, the magistrates and all the rulers of the
provinces to come to the dedication of the image that
Nebuchadnezzar the king had set up. . .Then the herald loudly
proclaimed: ". . .O peoples, nations and men of every language,
that you are to fall down and worship the golden image that
Nebuchadnezzar the king has set up." Daniel 3:2, 4-5*

Although King Nebuchadnezzar had witnessed God's power
and even acknowledged it, he had now retreated to unbelief.

In fact, the king had now slipped into total egotism,
making an image of gold which represented himself and then
demanding worship from the people. The king's advisors
used this proclamation to entrap Daniel's friends, who refused
to bow down to any king but the Lord. Therefore, Shadrach,
Meshach, and Abednego were bound and then thrown into
a fiery furnace and it was heated "seven times more than it
was usually" (Daniel 3:19-20).

But when the king looked into the furnace he saw a
fourth person in the midst of the fire. " 'Look! I see four men
loosed and walking about in the midst of the fire without
harm, and the appearance of the fourth is like a son of the
gods!' " (Daniel 3:25) So the king ordered them out again.

Jesus was with Daniel's friends in the fire. " 'When you
walk through the fire, you will not be scorched, nor will the
flame burn you. For I am the Lord your God, the Holy One
of Israel, your Savior' " (Isaiah 43:2-3).

Prayer — Lord, be my faithful God, just as You were to
Daniel's friends. Keep me from harm as I walk through the
fires in my own life.

Announced by the Prophets

"But the things which God announced beforehand by the mouths of all the prophets, that His Christ should suffer, He has thus fulfilled. Repent therefore and return, that your sins may be wiped away." Acts 3:18-19

If the Jews hadn't been told about their suffering Messiah they wouldn't have been accountable. However, this age-old singular message had been presented by every one of Israel's prophets. "Moses said, 'The Lord God shall raise up for you a prophet like me from your brethren; to Him you shall give heed in everything he says to you. And it shall be that every soul that does not heed that prophet shall be utterly destroyed from among the people.'" (Acts 3:22-23).

But the Jews had refused to listen to both the message and the messenger. Jesus said, " 'Elijah already came, and they did not recognize him, but did to him whatever they wished. So also the Son of Man is going to suffer at their hands.' Then the disciples understood that He had spoken to them about John the Baptist" (Matthew 17:12-13).

Both Jesus and John the Baptist had been killed for preaching the truth about God and the Messiah. Even as Peter and John now spoke, they were arrested (Acts 4:1-3).

Was their message wasted? Not at all. There will always be a remnant who hears and responds.

Prayer — Oh Lord, let me not also be guilty of rejecting the truth of God. Our Messiah has come! Hallelujah!

A True Mother's Love

"And now, O Lord my God, Thou hast made Thy servant king in place of my father David, yet I am but a little child; I do not know how to go out or come in. And Thy servant is in the midst of thy people which Thou hast chosen, a great people who cannot be numbered or counted for multitude. So give Thy servant an understanding heart to judge Thy people to discern between good and evil. For who is able to judge this great people of Thine?" 1 Kings 3:7-9

Shortly after King Solomon had asked the Lord for wisdom, two harlots brought their case before him.

Each woman stated that one particular infant belonged to her. Obviously one of them was lying. You see, one woman's child had died shortly after his birth and she had taken the other woman's live baby, laying her dead son in the other mother's arms.

As they stood arguing and shouting, Solomon said, " 'Get me a sword.' So they brought a sword before the king. And the king said, 'Divide the living child in two, and give half to the one and half to the other' " (1 Kings 3:24-25). Solomon knew that the child's true mother would come to the baby's defense.

Within minutes the issue was resolved and the real mother held her child again. "When all Israel heard of the judgment which the king had handed down, they feared the king; for they saw that the wisdom of God was in him to administer justice" (1 Kings 3:28).

Prayer — Lord, how I pray that such wisdom would be given to lawmakers. I also need Your guidance for my family. Help me remember to turn to You in my dilemmas.

Daniel's Deliverance

Then the commissioners and satraps began trying to find a ground of accusation against Daniel in regard to government affairs; but they could find no ground of accusation or evidence of corruption. Daniel 6:4

Jealousy unchecked renders men and women capable of untold evil. And now that Daniel had been appointed as one of the "commissioners," they plotted against Daniel.

"Then these commissioners and satraps came by agreement to the king and spoke to him as follows: 'King Darius, live forever! All the commissioners of the kingdom, the prefects and the satraps, the high officials and the governors have consulted together that the king should establish a statue and enforce an injunction that anyone who makes a petition to any god or man besides you, O king, for thirty days, shall be cast into the lions' den. Now, O king, establish the injunction and sign the document so that it may not be changed, according to the law of the Medes and Persians, which may not be revoked'" (Daniel 6:6-8).

The king signed the document into law.

The ink wasn't even dry when "these men came by agreement and found Daniel making petition and supplication before his God" (Daniel 6:11). They tattled on Daniel. Daniel was then thrust into the lions' den.

Prayer — Lord, I praise You that the next morning, the king found evidence of Your abiding love: " 'My God sent His angel and shut the lions' mouths and they have not harmed me,' " shouted Daniel! (Daniel 6:22)

Saul and Stephen

*And they went on stoning Stephen as he called upon the Lord
and said, "Lord Jesus, receive my spirit!" And falling on his
knees, he cried out with a loud voice, "Lord, do not hold this sin
against them!" And having said this, he fell asleep. And Saul
was in hearty agreement with putting him to death. And on
that day a great persecution arose against the church in
Jerusalem. Acts 7:59-60; 8:1*

Have you ever committed an action so despicable that you
can't imagine God could ever forgive you? Saul—who would
soon be acclaimed as the fearless apostle Paul—had been
persuaded by his own pious intentions to stamp out the
Gospel's heresy. After the stoning of Stephen, Saul entered
home after home and dragged Christians off to prison.

And then the powerful hand of the Lord God
intervened.

"Suddenly a light from heaven flashed around him; and
he fell to the ground, and heard a voice saying to him, 'Saul,
Saul, why are you persecuting Me?' And he said, 'Who art
Thou, Lord?' And He said, 'I am Jesus whom you are persecuting, but rise, and enter the city, and it shall be told you
what you must do'" (Acts 9:3-6).

Blinded for three days by God's incredible power, Saul
had to be led into the city of Damascus. There, a disciple
named Ananias, to whom God gave a message, would
intervene.

Prayer — Thank You, God, for changing Saul into Paul!

The Whirlwind of Elijah

And it came about when the Lord was about to take up Elijah by a whirlwind to heaven, that Elijah went with Elisha from Gilgal. And Elijah said to Elisha, "Stay here please, for the Lord has sent me as far as Bethel." But Elisha said, "As the Lord lives and as you yourself live, I will not leave you." So they went down to Bethel. 2 Kings 2:1-2

The movie *Twister's* heart-pumping terror pales in comparison with the real-life adventure of Elijah, who ascended into heaven in a whirlwind.

Elisha and Elijah stood together at the edge of the Jordan River. A large group looked on as the two men conversed.

"And Elijah took his mantle and folded it together and struck the waters, and they were divided here and there, so that the two of them crossed over on dry ground. Elijah said to Elisha, 'Ask what I shall do for you before I am taken from you.' And Elisha said, 'Please, let a double portion of your spirit be upon me'" (2 Kings 2:8-9). Elijah's successor sought confirmation that God's Spirit was with him.

"And he said, 'You have asked a hard thing. Nevertheless, if you see me when I am taken from you, it shall be so for you; but if not, it shall not be so.' Then. . .behold there appeared a chariot of fire and horses of fire which separated the two of them. And Elijah went up by a whirlwind to heaven. And Elisha saw it" (2 Kings 2:10-12).

Now Elisha took Elijah's mantle, which had fallen from him and struck it on the waters to divide them again. Elisha had received God's Spirit.

Prayer — Lord, You have such a flair for the dramatic! I love it!

Daniel Sees Four Beasts

Daniel saw a dream and visions in his mind as he lay on his bed. "And four great beasts were coming up from the sea, different from one another. The first was like a lion and had the wings of an eagle. I kept looking until its wings were plucked, and it was lifted up from the ground and made to stand on two feet like a man; a human mind also was given to it. And behold, another beast, a second one, resembling a bear. And it was raised up on one side, and three ribs were in its mouth between its teeth; and thus they said to it, 'Arise, devour much meat!' " Daniel 7:1-5

As this vision continued, Daniel saw another beast, "like a leopard" with "four heads, and dominion was given to it" (Daniel 7:6).

Daniel saw "a fourth beast, dreadful and terrifying and extremely strong;. . .and it was different from all the beasts that were before it, and it had ten horns" (Daniel 7:7). God made Daniel the recipient of but some of the pieces of this prophetic puzzle.

A nearly identical vision was given to John, who recorded it in the Book of Revelation.

"And I saw a beast coming up out of the sea, having ten horns and seven heads, and on his horns were ten diadems, and on his heads were blasphemous names. And the beast which I saw was like a leopard, and his feet were like those of a bear, and his mouth like the mouth of a lion." (Revelation 13:1-2).

Prayer — Lord, I know from Your Word that this last, terrible beast will be the antichrist. Do not let me be deceived by him.

James Is Martyred

Now about that time Herod the king laid hands on some who belonged to the church, in order to mistreat them. And he had James the brother of John put to death with a sword.
Acts 12:1-2

Perhaps John's own memories now returned to the days when he and his brother James first responded to the Lord's call to follow.

"He saw two other brothers, James the son of Zebedee, and John his brother, in the boat with Zebedee their father, mending their nets; and He called them. And they immediately left the boat and their father, and followed Him" (Matthew 4:19, 21-22).

John must also have considered the time when Jesus had been teaching the disciples about the kingdom of heaven. "Then the mother of the sons of Zebedee came to Him with her sons, bowing down, and making a request of Him. And He said to her, 'What do you wish?' She said to Him, 'Command that in Your kingdom these two sons of mine may sit, one on Your right and one on Your left.' But Jesus answered and said, 'You do not know what you are asking for. Are you able to drink the cup that I am about to drink?' They said to Him, 'We are able'" (Matthew 20:20-22).

His heart filled with grief for a martyred brother, John contemplated this promise of commitment and then went on with his ministry. The Lord's message and example must have echoed through his mind (Mark 10:40-45).

Prayer — Lord, I know that although James paid the ultimate price, he now worships before Your heavenly throne. Help me serve You as well.

A House Divided Disintegrates

*And they forsook all the commandments of the Lord their God
and made for themselves molten images, . . .and served Baal.
Then they made their sons and their daughters pass through the
fire, . . .and sold themselves to do evil in the sight of the Lord,
provoking Him. So the Lord was very angry with Israel.
2 Kings 17:16–18*

Baal worship was the besetting sin of Israel. Each time a new
king ascended the throne, the Israelites held the hope of
change. However, the records of their downward slide into
idolatry are clear. And although some of the kings fostered
true worship of the Lord for a time, none of them squelched
the worship of Baal.

Remember that it was for this reason "the Lord rejected
all the descendants of Israel and afflicted them and gave
them into the hand of plunderers, until He had cast them
out of His sight. . .And the sons of Israel walked in all the
sins of Jeroboam which he did; they did not depart from
them, until the Lord removed Israel from His sight, as He
spoke through all His servants the prophets. So Israel was
carried away into exile from their own land to Assyria until
this day" (2 Kings 17:20, 22-23). What then will happen to
our own civilization if we fail to turn the tide of idolatry in
which we too are steeped?

Prayer — Lord, what things keep me from Your presence?
Is my job more important than You? Is my husband, kids, or
house? Please bring me back into true worship that I might
not be led astray.

Seventy Weeks Have Been Decreed

"Seventy weeks have been decreed for your people and your holy
city. . .From the issuing of a decree to restore and rebuild
Jerusalem until Messiah the Prince there will be seven weeks
and sixty-two weeks; it will be built again, with plaza and
moat, even in times of distress. Then after the sixty-two weeks
the Messiah will be cut off and have nothing, and the people of
the prince who is to come will destroy the city and the
sanctuary." Daniel 9:24-26

Daniel was the recipient of some of the most critical
prophecies concerning the coming Messiah, the antichrist
who would follow, and also the timetable for these events.

The word "weeks" in Hebrew is *shabuim*, which means
"sevens." Therefore, one week is actually a period of seven
years.

The kickoff on these hands of time was the "decree
to restore and rebuild Jerusalem." King Artaxerxes of
Medo-Persia issued just such a pronouncement in 445
B.C. (Nehemiah 1:1-2:8).

Messiah's birth, heralded by a brilliant star in the heavens
and announced by angels, fulfilled Isaiah 7:14: "Behold, a
virgin will be with child and bear a son, and she will call His
name Immanuel."

Christ's death fulfilled another part of the prophecy.
"By oppression and judgment He was taken away; and as for
His generation, who considered that He was cut off out of
the land of the living, For the transgression of my people to
whom the stroke was due?" (Isaiah 53:8)

Prayer — Jesus, I await Your second coming and the
eventual demise of the evil one.

Aquila and Priscilla, Tentmakers

And he found a certain Jew named Aquila, a native of Pontus, having recently come from Italy with his wife Priscilla, because Claudius had commanded all the Jews to leave Rome. He came to them, and because he was of the same trade, he stayed with them and they were working; for by trade they were tentmakers. Acts 18:2-3

Every year we receive a myriad of requests for financial support from individuals entering various full-time ministries. My husband and I prayerfully consider these entreaties and support those we feel led to by God.

Paul worked as a tentmaker so that he might support his travels within his ministry. Aquila and Priscilla not only assisted him in this task, but they also accompanied Paul on his missionary journey to Syria (Acts 18:18). This married couple also encouraged new believers in teaching "the way of God more accurately" (Acts 18:26).

In the Book of Romans, we discover more about Aquila and Priscilla's depth of commitment and character. Paul admonishes the believers in Rome: "Greet Prisca and Aquila, my fellow workers in Christ Jesus, who for my life risked their own necks, to whom not only do I give thanks, but also the churches of the Gentiles; also greet the church that is in their house" (Romans 16:3-4).

Note that in these last Scripture verses Paul uses the nickname *Prisca* as though they have become dear friends.

Prayer — Lord, show me today how I might serve You and present the Gospel message to others.

God Designates the Temple Site

*Then the angel of the Lord commanded Gad to say to David,
that David should go up and build an altar to the Lord on the
threshing floor of Ornan the Jebusite. . .Then David said to
Ornan, "Give me the site of this threshing floor, that I may
build on it an altar to the Lord; for the full price you shall give
it to me, that the plague may be restrained from the people."*
1 Chronicles 21:18, 22

King David's disobedience to the Lord brought about a siege
of pestilence on the land: "Then Satan stood up against
Israel and moved David to number Israel" (1 Chronicles
21:1). David desired to take a census and find out how many
people he ruled over. But the Lord had already promised to
"multiply Israel as the stars of heaven" (1 Chronicles 27:23).
David was simply to take God at His Word, but instead he
sought proof.

David's impetuous act cost Israel dearly. "So the Lord sent
a pestilence on Israel; 70,000 men of Israel fell" (1 Chronicles
21:14-15).

Directly following this incident God commanded David
to obtain this particular property, where Ornan was threshing
wheat, for the temple. "Then David built an altar to the Lord
there, and offered burnt offerings and peace offerings. And
he called to the Lord and He answered him with fire from
heaven on the altar of burnt offering" (1 Chronicles 21:26).

There stood the altar, the first glimmer of the magnificent temple which would stand on this site.

Prayer — Lord, let me not test Your patience!

Good Angels or Bad Angels?

*Then he said to me, "Do not be afraid, Daniel, for from the first
day you set your heart on understanding this and on humbling
yourself before God your words were heard, and I have come in
response to your words. But the prince of the kingdom of Persia
was withstanding me for twenty-one days; then behold,
Michael, one of the chief princes, came to help me, for I had
been left there with the kings of Persia. Now I have come to
give you an understanding of what will happen to your people
in the latter days, for the vision pertains to the days yet future."*
Daniel 10:12-14

Have you ever wondered why your prayers seem to take so
long to get answered? Well, consider Daniel's plight. God
had just revealed to him that antichrist was going to cause a
"complete destruction" in Jerusalem. Consequently, Daniel
prayed for three solid weeks before relief finally came.

"I, Daniel, had been mourning for three entire weeks. . .
I lifted my eyes and looked, and behold, there was a certain
man dressed in linen, whose waist was girded with a belt of
pure gold of Uphaz" (Daniel 10:2, 5).

Now Daniel is further weakened by the vision of this
angel. "So I was left alone and saw this great vision; yet no
strength was left in me, for my natural color turned to a
deathly pallor, and I retained no strength" (Daniel 10:8).
Daniel then fell into a deep sleep but could hear the sound
of the angel's words. "Then behold, a hand touched me and
set me trembling on my hands and knees" (Daniel 10:10).

Prayer — Lord, let Your angels protect and enlighten me to
truth.

Paul's Mission in Life

Paul, a bond-servant of Christ Jesus, called as an apostle, set apart for the gospel of God, which He promised beforehand through His prophets in the holy Scriptures, concerning His Son, who was born of a descendant of David according to the flesh, who was declared the seed with power to be the Son of God by the resurrection from the dead, according to the Spirit of holiness, Jesus Christ our Lord, through whom we have received grace and apostleship to bring about the obedience of faith among all the Gentiles, for His name's sake, among whom you also are the called of Jesus Christ; to all who are beloved of God in Rome, called as saints: Grace to you and peace from God our Father and the Lord Jesus Christ.
Romans 1:1-7

Paul had come to know the true source of life. And with this knowledge came a mission for the rest of his days on earth. Notice in the verse above that he claims to have been "set apart for the gospel of God." Now remember that this great persecutor of the church had been specifically called by God, who changed not only Paul's life but also his name and priorities.

A sense of holy terror had stricken Ananias as God told him to find Saul/Paul and speak to him. For Paul's reputation as a ruthless butcher had preceded him. But the Lord said to Ananias, " 'Go, for he is a chosen instrument of Mine, to bear My name before the Gentiles and kings and the sons of Israel; for I will show him how much he must suffer for My name's sake' " (Acts 9:15-16).

Prayer — Paul stressed the inward cleansing the Lord could provide to the repentant sinner. Lord, cleanse me and refocus my spiritual walk this fall.

All the King's Horses

*And Solomon amassed chariots and horsemen. He had 1, 400
chariots, and 12,000 horsemen, and he stationed them in the
chariot cities and with the king at Jerusalem. . .And Solomon's
horses were imported from Egypt and from Kue; the king's
traders procured them from Kue for a price. And they imported
chariots from Egypt for 600 shekels of silver apiece, and horses
for 150 apiece, and by the same means they exported them to all
the kings of the Hittites and the kings of Aram.*
2 Chronicles 1:14, 16-17

Solomon's horses were the finest that money could buy. But
they weren't just for pleasure. These valiant steeds helped
defend his kingdom and also provided revenue as they were
sold or loaned to other kings.

Solomon's horses were stationed in strategic cities, ready
to guard and protect the kingdom. And in 1 Kings 4:26
we see that "Solomon had 40,000 stalls of horses for his
chariots." He also had deputies who "brought barley and
straw for the horses and swift steeds to the place where it
should be, each according to his charge" (1 Kings 4:28).

Long before Israel even had a king, the Lord had established certain standards for this monarch. He was not to multiply horses for himself, nor cause the people to return to
Egypt to get horses (Deuteronomy 17:14-16). God didn't
want the king's heart to turn away from following Him.

Prayer — Had Solomon followed God's commands his
kingdom would have been assured of survival. Lord, help
me to remain faithful.

Antichrist, the Ruler to Come

"And in his place a despicable person will arise, on whom the honor of kingship has not been conferred, but he will come in a time of tranquility and seize the kingdom by intrigue. And the overflowing forces will be flooded away before him and shattered, and also the prince of the covenant. And after an alliance is made with him he will practice deception, and he will go up and gain power with a small force of people. In a time of tranquility he will enter the richest parts of the realm, and he will accomplish what his fathers never did, nor his ancestors; he will distribute plunder, booty, and possessions among them, and he will devise his schemes against strongholds, but only for a time." Daniel 11:21-24

The antichrist is a real person who will one day deviously slither onto the scene right on cue. He will appear indispensable at a time of worldwide, unsolvable chaos. His allies will be the foes of God.

His deception will be so great that people will fail to see his face of evil until "the abomination of desolation" takes place (Matthew 24:15). Three and one-half years after he comes on the scene, the antichrist will enter the rebuilt temple in Jerusalem, declare himself god, and demand worship and allegiance from the world. Jesus Himself warned the Jews about this diabolical person, telling them that when they saw him to " 'let those who are in Judea flee to the mountains' " (Mark 13:14).

Prayer — Lord, compel me with new urgency to study Your powerful Word, that I might bring it to others.

Judge Not, Lest Ye Be Judged

And do you suppose this, O man, when you pass judgment upon those who practice such things and do the same yourself, that you will escape the judgment of God? Romans 2:3

Those who know precious little about the Word of God seem to parade about this particular verse. However, they could not tell you that Paul was addressing hypocrites, those who "know the ordinance of God," and yet practice things which are "worthy of death" (Romans 1:32).

These people recite this verse to those who have the audacity to suggest they obey. It cuts off the tongue which has spoken the truth which they refuse to hear.

Just prior to these verses Paul had been addressing the issue of sin. "For the wrath of God is revealed from heaven against all ungodliness and unrighteousness of men, who suppress the truth in unrighteousness, because that which is known about God is evident within them; for God made it evident to them. For since the creation of the world His invisible attributes, His eternal power and divine nature, have been clearly seen, being understood through what has been made, so that they are without excuse" (Romans 1:18-20).

A news report the other day said that only five percent of Americans say they don't believe in God. So, if ninety-five percent supposedly believe in God, then it makes me wonder which god they believe in.

_____

Prayer — Enlighten my heart so I can truly worship You.

Hezekiah Restores Worship

*Hezekiah became king when he was twenty-five years old; and
he reigned twenty-nine years in Jerusalem. . .And he did right
in the sight of the Lord, according to all that his father David
had done. In the first year of his reign, in the first month, he
opened the doors of the house of the Lord and repaired them.
And he brought in the priests and the Levites, and gathered
them into the square on the east. Then he said to them, "Listen
to me, O Levites. Consecrate yourselves now, and consecrate the
house of the Lord, the God of your fathers, and carry the
uncleanness out from the holy place."*
2 Chronicles 29:1-5

Did you notice that Hezekiah was only twenty-five years old
when he became king of Judah?

Instead of following in his father's footsteps, this young
king did what was right before the Lord.

During the very first month worship was reestab-
lished. Hezekiah removed "the high places and broke down
the sacred pillars and cut down the Asherah. He also broke
in pieces the bronze serpent that Moses had made, for until
those days the sons of Israel burned incense to it; and it was
called Nehushtan. He trusted in the Lord, the God of
Israel; so that after him there was none like him among all
the kings of Judah, nor among those who were before him"
(2 Kings 18:4-5).

Just four years later Israel was taken into exile. But
King Hezekiah hearkened to God's voice and his kingdom
survived (2 Kings 18:11).

Prayer — Lord, help me learn to abide in You completely.

Michael Stands Guard

"Now at that time Michael, the great prince who stands guard over the sons of your people, will arise. And there will be a time of distress such as never occurred since there was a nation until that time; and at that time your people, everyone who is found written in the book, will be rescued." Daniel 12:1

The prophet Daniel spoke of the archangel Michael because he wanted Israel to be aware that God had already given them a great prince who stands guard over them. Those whose names are written in the book will be spared. God writes the names in His book. It's called the Lamb's book of life. "And the city has no need of the sun or of the moon to shine upon it, for the glory of God has illumined it, and its lamp is the Lamb. . .and nothing unclean and no one who practices abomination and lying, shall ever come into it, but only those whose names are written in the Lamb's book of life" (Revelation 21:23, 27). When we come to believe in the Lamb, Jesus Christ, we are cleansed from our sins.

It is these, whose names are written in the book, who will be rescued from destruction: " 'These are the ones who come out of the great tribulation, and they have washed their robes and made them white in the blood of the Lamb. For this reason, they are before the throne of God; and they serve Him day and night in His temple; and He who sits on the throne shall spread His tabernacle over them' " (Revelation 7:14-15).

Prayer — Lamb of God, who takes away sin, I want to know my name is written in Your book!

But What About the Jews?

For if Abraham was justified by works, he has something to boast about; but not before God. For what does the Scripture say? "And Abraham believed God, and it was reckoned to Him as righteousness." Romans 4:2-3

Our work ethic is as old as the Garden of Eden. Because of sin Adam's free ride was over and he would now have to earn a living. But God said, " 'Because you have listened to the voice of your wife, and have eaten from the tree about which I commanded you, saying, "You shall not eat from it"; Cursed is the ground because of you; In toil you shall eat of it all the days of your life' " (Genesis 3:17).

Somehow men and women have transferred this attitude about working for things to salvation. However, salvation is not based on our "goodness," but rather on Christ's. For no matter how diligently we try to keep those Ten Commandments, we're going to fail.

God made Abraham, the one the Jews claim as their father, a promise and he believed God.

His belief wasn't merely an intellectual assent. The "Supreme God of the Universe," who made absolutely everything that Abraham now saw in his world, had deigned not only to speak to him, but He promised him an heir. The reason that Abraham could place his trust in God was because God kept His promises. No matter how impossible the situation looks, God always comes through.

Prayer — I thank You that I worship a God whose Word can be trusted. I know Jesus will always be there for me.

The Temple Is Rebuilt

Now. . .the Lord stirred up the spirit of Cyrus king of Persia, so that he sent a proclamation throughout all his kingdom, and also put it in writing, saying, "Thus says Cyrus king of Persia, 'The Lord, the God of heaven, has given me all the kingdoms of the earth, and He has appointed me to build Him a house in Jerusalem, which is in Judah. Whoever there is among you of all His people, may his God be with him! Let him go up to Jerusalem which is in Judah, and rebuild the house of the Lord, the God of Israel; He is the God who is in Jerusalem.'" Ezra 1:1-3

Is there a Christmas which really stands out in your memory, one for which the anticipation nearly drove you crazy?

Now transfer that degree of excitement to how Israel felt when this proclamation finally went out. The Israelites were on the fringe of being brought back to the land God had given them, and now, their center of worship was about to be restored! Thus, the prophecy recorded in Jeremiah was fulfilled: " 'For thus says the Lord, "When seventy years have been completed for Babylon, I will visit you and fulfill My good word to you, to bring you back to this place"'" (Jeremiah 29:10-11).

Approximately 175 years before King Cyrus was even born, God had spoken through the prophet Isaiah concerning him. "Thus says the Lord,. . .'It is I who says of Cyrus, "He is My shepherd! And he will perform all My desire." ' And he declares of Jerusalem, 'She will be built,' And of the temple, 'Your foundation will be laid'" (Isaiah 44:24, 28).

Prayer — Lord, my world is filled with uncertainty. But I can be absolutely sure that what You have said will come to pass.

Gomer, a Picture of Israel

*The Lord said to Hosea, "Go, take to yourself a wife of harlotry,
and have children of harlotry; for the land commits flagrant
harlotry, forsaking the Lord." So he went and took Gomer the
daughter of Diblaim, and she conceived and bore him a son.*
Hosea 1:2-3

Do you have a child who has wandered away from every
good thing you tried to give him? Your heart has broken as
that child perhaps chose a lifestyle that so contradicted your
own. Now imagine God going through this same kind of
pain as an entire nation, one He dearly loved, refused to walk
with Him.

Why would God ask the prophet Hosea to enter into an
unwholesome alliance? Because He wanted Israel to understand what it was like to observe the one to whom they were
betrothed go off and play the harlot. When Israel entered into
the covenant with God, the people had promised fidelity to
Him. But this beloved nation had "prostituted" themselves in
worship of false gods, forsaking their true God.

The Book of Hosea reveals the brokenness of God's
own heart as He watched Israel wander away. Now God was
forced to take action against the people He loved, in order
to bring them back to Him.

Prayer — " 'And I will say to those who were not My people,
"You are My people!" ' " (Hosea 2:23) Lord, thank You for
Your unique invitation.

Peace Despite Our Trials

*Therefore having been justified by faith, we have peace with
God through our Lord Jesus Christ, through whom also we
have obtained our introduction by faith into this grace in
which we stand; and we exult in hope of the glory of God. . .
For while we were still helpless, at the right time Christ died
for the ungodly. Romans 5:1-2, 6*

People have scoured every nook and cranny of the globe in
search of peace. From yoga and transcendental meditation to
new age tranquility tapes and self-empowerment courses,
people will try just about anything. But do these methods
work?

Of course not! Instead, each new road eventually leads
to the dead ends of dissatisfaction and emptiness. "I have
seen all the works which have been done under the sun, and
behold, all is vanity and striving after the wind" (Ecclesiastes
1:14). The promises of peace which this world has to offer are
nothing more than vapors of an expensive fragrance.

Enduring tranquility cannot be found outside a relationship with Christ. So why can't we just believe it's that
simple?

Maybe we're simply afraid to end the search. Before I
became a Christian I can recall thinking of God as my "ace
in the hole." If all else failed, I'd try religion. And when all the
other inlets I traveled led to dry lake beds, I did reach out for
religion. However, this too was but an attempt on my part to
"be good enough for God." Human effort doesn't bring
peace.

Prayer — Lord, I know the only true and lasting peace
comes from Jesus Christ.

Construction Is Halted

Now when the enemies of Judah and Benjamin heard that the people. . .were building a temple to the Lord. . .they said to them, "Let us build with you, for we, like you, seek your God; and we have been sacrificing to Him since the days of Esarhaddon king of Assyria, who brought us up here." But Zerubbabel and Jeshua and the rest of the heads of fathers' households of Israel said to them, "You have nothing in common with us in building a house to our god; but we ourselves will together build to the Lord God of Israel, as King Cyrus, the king of Persia has commanded us." Then the people of the land discouraged the people of Judah, and frightened them from building, and hired counselors against them to frustrate their counsel. Ezra 4:1-5

Can you imagine receiving a loud clear call from the Lord to take action on your life's work and then have such discouragement? How did the people of Israel keep going? By trusting God instead of rumors, rulers, or rivalry.

The final straw was the letter a few wicked leaders sent to King Artaxerxes. " 'Now let it be known to the king, that the Jews. . .are rebuilding the rebellious and evil city, and are finishing the walls and repairing the foundations. . .if that city is rebuilt and the walls are finished, they will not pay tribute, custom, or toll, and it will damage the revenue of the kings. . .therefore we have sent and informed the king. . .if that city is rebuilt. . .you will have no possession in the province beyond the River" (Ezra 4:12-14, 16).

Prayer — Lord, You always cause the wicked to stumble. Thank You!

Yet God Loves Them

Return, O Israel, to the Lord your God, for you have stumbled because of your iniquity. Take words with you and return to the Lord. Say to Him, "Take away all iniquity, and receive us graciously, that we may present the fruit of our lips. . ." I will heal their apostasy, I will love them freely, For My anger has turned away from them. Hosea 14:1-2, 4

During one presidential debate of 1996, Bob Dole asked President Bill Clinton if he had plans to pardon those who were involved in the Whitewater scandal. Dole went on to suggest that this action would be ill-advised. How heartily I agree. For if a pardon is granted to those who have already been found guilty, it removes their obligation to suffer for the wrong they've done.

But isn't that what all of us are seeking from God? We have sinned. And our holy God is not obligated to forgive us. Yet what hope would we have for change if God didn't wipe the slate of our past failures clean and then provide us with the strength to start afresh?

We don't deserve a pardon from God; we deserve death. However, He who created us is ready to meet us at the point of repentance and infuse us with such incredible love that we want to love Him back.

Just as we forgive our children when they go astray, so God forgives us, His stupid little sheep who wander away from the all-loving Shepherd.

_____

Prayer — "Praise the Lord in song, for He has done excellent things; let this be known throughout the earth" (Isaiah 12:5).

Safety Net

There is therefore now no condemnation for those who are in Christ Jesus. For the law of the Spirit of life in Christ Jesus has set you free from the law of sin and death. For what the Law could not do, weak as it was through the flesh, God did: sending His own Son in the likeness of sinful flesh and as an offering for sin, He condemned sin in the flesh, in order that the requirement of the Law might be fulfilled in us, who do not walk according to the flesh, but according to the Spirit.
Romans 8:1–4

Now that our children are older, my husband and I look back on some of their episodes of outright disobedience with a different perspective. We can see that even as they responded to our discipline with absolute hostility, these incidents became turning points in their lives.

With reckless abandon their flesh cried out with insolence, "Don't tell me what to do!" Fifteen or twenty years earlier we wanted to say the same things to our parents.

The "Law" Paul speaks of here is God's law, given to Moses and the Israelites in the entirety of what has been recorded in the Bible. It's the law which requires that we "love our enemies and do good to those who hate us." And it's also the law that says, " 'Come to me, all who are heavy laden and I will give you rest.' " To be out of control is such a weighty burden, one which we were never meant to carry.

God's rules provide for us a huge safety net. When we bounce against its sides, we become aware of the need to change our direction.

———————

Prayer — I rejoice that I am a child of God and heir to the kingdom! Hallelujah!

An Evil Plan Backfires

*"And now the document which you sent to us has been translated
and read before me. And a decree has been issued by me, and a
search has been made and it has been discovered that the city has
risen up against the kings in past days, that rebellion and revolt
have been perpetrated in it, that mighty kings have ruled over
Jerusalem, governing all the provinces beyond the River, and
that tribute, custom, and toll were paid to them." Ezra 4:19-20*

In *The Music Man*, the people of River City only become
aware that there's trouble in their town when the music man,
Professor Harold Hill, tells them how bad off they really are.
In today's Scripture, King Artaxerxes is just about as unaware
of a problem until this same kind of scenario tickles his ears.

The enemies of Judah and Benjamin worry him over the
potential of lost revenue. Next, they speak of how horrific it
would be to see the king dishonored. Finally, they intimate
that past problems with the Israelites can be proven by
obtaining the record books.

"Then as soon as the copy of King Artaxerxes' document
was read before Rehum and Shimshai the scribe and their
colleagues, they went in haste to Jerusalem to the Jews and
stopped them by force of arms. Then the work on the house of
God in Jerusalem ceased, and it was stopped until the second
year of the reign of Darius king of Persia" (Ezra 4:23-24).

"But the eye of their God was on the elders of the Jews,
and they did not stop them until a report should come to
Darius, and then a written reply he returned concerning it"
(Ezra 5:5). When the inquiry was made, it gave the Israelites
a chance to expound on how the decree had gone out by
Cyrus, king of Babylon, to rebuild the house of God (Ezra
5:6-13).

_____

Prayer — Lord, I read that shortly after King Darius issued
a decree, work began again to finish Your temple. Your will is
always done!

Joel and a Plague of Locusts

What the gnawing locust has left, the swarming locust has eaten; and what the creeping locust has left, the stripping locust has eaten. Joel 1:4

Joel's words could provide a great plot line for a sci-fi thriller. The worst thing about this plague is that it seemingly came upon the people without warning and was more devastating than anything they'd ever witnessed (Joel 1:1-7). Other catastrophes would follow.

The apostle Peter explained Pentecost in light of Joel's prophecy: " 'This is what was spoken of through the prophet Joel: "And it shall be in the last days," God says, "That I will in those days pour forth of My Spirit and they shall prophesy. And I will grant wonders in the sky above, And signs on the earth beneath, . . .Before the great and glorious day of the Lord shall come. And it shall be, that everyone who calls on the name of the Lord shall be saved" ' " (Acts 2:16-21).

The information contained in the book of Joel is referred to as eschatology, or a study of the end times, and parallels other passages in Scripture. When Jesus spoke to His disciples He too quoted this prophetic passage, providing additional clarity.

Prayer — Lord, I rejoice in Your Word: " 'But immediately after the tribulation. . .the sign of the Son of Man will appear in the sky, . . .and they will see the Son of Man coming on the clouds of the clouds of the sky with power and great glory' " (Matthew 24:29-30).

Paul's Prayer for the Jews

*Brethren, my heart's desire and my prayer to God for them is
for their salvation. Romans 10:1*

Is the deepest concern of your heart that those whom you
love will share heaven with Christ? The deepest longing of
Paul's soul was that the Jews might know their Messiah.

Paul longed for the Israelites, "to whom belongs the
adoption as sons and the glory and the covenants and the
giving of the Law and the temple service and the promises,"
to understand that Christ had come to save them (Romans
9:4-5).

The Jews couldn't truly be God's children until they
partook of the light of truth. "For the Scripture says, 'Whoever believes in Him will not be disappointed.' For there is no
distinction between Jew and Greek; for the same Lord is
Lord of all, abounding in riches for all who call upon Him;
for 'Whoever will call upon the name of the Lord will be
saved' " (Romans 10:11-13).

Paul presents the simple process by which they can
become cleansed of their sins. "But what does it say? 'The
word is near you, in your mouth and in your heart'—that is,
the word of faith which we are preaching, that if you confess
with your mouth Jesus as Lord, and believe in your heart that
God raised Him from the dead, you shall be saved; for with
the heart man believes, resulting in righteousness, and with
the mouth he confesses, resulting in salvation" (Romans
10:8-10).

Prayer —Lord, clarify Your Word, that women may yield
in faith.

Nehemiah and the Walls of Jerusalem

*While I was in Susa the capitol, . . .Hanani, one of my brothers,
and some men from Judah came; and I asked them concerning
the Jews who had escaped and had survived the captivity, and
about Jerusalem. And they said to me, "The remnant there in the
province who survived the captivity are in great distress and
reproach, and the wall of Jerusalem is broken down and its gates
are burned with fire." Now it came about when I heard these
words, I sat down and wept and mourned for days; and I was
fasting and praying before the God of heaven. Nehemiah 1:1-4*

Nehemiah records the events which took place as Jerusalem's
walls were repaired. Fortified walls were necessary not only to
guard the perimeter of the great city, but also to demonstrate
the renewed pride and unity of its citizens.

Although Nehemiah was in Susa, the Persian capital,
which was 600 miles away, he couldn't forget either his
beloved city or its people. So, he poured out heartfelt prayers
to the Lord, seeking His wisdom for this great renovation
project. And God's reply caused him to mourn, fast and
weep, as the solution to Israel's problem crystallized: " 'We
have sinned against Thee; I and my father's house have
sinned' " (Nehemiah 1:6).

Then Nehemiah requested that King Artaxerxes send
him to Judah that he might rebuild the walls. And all of
Nehemiah's time of fasting and prayer were answered as the
king wrote letters of safe passage for him to all "the governors
of the provinces beyond the River" (Nehemiah 2:7). In God's
timing Nehemiah shared his plan with the remnant of Israel.

Prayer — Lord, let me learn from Nehemiah's example. Let
me seek Your will through prayer and study, never losing sight
of Your Son.

Joel Prophesies a Final Judgment

Hasten and come, all you surrounding nations, and gather yourselves there. Bring down, O Lord, Thy mighty ones. Let the nations be aroused and come up to the valley of Jehoshaphat, for there I will sit to judge all the surrounding nations. Joel 3:11-12

Jerusalem will be the site of the world's last and greatest battle as all the surrounding nations rage against the Holy City. However, the powerful, almighty God of the universe will intervene on Israel's behalf.

"And the Lord roars from Zion and utters His voice from Jerusalem, and the heavens and the earth tremble. But the Lord is a refuge for His people and a stronghold to the sons of Israel. Then you will know that I am the Lord your God, dwelling in Zion, My holy mountain. So Jerusalem will be holy, and strangers will pass through it no more" (Joel 3:16-17).

God gave the prophet Isaiah a similar message: "For the law will go forth from Zion, and the word of the Lord from Jerusalem. And He will judge between the nations" (Isaiah 2:3-4).

When will this last and greatest battle take place? At the end of the age, when Christ comes back to conquer all those who have attempted to ravage His people and their city. "And I looked, and behold, a white cloud, and sitting on the cloud was one like a son of man, having a golden crown on His head, and a sharp sickle in His hand" (Revelation 14:14).

Prayer — Lord, I don't like to consider the brutality of this final judgment. However, I know that You are fair and just and have given men and women ample time and warning to repent.

Renewing Our Minds

*Present your bodies a living and holy sacrifice, acceptable to
God, which is your spiritual service of worship. And do not be
conformed to this world, but be transformed by the renewing of
your mind, that you may prove what the will of God is, that
which is good and acceptable and perfect. Romans 12:1-2*

Mary had lived an exemplary life and was betrothed to
Joseph. Then an angel came with an announcement that
would cast a shadow of doubt on her impeccable character.
God had asked Mary to bear His Son.

Leaving the results of this decision in the hands of her
powerful God, Mary accepted her role as the mother of the
Messiah. And during the difficult days which followed, she
allowed the Word of God to renew her mind. But was that
enough to give her sufficient power to obey the Lord?

The apostle Paul answers this question for us. "For
though we walk in the flesh, we do not war according to the
flesh, for the weapons of our warfare are not of the flesh, but
divinely powerful for the destruction of fortresses. We are
destroying speculations and every lofty thing raised up against
the knowledge of God, and we are taking every thought
captive to the obedience of Christ" (2 Corinthians 10:3-5).

The weapons which God provides for us are spiritual.
We must become proficient with such an arsenal before
such can be effective. So, if the Lord says His Word is a
weapon to be used against the enemy, we've got to read it,
know it, and follow it.

Prayer — Lord, I am grateful for Mary's example.

The Gathering at the Water Gate

*And all the people gathered. . .at the square and they asked
Ezra the scribe to bring the book of the law of Moses which the
Lord had given to Israel. Then Ezra the priest brought the law
before the assembly. . .on the first day of the seventh month.
And he read from it before the square. . .and all the people
were attentive to the book of the law. Nehemiah 8:1-3*

Through inspired teamwork, Nehemiah and the remnant of
Israel finished rebuilding the wall in only fifty-two days
(Nehemiah 6:15). Even their enemies lost the will to fight,
recognizing this accomplishment as coming from the hand of
Israel's God. Four times Sanballat and Geshem sent messages
to Nehemiah, hoping to drag him away from finishing his
task. And each time Nehemiah responded by saying " 'I am
doing a great work and I cannot come down' " (Nehemiah
6:3). Sanballat accused Nehemiah of appointing prophets to
proclaim that a king was in Judah.

Still, Nehemiah, refused to become agitated or frightened. Instead, he relied on God's strength. God put it in his
heart "to assemble the nobles, the officials, and the people to
be enrolled by genealogies. Then I found the book of the
genealogy of those who came up first. . .from the captivity of
the exiles whom Nebuchadnezzar the king of Babylon had
carried away, and who returned to Jerusalem and Judah, each
to his city" (Nehemiah 7:5-6). They searched for records
prior to the captivity, to prove their lineage and family ties,
but none could be found. In response, the people grieved.

Prayer — Lord, let Nehemiah be an example of trust for me.

Amos the Prophet

Thus says the Lord, "For three transgressions of Damascus and for four I will not revoke its punishment, Because they threshed Gilead with implements of sharp iron. . .I will also break the gate bar of Damascus, And cut off the inhabitant from the valley of Aven, And him who holds the scepter, from Beth-eden; So the people of Syria will go exiled to Kir," Says the Lord.
Amos 1:3, 5

Throughout the Old Testament we've read accounts of God's wrath and fury directed toward those whom He loved who were flagrantly disobedient. But God also extended His loving hand of protection to those who walked in obedience.

Amos was a simple sheepherder from a small city about ten miles south of Jerusalem. He was called by God to deliver a warning to these stiff-necked, idol-worshiping people of the northern kingdom of Israel: " 'I am not a prophet, nor am I the son of a prophet; for I am a herdsman and a grower of sycamore figs. But the Lord took me from following the flock and the Lord said to me, "Go prophesy to My people Israel" ' " (Amos 7:14).

Contained within the nine chapters of this book is a list of the cities and peoples which God considers ripe for judgment, along with the specific warnings. As angry as God already was, He still gave these people two years to repent before the great earthquake came. Still, the people refused to listen.

***

Prayer — Lord, thank You for Amos's prophecy : " 'Also I will restore the captivity of My people Israel, And they will rebuild the ruined cities and live in them' " (Amos 9:14).

Phoebe, Servant of the Church

*I commend to you our sister Phoebe, who is a servant of the
church which is at Cenchrea; that you receive her in the Lord in
a manner worthy of the saints, and that you help her in
whatever matter she may have need of you; for she herself has
also been a helper of many, and of myself as well.*
Romans 16:1-2

The apostle Paul singled Phoebe out as having been a great
help both to the church at Cenchrea and to him personally.
In bestowing this honor upon her, Paul showed to the ages
the depth of Phoebe's Christian commitment.

Paul viewed dedicated people as living testimonies to
all that God's Spirit could accomplish in one's character.
Paul deeply appreciated those who walked in step with him
to teach and nurture others in order to bring the Gospel
message to many.

Paul also requested that other believers receive Phoebe
"in a manner worthy of the saints." Obviously Christ within
her shone out to others like a beacon of light to a needy
world. And he asked that they assist her.

Some Bible translations also refer to her as a deaconess
at the church in Cenchrea. At any rate, she was no ordinary
woman.

Prayer — Lord, as a woman, let my life, as Phoebe's, shine
before others.

Queen Vashti Spurns the King

In those days as King Ahasuerus sat on his royal throne. . .he gave a banquet for all his princes and attendants, the army officers of Persia and Media, the nobles, and the princes of his provinces being in his presence, when he displayed the riches of his royal glory and the splendor of his great majesty for many days, 180 days. And when these days were completed, the king gave a banquet lasting seven days. Esther 1:2-5

Can you imagine a party that went on for 187 days? At the same time Queen Vashti had been giving her own banquet for the women (Esther 1:9). And things were going along quite nicely until. . .

"On the seventh day, when the heart of the king was merry with wine, he commanded. . .the seven eunuchs. . .to bring Queen Vashti before the king with her royal crown in order to display her beauty" (Esther 1:10-11). Queen Vashti, however, refused to appear on cue (Esther 1:12-13).

So the king sought out his legal advisers to discover how he could retaliate against the queen.

" 'For the queen's conduct will become known to all the women causing them to look with contempt on their husbands by saying, "King Ahasuerus commanded Queen Vashti to be brought in to his presence, but she did not come." And this day the ladies of Persia and Media who have heard of the queen's conduct will speak in the same way to all the king's princes, and there will be plenty of contempt and anger' " (Esther 1:17-18).

Prayer — Thank You, Lord God, King of all Kings, that You forgive me when I fail to come into Your presence.

The Apple of God's Eye

"For the day of the Lord draws near on all the nations. As you have done, it will be done to you. Your dealings will return on your own head. Then the house of Jacob will be a fire and the house of Joseph a flame; but the house of Esau will be as stubble. And they will set them on fire and consume them, so that there will be no survivor of the house of Esau," for the Lord has spoken. Obadiah 1:15, 18

Obadiah is such a tiny Old Testament book that you've probably overlooked it. Yet there are prophecies and promises for Israel here which can't be missed.

Israel, the people God had chosen, began to feel so overconfident that they considered themselves invincible. But it wasn't this choosing which made them special. Instead, it was the protection of God that rendered them unique as a people. Now their arrogance and lack of true worship rendered them vulnerable to attack. Obadiah calls Israel back to worship their God, but also issues a warning to Edom, the nation intent on wiping them out.

Scholars have divided opinions as to whether this incident is referring to the time when the Philistines and Arabs invaded Jerusalem in 853-841 B.C., or during the Babylonian sieges, between 605 and 586 B.C. Closing the gap on this date is much less critical than hearing the message.

Prayer — Lord, let me remember that it is Christ who is the head of His Church and I am but a member of the Body.

Wanted: Saints, Dead or Alive?

Those who have been sanctified in Christ Jesus, saints by calling, with all who in every place call upon the name of our Lord Jesus Christ, their Lord and ours. 1 Corinthians 1:2

Car statues are what's happening in the Midwest. I'd forgotten all about them until a few months ago when I traveled back to my roots in Missouri and Illinois.

We might call these statues "saints," but who are the saints to whom Paul addresses this first letter of Corinthians? How about real, live, walking, talking people who "call upon the name of our Lord Jesus Christ" as their Lord and Savior! (1 Corinthians 1:2)

As Christians, we've not only been "called into fellowship with His Son," but Christ "shall confirm us to the end, blameless" as we stand before His throne at the conclusion of our earthly lives (1 Corinthians 1:8-9). Does this intimate that because we belong to Christ we're perfect here on earth? Absolutely not! It just means that because God is faithful, He looks at us and sees the blood of His Son and declares us cleansed from sin.

These Corinthians, whom Paul addressed as saints, were far from model citizens, but he wasn't ashamed to call them brothers. "Now I exhort you, brethren, by the name of our Lord Jesus Christ, that you all agree, and there be no divisions among you, but you be made complete in the same mind and in the same judgment" (1 Corinthians 1:10).

Prayer — Lord, Am I truly Your disciple?

Esther Is Chosen

Then the king's attendants, who served him said, "Let beautiful young virgins be sought for the king. And let the king appoint overseers in all the provinces of his kingdom that they may gather every beautiful young virgin to Susa the capital, to the harem, into the custody of Hegai, the king's eunuch, who was in charge of the women; and let their cosmetics be given them. Then let the young lady who pleases the king be queen in place of Vashti." Esther 2:2–4

The search was on for "the fairest maiden of them all."

The Book of Esther is a beautiful story of a woman's absolute faith and trust in her God. God placed Esther in a position of authority—in order to save the people of Israel.

Mordecai, a Jew in Susa, had returned from the Babylonian exile and was raising his orphaned niece, Esther. And she was "beautiful of form and face. . . Esther was taken to the king's palace" (Esther 2:5-8).

Wisely, "Esther did not make known her people or her kindred" (Esther 2:10). Esther lived in the ultimate spa resort where, for over twelve months, she received beauty treatments and perfume baths.

Finally, "Esther was taken to King Ahasuerus. . . And the king loved Esther more than all the women, and she found favor and kindness with him, so that he set the royal crown on her head and made her queen instead of Vashti" (Esther 2:16-17).

Prayer — In the beginning, Esther was unaware of how God would use her life. Lord, let me be as available and obedient to You.

Jonah Flees God's Call

*The word of the Lord came to Jonah the son of Amittai saying,
"Arise, go to Nineveh the great city, and cry against it, for their
wickedness has come up before Me." But Jonah rose up to flee to
Tarshish from the presence of the Lord. So he went down to
Joppa, found a ship which was going to Tarshish, paid the fare,
and went down into it to go with them to Tarshish from the
presence of the Lord. Jonah 1:1-3*

Jonah flat out didn't want this job, no way, no how! Therefore, he decided to "get out of Dodge." And the quickest
route happened to be on the next boat sailing.

God had solicited Jonah's help in bringing a message to
Nineveh. However, Jonah's fear of these Ninevites loomed
far greater than his fear of the Lord.

But God always gives men and women a chance to
change, and now He set about the task of getting Jonah's
attention. First, "the Lord hurled a great wind on the sea
and there was a great storm. . .so that the ship was about to
break up" (Jonah 1:4). While the other passengers began
frantically praying to their own gods as they threw the cargo
overboard, Jonah went below and fell asleep.

"So the captain approached him and said, 'How is it
that you are sleeping? Get up, call on your god. Perhaps your
god will be concerned about us so that we will not perish' "
(Jonah 1:6). What a joke! Jonah couldn't pray because he
knew exactly who was causing this oceanic disturbance.

Prayer — Lord, I know that finally Jonah responded in
faith. Please help me take responsibility for the areas You're
ready to work on in my life.

Hearing God's Spirit Speak

For to us God revealed them through the Spirit; for the Spirit searches all things, even the depths of God. . . Now we have received, not the spirit of the world, but the Spirit who is from God, that we might know the things freely given to us by God.
1 Corinthians 2:10, 12

Have you ever tried to learn a foreign language? In high school I decided to take Spanish, and although I met the class requirements, I certainly didn't display unusual proficiency. Years later, God brought many Spanish-speaking people into my life. After taking a "Speed Spanish" course at the local junior college, my skills were rejuvenated enough so I could speak on a rudimentary level. Later I took a more in-depth class, and as long as I practiced, the ability to speak and understand Spanish came fairly easily.

This is exactly how to understand the things of God. You can't rely totally on what you received in your early education.

If you came to Christ as an adult then it's probably necessary to start from the beginning, using the Bible, not your memory. Find out what you believe and know why. If you never arrive at this understanding, how on earth can you share your faith with others?

Here's an excuse heard often: "We can't try to interpret the Bible ourselves because we'll get confused." But to refuse the Holy Spirit the opportunity to instruct you, as He promised He would, is to refuse true understanding.

Prayer — Lord, fill my mind and heart with true understanding.

Esther Thwarts a Royal Plot

*In those days, while Mordecai was sitting at the king's gate,
Bigthan and Teresh, two of the king's officials from those who
guarded the door, became angry and sought to lay hands on
King Ahasuerus. But the plot became known to Mordecai, and
he told Queen Esther, and Esther informed the king in
Mordecai's name. Esther 2:21–22*

Overhearing a private conversation in which a murder plot
is discussed, Esther's uncle, Mordecai, a Jew, channeled this
information back to his niece, whom the king trusted.

An official, Haman, had been promoted shortly after
this incident had taken place. The king had commanded that
all who were at the king's gate bow down and pay homage to
Haman. However, Mordecai refused and "Haman was filled
with rage" (Esther 3:5).

Therefore, Haman set an evil plan in motion. First came
his accusation to the king: " 'There is a certain people scattered
and dispersed among the peoples in all the provinces of your
kingdom; their laws are different from those of all other
people, and they do not observe the king's laws, so it is not in
the king's interest to let them remain' " (Esther 3:8).

Then Haman talked the king into issuing a decree that
this people, the Jews, be destroyed. He even offered to pay
10,000 talents of silver to those who carried out what he
termed as " 'the king's business' " (Esther 3:9).

Prayer — Lord, what a dark hour this was for Your people,
but You had already put a plan into action.

Jonah Is Swallowed by a Great Fish

So they said to him, "What should we do to you that the sea may become calm for us?"—for the sea was becoming increasingly stormy. And he said to them, "Pick me up and throw me into the sea. Then the sea will become calm for you, for I know that on account of me this great storm has come upon you." However, the men rowed desperately to return to land but they could not, for the sea was becoming even stormier against them. Jonah 1:11-13

The storm-tossed sailors have two options and neither one sounds like the right one.

Although these men were mad at Jonah for involving them in his duel with God, they were also aware that tossing him overboard like unwanted cargo would almost certainly spell his death. It wasn't until they had no other option that they finally complied with his request.

All they could do now was hope that God allowed him the time to live and speak. The sailors even prayed to Jonah's God.

As soon as they threw Jonah into the water, the sea stopped raging. "Then the men feared the Lord greatly, and they offered a sacrifice to the Lord and made vows. And the Lord appointed a great fish to swallow Jonah, and Jonah was in the stomach of the fish three days and three nights" (Jonah 1:16-17).

Prayer — Lord, You alone have the ability to deliver a great fish to swallow a man whole and not harm him. Help me trust You for creative solutions to all my problems.

Our Bodies, God's Temple

Do you not know that you are a temple of God, and that the Spirit of God dwells in you? If any man destroys the temple of God, God will destroy him, for the temple of God is holy, and that is what you are. 1 Corinthians 3:16-17

While people were living out the Old Testament times, God dwelt in His tabernacle. At first this was a traveling altar, known as the ark of the covenant, which the people carried with them from the time of Moses, through all the lands in which they wandered. When God's Son, Jesus Christ, came to earth He fulfilled God's requirements for sinful man through His death on the cross. Now God could cleanse man that He might indwell him, for God's temple is to be a holy place.

As we go about the business of life perhaps it's hard to remember that God indwells us. The apostle Paul constantly wrestled with desiring to do the right thing but having his flesh at war with his spirit. "For I know that nothing good dwells in me, that is, in my flesh; for the wishing is present in me, but the doing of the good is not. For the good that I wish, I do not do; but I practice the very evil that I do not wish" (Romans 7:18-19).

"However, you are not in the flesh but in the Spirit, if indeed the Spirit of God dwells in you. . . And if Christ is in you, though the body is dead because of sin, yet the spirit is alive because of righteousness" (Romans 8:9-10).

Prayer — Lord, let me live as though I believe You are permeating my very being. Amen.

Queen Esther Learns of a New Deception

And letters were sent by couriers to all the king's provinces to destroy, to kill, and to annihilate all the Jews, . . .in one day, the thirteenth day of the twelfth month, which is the month Adar, and to seize their possessions as plunder.
Esther 3:12-13

The people of Israel had only eleven months to get ready for their extinction. What could they do?

Esther summoned Hathach, one of the king's eunuchs, and ordered him to go to Mordecai and learn what was going on (Esther 4:5).

Mordecai then told Hathach and gave him a copy of the edict so that he would show it to Esther and she might implore the king for mercy. Esther knew that if she entered the king's presence without being summoned she would be killed. So she sent back a message to this effect to Mordecai.

And Mordecai replied, " 'For if you remain silent at this time, relief and deliverance will arise for the Jews from another place and you and your father's house will perish. And who knows whether you have not attained royalty for such a time as this?' " (Esther 4:14)

So three days later, Esther got all "gussied up" and walked around "the inner court of the king's palace in front of the king's rooms." And he saw her and bid her to come near his throne. " 'What is troubling you, Queen Esther? Even to half of the kingdom it will be given to you' " (Esther 5:3).

Prayer — Esther trusted God. I praise Him!

Jonah and God Reach Agreement

"I called out of my distress to the Lord, And He answered me. I cried for help from the depth of Sheol; Thou didst hear my voice. For Thou hadst cast me into the deep. . . All Thy breakers and billows passed over me. So I said, 'I have been expelled from Thy sight. Nevertheless I will look again toward Thy holy temple.' Water encompassed me to the very soul. . .Weeds were wrapped around my head. . . The earth with its bars was around me forever, But Thou hast brought up my life from the pit, O Lord my God. While I was fainting away, I remembered the Lord; And my prayer came to Thee, into Thy holy temple." Jonah 2:2-7

Can't you just see poor Jonah? No human hand can pluck him from the depths as the seaweed wraps around his body and begins to suck him down into the cold dark mire.

There in the belly of the fish, Jonah finally stopped running. Jonah finally pledges allegiance to his God. " 'But I will sacrifice to Thee with the voice of thanksgiving. That which I have vowed I will pay. Salvation is from the Lord' " (Jonah 2:9). Jonah's ears were finally ready to listen to God.

"Then the Lord commanded the fish, and it vomited Jonah up onto the dry land" (Jonah 2:10). And now the Lord issued a fresh call to Jonah, that he might get the response right this time. " 'Arise, go to Nineveh the great city and proclaim to it the proclamation which I am going to tell you' " (Jonah 3:2).

Prayer — Lord, if I'm as author Patsy Clairmont says, "sporting a 'tude," help me take it off today.

The Need for Godly Judges

Does any one of you, when he has a case against his neighbor, dare to go to law before the unrighteous, and not before the saints? Or do you not know that the saints will judge the world? And if the world is judged by you, are you not competent to constitute the smallest law courts? Do you not know that we shall judge angels? How much more, matters of this life? 1 Corinthians 6:1-3

God meant for His Church to govern themselves so that true justice would be served. But He also intended that the believers work out their differences in love. Today men and women have quit counting on the power of God to rule in their lives and have turned instead to the "courts of the unbelievers," where they have not found justice.

Perhaps we should adjust the scales on the statue of the woman who has come to symbolize justice. Spend some time talking to people whose children have been victimized and you will find that their hearts were broken once by the initial crime and then all over again by the judicial system. Our laws must be rewritten with the victim in mind.

The verses above are meant to give you hope. For the saints of God will one day judge those who operate within this world system of injustice. As God brings down His own pair of legal scales to weigh and measure, they will be held accountable to Him.

Prayer — Lord, help me remember the meaning of justice. May my court of law be governed by Your Holy Spirit in my heart.

Queen Esther's Shining Moment

*"If I have found favor in the sight of the king, may the king
and Haman come to the banquet which I shall prepare for
them, and tomorrow I will do as the king says." Esther 5:7-8*

Haman dined with the king and queen. How prestigious!
Then he went out of the gate and saw Mordecai, the Jew
who refused to "tremble at his very presence."

"Haman controlled himself, however, went to his house,
and sent for his friends and his wife Zeresh" (Esther 5:10).
Then he recounted the glory of his riches, and every instance
in which the king had magnified or promoted him. Last but
not least, Haman bragged and gloated about having dined in
the private audience of the king and queen (Esther 5:11-12).
But it still bothered Haman that Mordecai wouldn't bow
down to him. So Haman's wife suggested that he have a
gallows prepared and hang Mordecai on it.

During the night the king couldn't sleep, so he grabbed
the book of records and chronicles and had someone read
them to him. And he found that Mordecai had never been
properly honored for saving the king's life. The king called
Haman and told him to make preparations for someone to
receive a "royal honor." Haman was absolutely shocked
when the king told him to bestow the gifts of a robe, crown,
and horse on Mordecai.

At the second banquet she gave, Queen Esther finally
related to the king the plot to kill all the Jews, reminding
him of his promise to give her anything she desired.

Prayer — Lord, thank You for giving Esther the wisdom
and courage to save her people and Your people, the Jews.

Jonah Learns Compassion

*When God saw their deeds, that they turned from their wicked
ways, then God relented concerning the calamity which He had
declared He would bring upon them. Jonah 3:10*

Have you ever petitioned God on behalf of someone who
deeply needed prayer, only to feel that they were ungrateful
when their life situation finally turned around? Jonah had
risked his life to bring this message to the people of Nineveh
that God was furious with them, and the people didn't even
bother to thank him. So he left the city and went where he
could watch the complete and utter annihilation of Nineveh.

Intruding on Jonah's pity party, God asked, " 'Do you
have good reason to be angry?' " (Jonah 4:4).

And Jonah responded by saying he'd risked life and
limb for nothing. God acted with kindness and compassion,
just as Jonah knew He would. And the Ninevites were never
punished.

"So the Lord God appointed a plant and it grew up
over Jonah to be a shade over his head to deliver him from
his discomfort. And Jonah was extremely happy about the
plant. But God appointed a worm when dawn came the
next day, and it attacked the plant and it withered. And it
came about when the sun came up that God appointed a
scorching east wind, and the sun beat down on Jonah's head
so that he became faint and begged with all his soul to die"
(Jonah 4:6-8).

Prayer — "Then the Lord said, 'Should I not have compassion on Nineveh, the great city in which there are more than
120,000 persons?' " (Jonah 4:10-11). I praise my compas-
sionate God!

To Marry or Stay Single?

It is good for a man not to touch a woman. But because of immoralities, let each man have his own wife, and let each woman have her own husband. Let the husband fulfill his duty to his wife, and likewise also the wife to her husband. But this I say by way of concession, not of command.
1 Corinthians 7:1-3, 6

Paul, a single man, was convinced his marital state enhanced his service to God. He could travel whenever God called him to go, without worrying about a family in tow. By his own admission, the advice he gives here to those in the church is merely a suggestion. Paul is by no means advocating that all who enter God's service should adhere to a vow of living a solitary life. "Yet I wish that all men were even as I myself am. However, each man has his own gift from God, one in this manner, and another in that" (1 Corinthians 7:7).

Paul's admonitions were to those already involved in helping to build God's church. Better than most, Paul knew the hardships which were ahead for all who put their lives on the line that the Gospel might go forward.

If a woman can best serve God as part of a married couple, then the Lord will provide the mate she seeks. And all the give and take which is required will be by mutual consent and respect.

Prayer — Single or married, show me how to make a difference, Lord.

Esther Requests a New Law

On that day King Ahasuerus gave the house of Haman, the enemy of the Jews, to Queen Esther; and Mordecai came before the king, for Esther had disclosed what he was to her. . . And Esther set Mordecai over the house of Haman. Then Esther spoke again to the king, fell at his feet, wept, and implored him to avert the evil scheme of Haman the Agagite and his plot which he had devised against the Jews. And the king extended the golden scepter to Esther. So Esther arose and stood before the king. Esther 8:1-4

When the king extended his scepter, it meant that the person before him had permission to speak. And Esther wasted no time in getting to the point. " 'If it pleases the king. . .let it be written to revoke the letters devised by Haman, which he wrote to destroy the Jews who are in all the king's provinces. For how can I endure to see the calamity which shall befall my people, and how can I endure to see the destruction of my kindred?' " (Esther 8:5-6)

Esther and Mordecai were among the few in the king's palace who had acted in the king's behalf. Everyone else desired personal gain. Esther had risked her life not only for her people but also for the king. Had it not been for God's intervention, Haman undoubtedly would have hanged Esther on that gallows right along with Mordecai.

Prayer — Lord, I thank You for this account of Esther's obedience, loyalty, and trust.

Micah Knew His God

The word of the Lord which came to Micah. . .Hear,
O peoples, all of you; Listen O earth and all it contains, And let
the Lord GOD be a witness against you, The Lord from His
holy temple. For behold, the Lord is coming forth from
His place. He will come down and tread on the high places
of the earth. Micah 1:1-3

Micah understood the Lord's awesome power. In fact, Micah's name means, "who is like Jehovah," forever reminding us that he understood the object of his faith. God used Micah to prophecy to the southern kingdom of Judah.

God's revelation to man was progressive. That's why it's so important to read the entire Bible, as each prophet unfolds another piece of God's end-time mystery. The events recorded in Micah would be fulfilled in the near and far-distant future.

"The mountains will melt under Him, And the valleys will be split, Like wax before the fire, Like water poured down a steep place. All this is for the rebellion of Jacob and for the sins of the house of Israel. . . For I will make Samaria a heap of ruins in the open country, Planting places for a vineyard. I will pour her stones down into the valley, And will lay bare her foundations" (Micah 1:4-6).

Why was God doing this to His people? Both Judah and Israel had forsaken their God, becoming steeped in idolatry.

_____

Prayer — Lord, keep me from following in the footsteps of the rebellious that I might not require bitter lessons of truth.

The Preacher's Livelihood

Who at any time serves as a soldier at his own expense? Who plants a vineyard, and does not eat the fruit of it? Or who tends a flock and does not use the milk of the flock? I am not speaking these things according to human judgment, am I? Or does not the Law also say these things? 1 Corinthians 9:7-8

Those who bring us the Word of God deserve a living wage. This is the point Paul is making. After all, the apostles had given up their homes and any semblance of normal family life in order to travel and present the Gospel. "Do we not have a right to eat and drink? Do we not have a right to take along a believing wife, even as the rest of the apostles, and the brothers of the Lord, and Cephas? Or do only Barnabas and I not have a right to refrain from working?" (1 Corinthians 9:4-6).

The word *apostle* means "one sent under commission." And if they had been called into service by God, weren't they entitled to the financial support from the body of believers? Paul chose to make tents for a living rather than have others support him.

So why did Paul choose to labor without receiving any wages? This way no one could accuse him of presenting the Gospel for personal gain. For Paul considered himself a servant for Jesus' sake (2 Corinthians 4:5).

Prayer — Lord, let me remember in my prayers, tithes, and offerings all those who labor to bring the Word of God to me and others.

The Reason for Job's Suffering

Job. . .was blameless, upright, fearing God, and turning away from evil. And seven sons and three daughters were born to him. His possessions also were 7,000 sheep, 3,000 camels, 500 yoke of oxen, 500 female donkeys, and very many servants. Job 1:1–3

This, of course, was life as Job used to know it, before his character was tested. "And the Lord said to Satan, 'Have you considered My servant Job? For there is no one like him on the earth, a blameless and upright man, fearing God and turning away from evil.' Then Satan answered the Lord, 'Does Job fear God for nothing? Hast Thou not made a hedge about him and his house. . .and all his possessions have increased in the land. But put forth Thy hand now and touch all that he has; he will surely curse Thee to Thy face' " (Job 1:8-11).

Satan intimated to God that Job only loved Him because of all the blessings Job had received. "Then the Lord said to Satan, 'Behold, all that he has is in your power, only do not put forth your hand on him' " (Job 1:12).

Job's life became an unwelcome ride on a trolley called tragedy. In one day he lost all his children and his house, servants, and livestock. And through all of this Job refused to blame God or sin.

Prayer — Lord, as a Christian, lead me so that I do not expect You to be my "celestial Santa Claus." Lead me so I continue to follow, no matter the circumstances. — Amen

The Content of Our Thoughts

Woe to those who scheme iniquity, Who work out evil on their beds! When morning comes, they do it, For it is in the power of their hands. They covet fields and then seize them, And houses, and take them away. They rob a man and his house, A man and his inheritance. Micah 2:1-2

Micah acknowledges that the source of evil thoughts is the human mind. Other portions of Scripture also bear out this truth.

"Transgression speaks to the ungodly within his heart; There is no fear of God before his eyes. For it flatters him in his own eyes, Concerning the discovery of his iniquity and the hatred of it. The words of his mouth are wickedness and deceit; He has ceased to be wise and do good. He plans wickedness upon his bed; He sets himself on a path that is not good; He does not despise evil" (Psalm 36:1-4).

Therein lies the problem, that we at some point begin to accept wickedness as good. And the things we devise in our minds then become the vehicle for our actions.

Part and parcel of idolatrous worship, for which Israel as a nation assumed guilt before God, was that of human sacrifice to pagan gods. Can you understand why this sin was so detestable to the Lord?

Prayer — Lord, guard my mind from evil that I might not ruminate on such things and be propelled into ungodly actions. Instead, let me turn to Your Word which acts as a cleansing agent.

God, Judge of Immorality Past and Present

For I do not want you to be unaware, brethren, that our fathers were all under the cloud, and all passed through the sea; and all were baptized into Moses in the cloud and in the sea; and all ate the same spiritual food; and all drank the same spiritual drink, for they were drinking from a spiritual rock which followed them; and the rock was Christ. Nevertheless, with most of them God was not well-pleased; for they were laid low in the wilderness. Now these things happened as examples for us, that we should not crave evil things, as they also craved. . . Nor let us act immorally, as some of them did, and twenty-three thousand fell in one day.
1 Corinthians 10:1-6, 8

By reading the entire Bible we have the privilege of learning from God's dealings with men and women throughout recorded history so we will not fall into the same traps. Twenty-three thousand people fell by the sword in one day because they joined themselves with pagan gods in sexual rituals, refusing to obey the true God.

How can we stop ourselves from falling into sin? By remembering: "No temptation has overtaken you but such as is common to man; and God is faithful, who will not allow you to be tempted beyond what you are able, but with the temptation will provide the way of escape also, that you may be able to endure it" (1 Corinthians 10:13).

Prayer — Father, help me avoid temptation by taking one step closer to You.

A Little Help from His Friends

"Remember now, who ever perished being innocent? Or where were the upright destroyed? According to what I have seen, those who plow iniquity And those who sow trouble harvest it. By the breath of God they perish, And by the blast of His anger they come to an end." Job 4:7-9

Thanks to Satan, the second wave of sorrows has been inflicted on Job. Now he's covered "with sore boils from the sole of his foot to the crown of his head" (Job 2:7).

At this point Job's wife asks, " 'Do you still hold fast your integrity? Curse God and die!' " (Job 2:9) Rather than "standing by her man," she accuses Job as she struggles with her own grief.

Just when things couldn't get worse, along comes Job's friend, Eliphaz, to put in his own two cents. Eliphaz drops a bomb at Job's feet: " 'For man is born for trouble, as sparks fly upward' " (Job 5:7).

"Then Job answered, 'Oh that my vexation were actually weighed, and laid in the balances together with my iniquity! For then it would be heavier than the sand of the seas, therefore my words have been rash. . . But it is still my consolation, And I rejoice in unsparing pain, that I have not denied the words of the Holy One' " (Job 6:1-3, 10).

Do we stand on the bedrock of knowledge about God's goodness, despite the circumstances? Or do we succumb to the taunting of cruel and unfeeling friends?

Prayer — Lord, sometimes I have been targeted by the misguided missiles of well-meaning friends. Show me that true relief is spelled J-E-S-U-S.

Bethlehem's Child Will Rule

*And He will arise and shepherd his flock In the strength of the
Lord, In the majesty of the name of the Lord His God. And
they will remain, Because at that time He will be great To the
ends of the earth. And this One will be our peace.*
Micah 5:4-5

In only two months you'll be into Christmas. Before
the tyranny of toys and tinsel vanquishes the true meaning
of this blessed time, let's reflect on whose birth we're preparing to celebrate.

As you read the next Scripture verse, keep Christ's
character in mind. "Then a shoot will spring from the stem
of Jesse, And a branch from his roots will bear fruit. And the
Spirit of the Lord will rest on Him. . . And He will delight
in the fear of the Lord. . .with righteousness He will judge
the poor, And decide with fairness for the afflicted of the
earth; And with the breath of his lips He will slay the wicked"
(Isaiah 11:1-4).

Christ's birth demanded worship or fear. After Jesus'
birth the magi inquired of King Herod, " 'Where is He who
has been born King of the Jews? For we saw His star in the
east, and have come to worship Him' " (Matthew 2:1-2). And
they quoted Micah 5:2 to Herod, who then decided to kill
this babe rather than face Him either as king or judge. But
God hid the child in Egypt until Herod's death (Matthew
2:14-15, 19-20).

Prayer — I rejoice because Christ is coming back! "He will
rule them with a rod of iron; . . . And on His robe and on
His thigh He has a name written, 'King of Kings, And Lord
of Lords' " (Revelation 19:15-16).

The Holy Spirit, Our Great Gift

*Therefore I make known to you, that no one speaking by the
Spirit of God says, "Jesus is accursed"; and no one can say,
"Jesus is Lord," except by the Holy Spirit.
1 Corinthians 12:3*

For twenty-nine years a desperate woman waded through the
motions of life, wondering whether the Creator really cared
for her at all. Her loneliness and despair seemed to confirm
to her that He didn't. And then came the day when the
Gospel message finally penetrated her soul with its extraordinary light and she began to call Him Lord.

I was that woman. When I heard today's Scripture the
truth flew straight and sure as an arrow to the deepest part
of my being.

It's no accident that despair caused me to succumb to
messages of doubt concerning God's nature and character.
The evil one is, after all, the author of confusion and lies.
However, as I tested the spirits the truth became clear. "By
this you know the Spirit of God: every spirit that confesses
that Jesus Christ has come in the flesh is from God; and
every spirit that does not confess Jesus is not from God; and
this is the spirit of the antichrist, of which you have heard
that it is coming, and now it is already in the world"
(1 John 4:2-3).

Prayer — Lord, I know if I'm listening to a message that
makes me depressed and defeated, that's from Satan. I know
the one that says I'm worth dying for is from Christ.

God Has Been There, Done That

"It is God who removes the mountains, . . .Who alone stretches out the heavens, And tramples down the waves of the sea; Who makes the Bear, Orion, and the Pleiades, And the chambers of the south; Who does great things, unfathomable, And wondrous works without number." Job 9:5, 8-10

In one theology class I took, the teacher asked us to examine the ways in which we attempt to stuff God into a box. As A. W. Tozer said, "We tend to reduce God to manageable terms."

As our human nature cries out to control what we don't understand, this feat becomes impossible. For the God who has created all that we see, hear, touch, taste, and smell has been there and done that.

When we accept this, our own importance seems diminished.

Even as Job screamed for relief from his pain, he recognized that both blessings and testing through trials flowed from the same loving hands. " 'Thy hands fashioned and made me altogether, And wouldst Thou destroy me? Remember now, that Thou has made me as clay; And wouldst Thou turn me into dust again? Thou hast granted me life and lovingkindness; And Thy care has preserved my spirit' " (Job 10:8-9, 12).

Prayer — I await the balm of good news from You, Lord. O may Thy lovingkindness comfort me, "According to Thy word to Thy servant. May Thy compassion come to me that I may live, For Thy law is my delight" (Psalm 119:76-77).

What Response Does God Require?

With what shall I come to the Lord And bow myself before the God on high? . . . He has told you, O man, what is good; And what does the Lord require of you But to do justice, to love kindness, And to walk humbly with your God?
Micah 6:6, 8

They drag themselves across the uneven pavement until their knees are bloodied and their exhausted bodies finally fall against the splintered wooden doors to the church. In this way, many in Mexico seek to do their yearly public penance for sin.

Christ has already paid the price that needed to be exacted for our sins. He took the whips, the lashes, the nailing to the cross, the verbal rebukes, and also the physical agony on our behalf. The God of this universe looked upon our futility and became a man, and then He sacrificed His life so that we who did not and could not ever deserve His mercy might obtain it. Jesus Christ did all this because He is both just and kind.

Isaiah prophesied the promise of Christ's cross. "Surely our griefs He Himself bore, And our sorrows He carried. . . But He was pierced through for our transgressions, He was crushed for our iniquities; The chastening for our well-being fell upon Him, And by His scourging we are healed" (Isaiah 53:4-5).

Prayer — Though I expend every effort, I can never rid myself of sin. You've already provided the only way in which I can be cleansed.

How to Know If You're in Love

If I speak with the tongues of men and of angels, but do not have love, I have become a noisy gong or a clanging cymbal.
1 Corinthians 13:1

"Although we love each other deeply, I know there will be times when we'll fail to be there for one another. That's when we'll go to the Lord to receive in abundance what we lack." These words of wisdom were spoken by a twenty-four-year-old woman who had just become engaged. If only more marriages began this way! For even though we've prayed for godly mates, and then relied on His guidance, there will still be times when our attempts to love are less than perfect.

However, if both man and woman turn back to God's blueprint, harmony can be restored. "Love is patient, love is kind, and is not jealous; love does not brag and is not arrogant, does not act unbecomingly; it does not seek its own, is not provoked, does not take into account a wrong suffered, does not rejoice in unrighteousness, but rejoices with the truth; bears all things, believes all things, hopes all things, endures all things. Love never fails" (1 Corinthians 13:4-8).

Why don't more people tap into this resource? To truly love someone means that we will always place that person's welfare above our own. This, after all, is how God loves us.

Prayer — Lord, help me exhibit true love.

True Environmentalists

"But now ask the beasts, and let them teach you; And the birds of the heavens, and let them tell you. Or speak to the earth, and let it teach you; And let the fish of the sea declare to you. Who among all these does not know That the hand of the Lord has done this, In whose hand is the life of every living thing, And the breath of all mankind?" Job 12:7-10

The news media regularly report how the earth's resources and species are diminishing rapidly. Perhaps we have forgotten that God also cares about every living thing.

While I was visiting with friends recently, one asked if animals go to heaven. I reminded her man alone is made in the image and likeness of God, and also the recipient of salvation. This pat answer seemed to leave my friends very disappointed. So, I offer another verse of Scripture as comfort: "And there is no creature hidden from His sight" (Hebrews 4:13).

"For in Him all things were created, both in the heavens and on earth. . .all things have been created through Him and for Him" (Colossians 1:16). It's important to remember that Christ created animals for our enjoyment. Therefore, be grateful to the Lord.

Prayer — Lord, I know that even if I didn't have Your written Word, the order and perfection of Your creation still prove Your existence!

The True Shepherd Will Return

And the earth will become desolate because of her inhabitants,
On account of the fruit of their deeds. Shepherd Thy people
with Thy scepter, The flock of Thy possession Which dwells by
itself in the woodland, in the midst of a fruitful field.
Micah 7:13-14

When David first received the Lord's call he was a simple shepherd boy. Yet God raised him up to become Israel's great king. Did the death of David mean the end of His rule?

First, let's consider the facts surrounding the promise from God to bring Israel back to their land. " 'And I shall bring Israel back to his pasture, and he will graze on Carmel and Bashan, and his desire will be satisfied in the hill country of Ephraim and Gilead. In those days and at that time,' declares the Lord, 'search will be made for the iniquity of Israel, but there will be none; for I shall pardon those whom I leave as a remnant' " (Jeremiah 50:19-20). Israel will return to their land during a time in which they are a surviving remnant and, more importantly, forgiven.

Jesus claimed to be the Good Shepherd. " 'I am the good shepherd; the good shepherd lays down His life for the sheep' " (John 10:11). The return of the Shepherd has to take place after He has already died for the sheep.

Furthermore, the Shepherd's return at the end of the age will be as judge. " 'For the Lamb in the center of the throne shall be their shepherd, and shall guide them to springs of the water of life; and God shall wipe every tear from their eyes' " (Revelation 7:17).

Prayer — I look forward to meeting my Shepherd!

By One Man Death,
By Another Man Life

But now Christ has been raised from the dead, the first fruits of those who are asleep. For since by a man came death, by a man also came the resurrection of the dead. For as in Adam all die, so also in Christ all shall be made alive.
1 Corinthians 15:20-22

Satan would love to seduce us into thinking that Christ never rose from the dead. If that were the case, the whole foundation of our faith would crumble. During Paul's time some men had already begun to teach such heresy. For this reason, God inspired Paul to provide proof of the Resurrection.

The first question Paul settled was whether or not the dead are actually raised. Although Christ had raised Lazarus, some had begun to waver on this truth. Christ had prophesied His own death and Resurrection (John 2:19). And after His Resurrection, Christ was seen by Mary Magdalene, Peter, John, James, and the rest of the disciples.

Another proof of the Resurrection was the testimony of all who had placed their trust in Christ, for He had transformed their lives. On Pentecost the disciples displayed such a metamorphosis. Furthermore, they continued to stand firm, proof of their genuine faith.

And lastly, we have the testament of Scripture itself. From man's beginning in the Garden of Eden, one Savior was promised (Genesis 3:15).

Prayer — Jesus Christ hung on the cross to save me.

His Fortunes Restored

And the Lord restored the fortunes of Job when he prayed for his friends, and the Lord increased all that Job had twofold. . . And the Lord blessed the latter days of Job more than his beginning, and he had 14,000 sheep, and 6,000 camels, and 1,000 yoke of oxen, and 1,000 female donkeys. And he had seven sons and three daughters. Job 42:10, 12-13

Don't you just love stories with happy endings? Reading through the Book of Job makes anyone cry out for a great finish.

In today's Scripture, we join up again with Job's two friends. Well, the long arm of God's justice finally caught up with them and the Lord called them to accountability. " 'Now therefore, take for yourselves seven bulls and seven rams, and go to My servant Job, and offer up a burnt offering for yourselves, and My servant Job will pray for you. For I will accept him so that I may not do with you according to your folly, because you have not spoken of Me what is right, as My servant Job has' " (Job 42:8).

Finally, Job received the Lord's public vindication. Revenge doesn't get any sweeter than that! And don't you know that Eliphaz and Temanite were "sweatin' it big time" as they awaited Job's eloquent prayer that would restrain God's hand of wrath!

Prayer — Lord, through Job's pain, agony, and loss You placed "wisdom in his innermost being" concerning deep and marvelous truths about Your character. When I am afflicted, remind me to turn toward You.

Nahum Proclaims Israel's Restoration

*Behold, on the mountains the feet of him who brings good
news, Who announces peace! Celebrate your feasts, O Judah;
Pay your vows. For never again will the wicked one pass
through you; He is cut off completely. Nahum 1:15*

No news could be sweeter than the confirmation that a
mighty enemy army was about to suffer a great demise. God
gave Nahum, the prophet, just such a vision concerning the
great Assyrian invaders who had devastated Judah. It had
been such a long time that these pagans began boasting no
god would be able to deliver the Israelites. However, the true
God of power and might was now ready to act against them
for enslaving His people. And they never saw it coming!

"The Lord takes vengeance on His adversaries, And
He reserves wrath for His enemies. The Lord is slow to
anger and great in power, And the Lord will by no means
leave the guilty unpunished. . . Bashan and Carmel wither;
The blossoms of Lebanon wither" (Nahum 1:2-4).

Nahum knows that if God is presenting a message then
He's ready to take action. So Nahum, whose name means
"comforter," is going to extol the virtues of His God to these
pagans. That way, when God does begin His judgment,
they'll know exactly whom they have encountered.

Prayer — Lord, You are a mighty foe indeed! Why do
people devise plots against You?

When Will Our Suffering Cease?

Blessed be the God and Father of our Lord Jesus Christ, the Father of mercies and God of all comfort; who comforts us in all our affliction so that we may be able to comfort those who are in any affliction with the comfort with which we ourselves are comforted by God. But if we are afflicted, it is for your comfort and salvation. 2 Corinthians 1:3-4, 6

An experienced mountain biker and triathelete, my son hit some debris in the street when he was riding recently and, before he could dislodge his shoe clips, was thrown from his bike and onto a pile of bricks. His knee took the brunt of the fall, requiring surgery to repair the breaks.

Yet he seems to be taking this whole episode in stride, with a graciousness one wouldn't think possible. He and his fiancée have learned to depend upon each other in a new way: She is providing the medical expertise he desperately needs, while he has learned to allow her to intervene. And both of them depend entirely on the Lord's sufficiency.

This is the purpose of our trials, that we might comfort one another and lean on the Lord's strength. Paul's own burdens had been borne with a view of Christ that few of us will ever know.

Prayer — Thank You, God, that in heaven all suffering will cease.

Slavery Is Nothing New

I appeal to you for my child, whom I have begotten in my imprisonment, Onesimus. . . And I have sent him back to you in person. . .without your consent I did not want to do anything, that your goodness should not be as it were by compulsion, but of your own free will. Philemon 1:10, 12, 14

While imprisoned in Rome, the apostle Paul wrote this letter to Philemon who was then in Colossae. Philemon's slave, Onesimus, robbed his master and then fled to Rome. He met Paul and was converted. However, according to Roman law he could still be put to death by his master.

This passage provides a clear picture of what the Father did for each of us by sending His Son, Jesus Christ.

Paul became the beloved friend to both Philemon and Onesimus, not wishing for either to harm the other. He spoke to them heart-to-heart.

This wasn't an isolated case. Millions of slaves lived throughout the region, and all were accustomed to being bought and sold like merchandise. If they did manage to escape, their names were posted on "wanted" lists. Anyone finding deserting slaves could keep them. Paul could have simply exercised his legal right.

Paul now approached Philemon as a burdened partner in ministry. "If then you regard me as a partner, accept him as you would me. But if he has wronged you in any way, or owes you anything, charge that to my account" (Philemon 1:17-18).

Prayer — Father, my sins have been charged to Christ's account. He paid the debt.

What Is Your Foundation?

"Woe to him who builds a city with bloodshed And founds a town with violence!" Habakkuk 2:12

No matter how many westerns are made, we still flood into movie theaters to see them. We're fascinated that people survived for a time without food, water, and shelter to conquer the western frontier.

Yet the first western settlements were as much founded on religious beliefs as they were on bloodshed.

Blazing new territories isn't just about conquering the land. Martin Luther was pierced by a verse in Habakkuk and his reaction changed the course of church history. " 'The righteous will live by his faith' " (Habakkuk 2:4). But in whom is this faith placed? If our faith is in Christ, we are established upon firm ground. But if it's in systems, programs, or even religion, it's doomed to fail.

The people of Judah were entering their darkest hour. The Babylonians had invaded this southern kingdom three times. During the final siege both Jerusalem and the temple were destroyed. Habakkuk is seeking assurance from the Lord that He will save them from extinction.

Prayer — Thank You, God, for Your promise to Habakkuk: " 'For the vision is yet for the appointed time; It hastens toward the goal, and it will not fail. Though it tarries, wait for it; For it will certainly come, it will not delay' " (Habakkuk 2:3).

Paul's Trip to Paradise

I know a man in Christ who fourteen years ago. . .was caught up into Paradise, and heard inexpressible words, which a man is not permitted to speak. On behalf of such a man I will boast; but on my own behalf I will not boast, except in regard to my weaknesses. 2 Corinthians 12:2, 4-5

God propelled Paul up to heaven for a glimpse of what was ahead for him and all believers.

But why does Paul present this vision as though it happened to someone else? Remember that he had been trained as a rabbi and had received a thorough knowledge of the law. Rabbis often refer to themselves in the third person, to refrain from sounding unduly prideful. Paul does clarify how he has handled pride. "To keep me from exalting myself, there was given me a thorn in the flesh, a messenger of Satan to buffet me—to keep me from exalting myself!" (2 Corinthians 12:7)

He never tells what that affliction was. But he did understand it as coming from the Lord. Paul chose not to dwell on his discomfort, clinging instead to the incredible and unforgettable things he saw and heard while in heaven.

Prayer — Lord, Your magnificent presence is all I need to provide me with the momentum to continue spreading Your Word.

We Still Have a High Priest

God. . . In these last days has spoken to us in His Son, whom He appointed heir of all things, through whom also He made the world. . . When He had made purification of sins, He sat down at the right hand of the majesty on high.
Hebrews 1:1-3

While the human author of the Book of Hebrews is unknown to us, the divine author is the Holy Spirit. Indeed, the messages contained in this volume are consistent with all the doctrine presented in the Wordof God.

This particular book confirms to those who had left the rituals of Judaism that they still had a high priest who could petition the Father for them. He is Jesus Christ, their Messiah, our Savior and Lord. For in Him the sacrificial offering for sin was made complete.

Once Christ had paid in full the debt man owed for sin, the infusion of God's Spirit became possible, taking place on the day of Pentecost. "And suddenly there came from heaven a noise like a violent, rushing wind, and it filled the whole house where they were sitting. . . And they were all filled with the Holy Spirit. . ." (Acts 2:2, 4).

Now God tabernacles among men, and Christ, God's perfect Lamb, also became our High Priest. "For we do not have a high priest who cannot sympathize with our weaknesses, but one who has been tempted in all things as we are yet without sin" (Hebrews 4:15).

Prayer — I, who believe in His Son, can enter into worship!

Woe to the Mediocre!

*"Then it will come about on the day of the Lord's sacrifice,
That I will punish the princes, the king's sons, And all who
clothe themselves with foreign garments. And I will punish on
that day all who leap on the temple threshold, Who fill the
house of their lord with violence and deceit. . . Wail,
O inhabitants of the Mortar, for all the people of Canaan
will be silenced." Zephaniah 1:8-9, 11*

Out in California we take our earthquakes in stride. But
most of us have a stash of water, canned goods, and at least
a small box of emergency first-aid supplies. We "hope for
the best, but prepare for the worst."

Zephaniah's call from the Lord involved dislodging
those who were indifferent to God. " 'I will search Jerusalem
with lamps, and I will punish the men who are stagnant in
spirit, who say in their hearts, "The Lord will not do good
or evil!" ' " (Zephaniah 1:12)

Look around, America! While the latest opinion polls
show that a majority of us claim to believe in God, the crime
rate soars, homosexuality (called sin by God) is accepted as
normal behavior, the divorce rate increases, and our teens
search in vain for godly role models. How is faith evidenced?

This is the same question God was posing to Israel.
And as surely as judgment fell upon them, it will ultimately
fall on us.

———————————

Prayer — Only my faith in You will save me.

Grace Versus the Law

I am amazed that you are so quickly deserting Him who called you by the grace of Christ, for a different gospel; which is really not another; only there are some who are disturbing you, and want to distort the gospel of Christ. Galatians 1:6-7

Christmas will be here before we know it. Perhaps there will be a big red package under the tree for you, perhaps a brand-new bathrobe? Doesn't your family know how comforting and warm your old robe is? Are they trying to rip away this "nucleus of your solace"? No, they just want to replace one that is threadbare, faded, and otherwise tacky with a better-looking model.

Jewish believers were transitioning from the Law, filled with regulations, and beginning to follow the Gospel of grace. However, they easily fell into the trap of "desiring their old robes back." A group called the Judaizers began wooing them back to the old covenant rites, including circumcision.

Therefore, Paul, God's apostle to the Gentiles, left on his missionary journeys to bring the Gospel of grace to those who were being seduced by this group.

Paul, teacher of the Law, now speaks to them of his own conversion. "The gospel which was preached by me is not according to man. For I neither received it from man, nor was I taught it, but I received it through a revelation of Jesus Christ" (Galatians 1:11-12).

Prayer — Paul played a central role in the "persecution of the church of God beyond measure." But seeing Christ, face-to-face, reduced him to heartfelt repentance. Lord, strengthen my own commitment to You.

Whom Do You Follow, Moses or Christ?

Therefore, holy brethren, partakers of a heavenly calling, consider Jesus, the Apostle and High Priest of our confession. He was faithful to Him who appointed Him, as Moses also was in all His house. For He has been counted worthy of more glory than Moses, by just so much as the builder of the house has more honor than the house. For every house is built by someone, but the builder of all things is God. Hebrews 3:1-4

Do you ever wake up thinking about someone you may not have seen in years? Well, that's a "God call." God may be prompting your heart to respond to that person's need for encouragement.

One of Paul's great gifts was that of being an encourager. Yes, he spoke the truth unabashedly, yet he tempered it with praise and hope. "As you therefore have received Christ Jesus the Lord, so walk in Him, having been firmly rooted and now being built up in Him and established in your faith, just as you were instructed, and overflowing with gratitude" (Colossians 2:6-7).

The writer of the Book of Hebrews spoke with the same conviction and understanding. "Encourage one another day after day, as long as it is still called 'Today,' lest any one of you be hardened by the deceitfulness of sin. For we have become partakers of Christ, if we hold fast the beginning of our assurance firm until the end" (Hebrews 3:13-14).

Prayer — Man's memory of his own disobedience is so quickly forgotten, Lord. The opportunity to follow Christ lays before me. Lord, help me respond.

A Day of Prayer

Gather yourselves together, yes, gather, O nation without shame. . . Seek the Lord, All you humble of the earth Who have carried out His ordinances; Seek righteousness, seek humility. Perhaps you will be hidden In the day of the Lord's anger.
Zephaniah 2:1, 3

Here Zephaniah is addressing those who have become totally turned off and unresponsive to God.

The majority of Zephaniah's audience will perish instead of listening with their hearts. Only a faithful few will be spared. " 'But I will leave among you a humble and lowly people, and they will take refuge in the name of the Lord. The remnant of Israel will do no wrong and tell no lies, nor will a deceitful tongue be found in their mouths; For they shall feed and lie down with no one to make them tremble. Shout for joy, O daughter of Zion!' " (Zephaniah 3:12-14)

The remnant which survived, long into Israel's future, saw the day of this prophecy's fulfillment. "Shout in triumph, O daughter of Jerusalem! Behold, your king is coming to you; He is just and endowed with salvation, humble, and mounted on a donkey, Even on a colt, the foal of a donkey" (Zechariah 9:9).

Prayer — Thank You, Father, that prayer can place me in Your presence.

For What Are You Zealous?

For am I now seeking the favor of men, or of God? Or am I striving to please men? If I were still trying to please men, I would not be a bond-servant of Christ. Galatians 1:10

"Save the Whales," "Save the Rain Forests," read the placards of our times. But where are the billboards which proclaim, "Save the Human Soul"? Paul carried such a sign every day.

He was a "Jew's Jew" and proficient at keeping the law of Moses. Then Paul's life took an unscheduled detour. "But when He who had set me apart, even from my mother's womb, and called me through His grace, was pleased to reveal His Son in me, that I might preach Him among the Gentiles, I did not immediately consult with flesh and blood, nor did I go up to Jerusalem to those who were apostles before me; but I went away to Arabia, and returned once more to Damascus" (Galatians 1:15-17).

Paul didn't sit around asking men for their opinions. Christ's call was sufficient. Therefore, he devoted himself to study, prayer, and meditation alone with his Lord. For although he'd known the Scriptures, he had approached them from the wrong perspective. Paul would spend three years allowing his Lord to instruct him correctly in all that he'd missed the first time.

Prayer — Lord, what are my own misconceptions concerning Your Word? Teach me the true meaning of the Scriptures.

Who Is the Rightful Heir?

Abraham had two sons, one by the bond woman and one by the free woman. But the son by the bondwoman was born according to the flesh, and the son by the free woman through the promise. Galatians 4:22

Sibling rivalry is at the crux of the quarrel between the Arabs and Israelis. Both peoples claim Abraham as their father and therefore feel entitled to his inheritance. However, God Himself made a great distinction between the two, calling Isaac the "son of promise" and Ishmael "the son of the slave woman."

God had promised Abraham a son but at eighty-six years old, Abraham had become weary of waiting (Genesis 16:16). To him, it was apparent that Sarah, his wife, was barren. So, at Sarah's urging, Abraham sought out the slave girl Hagar, and she conceived. Abraham's action led to much dissension within his home. And by the time Sarah conceived the son of promise, the household was in a complete upheaval. God promised to make both sides great nations (Genesis 21:9-13).

Paul now uses these two sons to illustrate the status of the unbeliever versus her changed relationship once she commits her life to Christ. Once we were slaves to sin. But with our redemption in Christ we become free.

Prayer — Lord, through the line of Isaac men and women are truly blessed. For Christ Himself would be that seed from whom Redemption would come (Galatians 3:13-18).

Get Those Hammers Ready

"Thus says the Lord of hosts, 'This people says, "The time has not come, even the time for the house of the Lord to be rebuilt." ' "
Then the word of the Lord came by Haggai the prophet saying,
"Is it time for you yourselves to dwell in your paneled houses while this house lies desolate?" Now therefore, thus says the Lord of hosts, "Consider your ways!"
Haggai 1:2-5

Since our winters here in California are fairly mild, a coat of paint can last about twenty years. The roof, however, is another story. When several severe rainstorms hit the coastline, we knew we'd ignored that roof long enough!

This same shabby state of affairs could be seen during the time of Haggai with God's temple. Although a small remnant had begun rebuilding, they had become overwhelmed. For about sixteen years the temple stood like a piece of unfinished furniture. Now God commissioned Haggai to bring His motivating Word to the people.

"So the Lord stirred up the spirit of Zerubbabel the son of Shealtiel, governor of Judah, and the spirit of Joshua the son of Jehozadak, the high priest, and the spirit of the remnant of the people; and they came and worked on the house of the Lord of hosts, their God" (Haggai 1:14).

The task loomed larger than life so the Lord spoke again: " '. . . take courage, . . .' declares the Lord, 'and work; for I am with you' " (Haggai 2:4).

Prayer — Lord, whatever task is overwhelming me today You have the strength to see it through to fulfillment.

Halloween, Day of Evil or Innocent Fun?

Therefore, let us fear lest, while a promise remains of entering His rest, any one of you should seem to have come short of it. For indeed we have had good news preached to us, just as they also; but the word they heard did not profit them, because it was not united by faith in those who heard. Hebrews 4:1-2

Halloween is here again. Time for Christians to espouse their polarized viewpoints concerning this mysterious and/or magical time of year. Halloween isn't just about dressing up and collecting candy. Today it's become an issue that each Christian must address.

Realizing that a child's objective is not to indulge in the occult but instead to have fun, Christian writers are exercising their creativity. To go along with the "harvest festival" idea, already fostered by many churches, is a drama book by Louis Merryman entitled *Halloween Alternatives,* containing ideas for reaching young minds with the Gospel. A book by Liz Curtis Higgs, *The Pumpkin Patch Parable,* relates how God plants the seed of belief in our hearts.

Today's Scripture is about "entering into God's rest," something which those who do not choose Him will never experience.

Prayer — Dear God, I know You have kept Your part of the bargain, in obtaining salvation for me through Christ's death on the cross. Whether I respond to this salvation or not is up to me.

Melchizedek, Priest of the Most High God

For this Melchizedek, king of Salem, priest of the Most High God, who met Abraham as he was returning from the slaughter of the kings and blessed him, to whom also Abraham apportioned a tenth part of all the spoils, was first of all, by the translation of his name, king of righteousness, and then also king of Salem, which is king of peace. Without father, without mother, without genealogy, having neither beginning of days nor end of life, but made like the Son of God, he abides a priest perpetually. Hebrews 7:1-3

Perhaps this is the first you've heard of Melchizedek. The meaning of his name is extremely significant. "King of righteousness" or "King of peace" is used for Christ alone.

Melchizedek is first mentioned in Genesis. This priest of the Most High God came out to meet Abraham as he returned from defeating all the kings in battle. Melchizedek brought him bread and wine, blessed him, and introduced himself as a priest of God Most High (Genesis 14:17-24). Abraham affirmed this king-priest by giving Melchizedek tithes and also receiving the blessing he gave.

Although Melchizedek is spoken of as a real man, there is no record of his genealogy. This is particularly significant because he was not from the tribe of Levi. Therefore, Melchizedek's priesthood is not only superior to that of Levi, but also a perpetual one. The Levitical priesthood, no longer necessary after Christ's death on the cross, ended when the temple was destroyed.

Prayer — Thank You for Your Word, Heavenly Father.

Zechariah, Messenger of Messiah's Triumph

I saw at night, and behold, a man was riding on a red horse, and he was standing among the myrtle trees which were in the ravine, with red, sorrel, and white horse behind him. Then I said, "My Lord, what are these?" And the angel who was speaking with me said to me, "I will show you what these are." And the man who was standing among the myrtle trees answered and said, "These are those whom the Lord has sent to patrol the earth." Zechariah 1:8-10

Zechariah's name means "God remembers." And the message he received from the Lord came at a time when Israel most needed to be reminded that their God still stood watch over them. For only a remnant of them had returned from the Babylonian captivity. The temple and the city walls were in ruins. Then the prophet Haggai brought them the Word of the Lord, telling them to rebuild the temple after their initial enthusiasm had waned and an interim of eighteen years had lapsed. They needed hope, and so, two months later, the Lord sent Zechariah.

Through a series of eight visions God unfolds His future plans for Israel and the completion of the temple to Zechariah.

Prayer — Lord, help to clarify this beautiful book of prophecy that I will look at it with eyes of wisdom.

The Fruit of the Spirit

But the fruit of the Spirit is love, joy, peace, patience, kindness,
goodness, faithfulness, gentleness, self-control; against such
things there is no law. Now those who belong to Christ Jesus
have crucified the flesh with its passions and desires. If we live
by the Spirit, let us also walk by the Spirit.
Galatians 5:22-25

When we become Christians we receive spiritual gifts as a result of our inward relationship with Jesus Christ. These gifts are known in the Bible as the fruit of the Spirit, but what does that really mean?

Inventoried in today's Scripture are qualities that, apart from God's power, would likely not be displayed in our character.

Take, for instance, joy. How many truly joyful people do you know? Most of us could probably count them on one hand. Joy is the inward peace and sufficiency which transcends life's circumstances.

So, what's the catch? Why is God showering us with these gifts? Because they prove that He can enter a human life and affect her or him with change, that others might also be won to Christ as they observe this miracle.

Prayer — Lord, my greatest gift from You is salvation, Your grace enables me to begin life with a fresh start. And with this transformation of character, fruit becomes the yield, shared as I serve the body of believers with my unique spiritual gifts.

James, Bond-Servant of God

James, a bond-servant of God and of the Lord Jesus Christ, to the twelve tribes who are dispersed abroad, greetings. Consider it all joy, my brethren, when you encounter various trials, knowing that the testing of your faith produces endurance.
James 1:1-3

As the Lord's half-brother, James had observed the life of Christ from a close vantage point, yet missed entirely the fact that someone within his own family was the Messiah.

Like so many others, James had taken Christ for granted. Jesus' sinless life had been lived out before him and yet James had not responded to the invitation for salvation.

James finally understood his position in Christ, that of a servant. He had successfully journeyed from a place of hindering the Gospel, unaware of the time constraints Christ had with the Father, to a place of understanding the true source of wisdom (John 7:1-5). The apostle Paul relates that James, along with Peter and John, became one of the chief leaders of the church in Jerusalem (Galatians 2:9).

Prayer — How grateful I am, Lord, that You're not willing that any should perish, especially those of Your own family.

The Divine Protector of Jerusalem

"Jerusalem will be inhabited without walls, because of the multitude of men and cattle within it. 'For I,' declares the Lord, 'will be a wall of fire around her, and I will be the glory in her midst.'" Zechariah 2:4-5

When we're in the midst of a crisis, God's reassurance means more to us. For this reason, the message of hope which Zechariah now received uplifted his soul.

An angel addressed him. We know from Zechariah 1:11-12, that this is the "angel of the Lord," Messiah, the preincarnate Christ.

At a time when only a remnant of Israel had returned to Jerusalem, the Lord is promising that at a future time they will become a great nation, having grown so large that conventional walls will be obsolete. Zechariah is being told that someday in the future walls won't be necessary and the Lord will be a ring of fire around the city.

In the Book of Revelation we see another description of this incredible city: "Its length is as great as the width; and he measured the city with the rod, fifteen hundred miles. . . And the material of the wall was jasper; and the city was pure gold, like clear glass. The foundation stones of the city wall were adorned with every kind of precious stone" (Revelation 21:16, 18-19).

Prayer — How grateful I am, Lord, to know that Your might and unlimited power protect Israel. How magnificent You are!

Chosen Before the Foundation of the World

Blessed be the God and Father of our Lord Jesus Christ, who has blessed us with every spiritual blessing in the heavenly places in Christ, just as he chose us in Him before the foundation of the world, that we should be holy and blameless before Him. Ephesians 1:3–4

The doctrine of predestination has baffled Christian theologians since the time the Bible was written. How can a woman have free will if God already knows what she'll choose? The fact that God knows the beginning from the end in no way diminishes our ability to choose.

To state this more simply, when God created the world He not only planned your place in it, but He also reserved a place in heaven for you. Now, you can either claim your ticket, by accepting Christ's salvation on your behalf, or you can cancel the reservation by never responding to God's offer.

Remember Paul's encounter with that blinding light? He knew when Christ appeared to him that God had intervened to change the very course of his life, "Paul, an apostle of Christ Jesus by the will of God. . ." (2 Corinthians 1:1). God extended to Paul the truth about Jesus Christ and he responded in commitment.

———————————

Prayer — Lord, help me and each woman reading this to enjoy the safety, protection, and sense of belonging that come from being chosen.

What Constitutes Dynamic Faith?

*You believe that God is one. You do well; the demons also
believe, and shudder. But are you willing to recognize, you
foolish fellow, that faith without works is useless? Was not
Abraham our father justified by works, when he offered up
Isaac his son on the altar? You see that faith was working with
his works, and as a result of the works, faith was perfected; and
the Scripture was fulfilled which says, "And Abraham believed
God, and it was reckoned to him as righteousness," and he was
called the friend of God.*
James 2:19–23

Abraham's faith was evident by his actions. The very
foundation of Abraham's faith was the Word of God. And no
matter what God required of him, Abraham obeyed God.
Therefore, all of his actions were born out of the call God
had on his life.

"Faith comes from hearing, and hearing by the word of
Christ" (Romans 10:17). This kind of dynamic faith involves
the whole person. If someone professes their belief in God
and yet does not take the Word to others, and does not
attend a weekly Bible study, and can't be bothered to help
those in obvious need, it makes me wonder whether that
faith is real. For there has to be some outward manifestation
of the change that takes place inwardly.

Prayer — Lord, show me by Your Word how to reflect
dynamic faith.

The "Holy Land" of Christ's Return

And the Lord will possess Judah as his portion in the holy land, and will again choose Jerusalem. "Be silent, all flesh, before the Lord; for He is aroused from His holy habitation."
Zechariah 2:12-13

With a history of wars on all its borders, Israel is far from being a holy land, and yet this is the way we refer to it today. Why? Because verse 12 of today's Scripture referred to it that way. This promise, however, has yet to be fulfilled.

True holiness cannot reign within Israel until the Messiah, Jesus Christ, comes to inhabit this nation. At the present, Israel is a secular, humanistic country. However, the future holds for Israel a time when the Lord Jesus Christ will reign from Jerusalem as King. "The portion of Jacob is not like these; for the maker of all is He, And Israel is the tribe of His inheritance; The Lord of hosts is His name" (Jeremiah 10:16).

The prophet Isaiah recorded a promise that is even more profound. "Thus He will sprinkle many nations, Kings will shut their mouths on account of Him; for what had not been told them they will see, And what they had not heard they will understand" (Isaiah 52:15). In other words, Jesus will finally reign as Israel's true King.

Prayer — David was also inspired by God to write concerning Israel's future. "For the Lord has chosen Zion; He has desired it for His habitation. 'This is My resting place forever; Here I will dwell, for I have desired it. I will abundantly bless her provision; I will satisfy her needy with bread' " (Psalm 132:13-15). I praise Him!

Sealed by the Holy Spirit

In Him, you also, after listening to the message of truth, the gospel of your salvation—having also believed, you were sealed in Him with the Holy Spirit of promise, who is given as a pledge of our inheritance, with a view to the redemption of God's own possession, to the praise of His glory.
Ephesians 1:13-14

Ornamental sealing waxes and metal impressions were used in the past as both a security measure and a statement of authenticity, especially by royalty. The king's signet ring was pressed into the hot melted wax, leaving an indelible and unique impression. Paul was inspired to use this image to describe how we, as believers, are sealed by God's Holy Spirit.

The apostle Paul penned the Book of Ephesians between A.D. 60 to 62 while he was a prisoner in Rome. Ephesus, the fourth largest city in the Roman Empire, was steeped in idolatrous worship.

Into this spiritual darkness God sent Paul. The Lord desired to use this cultural setting to call out for Himself a church so that He could shine the light of truth upon this evil place.

Prayer — Lord, there are dark places today that cry out for Your redeeming light. Lead me to share Your Word where it is needed desperately.

Oh, That "Biting Tongue"

So also the tongue is a small part of the body, and yet it boasts
of great things. Behold, how great a forest is set aflame by such
a small fire! And the tongue is a fire, the very world of
iniquity; the tongue is set among our members as that which
defiles the entire body, and sets on fire the course of our life, and
is set on fire by hell. James 3:5-6

Liz Curtis Higgs spoke at the Southern California Christian Women's Retreat in Irvine, California, a few years ago. I'll never forget her hilarious presentation on "taming the tongue." She revealed that before becoming a Christian she suffered from "fits of unsavory verbiage." After making her Christian commitment she became convicted that this bad habit didn't reflect well on the Lord and it had to go. Therefore, she developed a system of numbering all her swear words. And whenever she got upset she'd just yell out one of these numbers that corresponded to a certain word.

Liz definitely came up with a creative solution to one of life's common maladies. For we all have difficulty either saying too much or not saying it right. I can remember one of my former Bible study leaders saying, "If your second remark is usually an apology for your first remark, you've got a problem!"

Prayer — Thank You, Jesus, for Your Words of infinite wisdom: " 'The mouth speaks out of that which fills the heart. The good man out of his good treasure brings forth what is good; and the evil man out of his evil treasure brings forth what is evil' " (Matthew 12:34-35).

Israel's Filthy Garments

*Now Joshua was clothed with filthy garments and standing
before the angel. And he spoke and said to those who were
standing before him saying, "Remove the filthy garments from
him." Again he said to him, "See, I have taken your iniquity
away from you and will clothe you with festal robes."
Zechariah 3:3-4*

Ah, life's embarrassing moments! It never fails, someone
always pops in for an unscheduled visit about an hour after
you've decided to weed the garden and are covered with mud.

This must have been how Joshua felt as he stood before
the Lord in filthy garments. A real priest of Israel, who had
returned to Jerusalem from the Babylonian exile, Joshua is
wearing robes that are filthy as a symbol of Israel's sins that
need to be cleansed by God.

To this day there has been no national repentance for
Israel's sins. Therefore, Satan stands ready before God accuing
them. And unfortunately, they are "guilty as charged" by this
evil foe who not only led them down the primrose path to
idolatry, but fed them the lie that God didn't care. So how can
God go on loving them? The same way He continues to love
the rest of us. He has provided the means for our atonement
and will do all in His power to lead us to the foot of the cross
that we might obtain it.

Prayer — "For it is impossible for the blood of bulls and
goats to take away sins" (Hebrews 10:4). Lord, I praise You
for obtaining my salvation and releasing me from the
impossible system of sacrifices.

A Husband's Love

Wives, be subject to your own husbands, as to the Lord. For the husband is the head of the wife, as Christ also is the head of the church, He Himself being the Savior of the body. But as the church is subject to Christ, so also the wives ought to be to their husbands in everything. Ephesians 5:22-24

Wives, our role is that of a helpmate, not doormat. It's critical to remember that God intended marriage to be a partnership. Thus, if each person vies for control, the union begins eroding until it simply dissolves. Instead, we need to build one another up.

"So husbands ought also to love their own wives as their own bodies. He who loves his own wife loves himself; for no one ever hated his own flesh, but nourishes and cherishes it, just as Christ also does the church, because we are members of His body" (Ephesians 5:28-29). If men truly loved their wives to this degree, there probably isn't a woman alive who'd run from it.

So what can we do to make things better? Pray. . .every single day. But especially when things are out of kilter. Know that God is vitally interested in the success of your marriage and act accordingly.

Prayer — Lord, I know that only You are capable of loving perfectly. So the next time my marriage feels like a 90/10 proposition, please remind me that You're giving 100 percent.

Peter, an Apostle of Jesus Christ

Peter, an apostle of Jesus Christ, to those who reside as aliens. . .who are chosen according to the foreknowledge of God the Father, by the sanctifying work of the Spirit, that you may obey Jesus Christ and be sprinkled with His blood: May grace and peace be yours in fullest measure. 1 Peter 1:1-2

The only true "superhero" is Jesus Christ, who will never fail us. He alone was fully God and fully man. Therefore, He alone possesses perfectly all the characteristics we most admire. For He remains faithful, just, loving, omnipotent, and eternal.

To credit Peter with a more elevated status than the one given to him by Christ is to add to the Scriptures. By his own admission Peter was the apostle to the Jews, just as Paul was the apostle to the Gentiles, and upon neither was the title "head of the church" conferred. Christ alone holds that title. "For the husband is the head of the wife, as Christ also is the head of the church, He Himself being the Savior of the body" (Ephesians 5:23).

Peter never seeks position or power. Instead, he humbly admonishes his hearers to "obey Christ," on whom Peter also depends.

———————————

Prayer — The name *Peter,* or *petra,* means "rock." Help my faith, Lord, to be rock solid and unwavering.

A Closer Walk with Thee

*And the angel of the Lord admonished Joshua saying, "Thus
says the Lord of hosts, 'If you will walk in My ways, and if you
will perform My service, then you will also govern My house
and also have charge of My courts, and I will grant you free
access among these who are standing here.' "
Zechariah 3:6-7*

Our world has seemingly become obsessed with angelic
beings. In addition to popular movies and a weekly television
show starring "angels," items saturate the marketplace with
supposed likenesses of the heavenly hosts. But such represen-
tations pale in comparison with an actual offer to walk
among the angels.

God Himself is making such a conditional promise to
Joshua, the High Priest. If he will "walk in God's ways,"
then the Lord will grant him free access to stroll through
His heaven with these angelic beings.

As incredible an offer as this might have been for Joshua,
an even more miraculous invitation awaits those who accept
Jesus Christ as their Lord and Savior. For immediately they
can enjoy the very presence of God every day of their lives.
When we make a commitment to Him, His Spirit comes to
indwell us. "However, you are not in the flesh but in the Spirit,
if indeed the Spirit of God dwells in you. But if anyone does
not have the Spirit of Christ, he does not belong to Him"
(Romans 8:9).

Prayer — *Immanuel* means "God with us." God's Spirit
resides in me!

The Meaning of True Christian Fellowship

I thank my God in all my remembrance of you, always offering prayer with joy in my every prayer for you all, in view of your participation in the gospel from the first day until now. . . For it is only right for me to feel this way about you all, because I have you in my heart, since both in my imprisonment and in the defense and confirmation of the gospel, you all are partakers of grace with me. Philippians 1:3-5, 7

Paul was confined to prison when he wrote his letter to the Philippians. Yet rather than wallowing in self-pity, we see him reaching out to those he loves and reminiscing about their joyful times of fellowship together. The sheer memory of them causes warmth to invade his lonely prison. And though he longs to be with them, he is content in the place Christ has called him.

Paul's joy is not dependent upon circumstances. Rather, it overflows from the content of his heart, where the true source of joy resides, Jesus Christ. And because of this indwelling, Paul senses a oneness with other believers, despite the fact that they are far from him. It is the love of Christ which binds them together.

Paul's only aim in life was to be where God wanted him—so that he might spread the Gospel to all who would listen. And if this aspiration required suffering and isolation on his part, then Paul gladly paid the price.

Prayer — Lord, might I pray as Paul, "I press on toward the goal for the prize of the upward call of God in Christ Jesus" (Philippians 3:14).

Born Again to a Living Hope

*In this you greatly rejoice, even though now for a little while, if
necessary, you have been distressed by various trials, that the
proof of your faith, being more precious than gold which is
perishable, even though tested by fire, may be found to result in
praise and glory and honor at the revelation of Jesus Christ.*
1 Peter 1:6-7

"Religious fanatics!" "Jesus freaks!" "Bible thumpers!" These
are just a few of the choice names hurled at those who dare
to share their Christian faith. What degree of persecution
are you willing to endure that the Gospel of truth might go
forward to a needy world?

Remember Nicodemus? He came to Jesus by night,
asking what he might do to be saved.

Although he continued to watch from afar, this encounter with Christ had stirred something within the heart of
Nicodemus. Christ's words had caused light to flood into his
soul: " 'He who believes in Me, as the Scripture said, "From
his innermost being shall flow rivers of living water" ' " (John
7:38). Then came the day when this Pharisee interceded for
Christ.

When the multitude became divided as to Christ's true
identity and many wanted to seize Jesus, Nicodemus, who
could no longer remain silent, reminded them that their law
couldn't judge a man without a proper hearing (John 7:51).
At the foot of the cross Nicodemus publicly declared his
belief.

———————

Prayer — Thank You, Jesus, for convicting my soul today.

Our Precious Cornerstone

" 'For behold, the stone that I have set before Joshua; on one stone are seven eyes. Behold, I will engrave an inscription on it,' declares the Lord of hosts, 'and I will remove the iniquity of that land in one day.' " Zechariah 3:9

During the 1970s an ingenious entrepreneur used gentle persuasion to convince the masses of the need to own a "pet rock." Amazingly, people raced to purchase these once garden-variety stones which were painted with faces and given costumes.

However, the rock which Zechariah describes here is Jesus Christ, Israel's Messiah. The prophet Daniel described Him as a "stone which was cut out of the mountain without hands and that it crushed the iron, the bronze, the clay, the silver, and the gold" (Daniel 2:45).

The Psalms present Messiah as "the stone which the builders rejected, [Who] has become the chief corner stone" (Psalm 118:22). Thus, when Messiah came to Israel, the Israelites were seeking a king, not a suffering Savior. Fulfilling Old Testament prophecy, they rejected this cornerstone.

Isaiah the prophet described Messiah as the foundation stone. "Therefore thus says the Lord God, 'Behold, I am laying in Zion a stone, a tested stone, A costly cornerstone for the foundation, firmly placed. He who believes in it will not be disturbed' " (Isaiah 28:16).

Prayer — Lord, help me cherish the truth that has been presented concerning Messiah's identity.

Being of One Mind

Do nothing from selfishness or empty conceit, but with humility of mind let each of you regard one another as more important than himself; do not merely look out for your own personal interests, but also for the interests of others. Philippians 2:3-4

While vacationing in the Midwest this past fall, my husband and I toured several Amish communities. How well these people live out the teaching of today's Scripture on unity. Forsaking the modern world that surrounds them, with a deep sense of community, the Amish labor together for the good of all.

As Christians we are called to encourage one another in the faith. Paul, who spent so much of his own life in prison, had a deep understanding of the need for the reassurance and hope which the Lord richly supplied. This reliance on God's abundant source of blessings overflowed from his heart, spilling out to his fellow Christians.

What if we used the greeting time in church, during the worship service, to find out the specific needs within the Body of Christ? Many of our brothers and sisters are wounded, both physically and spiritually. Yet they come to Sunday services with a deceptive smile on their faces, their return trip home as lonely as the rest of their week will probably be. Do you care?

Prayer — Who is my source of strength? Lord, help me encourage others.

Babes in Christ

*Therefore, putting aside all malice and all guile and hypocrisy
and envy and all slander, like newborn babes, long for the pure
milk of the word, that by it you may grow in respect to
salvation, if you have tasted the kindness of the Lord.*
1 Peter 2:1-3

When you have a new baby, you're starting with a clean slate.
And although babies have inherited Adam's bent toward sin-
ning, they haven't as yet exercised this "family affliction."

If we grow physically but ignore our spiritual needs, the
potential for becoming a well-rounded human being is
severely diminished, if not permanently stunted. This is the
issue which Peter addresses in this passage.

As mothers, grandmothers, stepmothers, and aunts, we
have a God-ordained call to teach children the Word of God
that they might someday enter the kingdom of God. Jesus
said: " 'Whoever causes one of these little ones who believe
in Me to stumble, it is better for him that a heavy mill-
stone be hung around his neck, and that he be drowned in
the depth of the sea' " (Matthew 18:6).

That's pretty strong language. But look at the stakes! A
child's whole life can be altered by someone who turns them
away purposely from the truth of Jesus Christ.

Prayer — Lord, lead me to spiritual growth, as I read "
'every Word that proceeds out of the mouth of God' "
(Matthew 4:4).

God's Glory, the Menorah of Heaven

And he said to me, "What do you see?" And I said, "I see, and behold, a lampstand all of gold with its bowl on the top of it, and its seven lamps on it with seven spouts belonging to each of the lamps which are on the top of it; also two olive trees by it, one on the right side of the bowl and the other on its left side." Zechariah 4:2–3

God's purpose for these visions was to prompt Zechariah to motivate the Israelites to rebuild the temple. The Lord was showing him the symbolism behind the earthly temple, which is a replica of the one God has in heaven.

The seven-branched lampstand in Zechariah's vision reminded him of the candelabra which the Jews call the menorah (Exodus 25:31-40). It was modeled after the salvia plant found in the Sinai Peninsula. The menorah was used in the temple as a natural light within the holy place.

John, who recorded the Book of Revelation, had a heavenly vision of these lampstands. " 'As for the mystery of the seven stars which you saw in My right hand, and the seven golden lampstands: the seven stars are the angels of the seven churches, and the seven lampstands are the seven churches' " (Revelation 1:20).

Prayer — Jesus, the Light of the world, illumine our souls!

Stand Firm and Receive the Crown

Therefore, my beloved brethren whom I long to see, my joy and crown, so stand firm in the Lord, my beloved. I urge Euodia and I urge Syntyche to live in harmony in the Lord.
Philippians 4:1-2

Church committee meetings can either be a blessing or a bear, depending, of course, upon whether the members are working together for a common goal. Evidently, two of the church women at Philippi, Euodia and Syntyche, were less than harmonious. Therefore, Paul admonished them.

It is significant that Paul took the time to address this issue. Left unchecked, such arguing would wreak havoc in the church. Perhaps you have encountered someone who, although she professes belief in Christ, has treated you without charity or love. Fast, pray for guidance, and then go to her and pray again. Failure to do so gives Satan an opportunity to get a foothold within the church, as the argument escalates and people choose sides.

Speaking like a proud father, Paul refers to these believers at Philippi as his "joy and crown." He brought the Gospel message to them. And then he stood back to watch them grow in their faith. He doesn't want it all to turn to ashes.

Prayer — Lord, help me to remember that You surrendered all Your rights that I might know true freedom. Please show me how to persevere, make amends, and live in harmony.

Should You Leave an Unbelieving Husband?

In the same way, you wives, be submissive to your own husbands so that even if any of them are disobedient to the word, they may be won. . .as they observe your chaste and respectful behavior. And let. . .your adornment be. . .the hidden person of the heart, with the imperishable quality of a gentle and quiet spirit, which is precious in the sight of God. For in this way in former times the holy women also, who hoped in God, used to adorn themselves, being submissive to their own husbands. 1 Peter 3:1-5

The most extreme case of an unbelieving spouse is one who is out of control. Nobody knows your circumstances like you. But if there's physical abuse in your marital relationship, get help immediately. God never intended for you to become the object of someone's angry blows. Leave the home if your safety or that of your children is at risk.

Living with an unbelieving spouse is a tremendous challenge. I was a Christian for thirteen years before my husband finally made his own commitment. These were extremely difficult and challenging times. However, they also included the cultivation of my own relationship with the Lord, as Bible study became a matter of daily survival. And when my husband eventually "saw the light," he had a family that already knew the Lord.

Prayer — Lord, show me Your way through my difficulties. If my spouse or boyfriend does not know You as his Savior, help me lead by example.

Two Olive Branches

Then I answered and said to him, "What are these two olive trees on the right of the lampstand and on its left?" And I answered the second time and said to him, "What are the two olive branches which are beside the two golden pipes, which empty the golden oil from themselves?" So he answered me saying, "Do you not know what these things are?" And I said, "No, my lord." Then he said, "These are the two anointed ones, who are standing by the Lord of the whole earth."
Zechariah 4:11-14

Zechariah sees two olive trees. And the angel says that these are "the two anointed ones." John, in the Book of Revelation, received more enlightenment concerning these two trees.

" 'I will grant authority to my two witnesses, and they will prophesy for twelve hundred and sixty days, clothed in sackcloth.' These are the two olive trees and the two lampstands that stand before the Lord of the earth" (Revelation 11:3-4).

While they are symbolically referred to as "olive branches," these are two men who spread the Gospel to the Jews during the tribulation period. The fact that they are referred to as olive branches, the symbol for Israel, shows they will be Jews. They have God's authority to speak as His prophets during one of the most trying periods of time in history. At the end of their allotted time, they will be murdered by the antichrist who comes on the scene to try and dominate the earth (Revelation 11:7).

Prayer — Lord, I pray that those in Israel will listen to the message of Your witnesses, that many might be saved.

Giving Thanks to God

We give thanks to God, the Father of our Lord Jesus Christ,
praying always for you, since we heard of your faith in Christ
Jesus and the love which you have for all the saints; because of
the hope laid up for you in heaven, of which you previously
heard in the word of truth, the gospel, which has come to you,
just as in all the world also it is constantly bearing fruit and
increasing, even as it has been doing in you also since the day
you heard of it and understood the grace of God in truth; just as
you learned it from Epaphras, our beloved fellow bond-servant,
who is a faithful servant of Christ on our behalf,
and he also informed us of your love in the Spirit.
Colossians 1:3-8

Paul is famous for his long sentences. His thoughts are one
long continuum and yet they flow beautifully. Here he thanks
those who have held to the truth of God's Word. The culture
of these people in Colossae was steeped in Oriental mysti-
cism. They lived along the main trade route, which made for
a wide variety of backgrounds and doctrines. Ungodly influences were rampant. Paul reaches out to this nucleus of
believers with God's truth that their foundation in Him might
remain strong enough to withstand the bombardment of
confusing thoughts which tore at them daily.

Prayer — Father, how grateful I am today that You sent
Jesus.

God's Precious Promises

*His divine power has granted to us everything pertaining to
life and godliness, through the true knowledge of Him who
called us by His own glory and excellence. For by these He has
granted to us His precious and magnificent promises, in order
that by them you might become partakers of the divine nature,
having escaped the corruption that is in the world by lust.*
2 Peter 1:3-5

From the moment a baby is conceived it has everything it
needs to grow into a complete human being, everything
except time. For time acts as a refiner. Our spiritual growth
is the same. From the moment we accept Christ, He infuses
His Spirit within us, giving us right standing with the Father
and making us a child of God. "He made Him who knew no
sin to be sin on our behalf, that we might become the
righteousness of God in Him" (2 Corinthians 5:21). As we
walk in step with Him, learning His ways, we will eventually
reflect these changes in our character.

Peter reminds us that Jesus Christ is the Savior. "Therefore, brethren, be all the more diligent to make certain about
His calling and choosing you; for as long as you practice these
things, you will never stumble; for in this way the entrance
into the eternal kingdom of our Lord and Savior Jesus Christ
will be abundantly supplied to you" (2 Peter 1:10-11).

Prayer — God promised me a Savior and He sent Jesus.
Hallelujah!

God Questions Israel's Motive for Rituals

Then the word of the Lord of hosts came to me saying, "Say to all the people of the land and to the priests, 'When you fasted and mourned in the fifth and seventh months these seventy years, was it actually for Me that you fasted?'" Zechariah 7:4-5

The Lord instituted several feasts for Israel to commemorate important events during which He had delivered their nation. He wanted these days observed that all the generations to come would know their heritage of rescue by the Lord. On these feast days of holy convocation—Passover, The Feast of Booths or Tabernacles, Pentecost, First Fruits, Unleavened Bread, and the Feast of Weeks—God wanted His people to celebrate joyously with a sense of gratitude to their God.

Instead, the Israelites had made nothing but rituals out of the days. Furthermore, they had added other days of fasting to commemorate some of their national calamities, until it had become a burden to keep them all. The Israelites questioned whether they needed to continue observing them.

Now, the Lord's answer was: " 'Dispense true justice, and practice kindness and compassion each to his brother; and do not oppress the widow or the orphan, the stranger or the poor; and do not devise evil in your hearts against one another'" (Zechariah 7:9-10).

Prayer — Lord, help me to love You with my whole heart.

The Image of the Invisible God

*He is the image of the invisible God, the first-born of all
creation. For in Him all things were created, both in the
heavens and on earth, visible and invisible, whether thrones or
dominions or rulers or authorities—all things have been created
by Him and for Him. Colossians 1:15-16*

A friend recently told me that she believed Jesus lived a life
much like ours, one that certainly wasn't perfect. Yet she is
a member of a church and celebrates Christmas and Easter
as though they have real meaning to her.

The entire Bible presents a singular message about
Christ's identity, one she'd missed completely. The first
verse of Genesis says it all: "In the beginning God created
the heavens and the earth" (Genesis 1:1). The word for *God*
in this passage is *Elohim* and it's plural—for there are three
distinct persons within the Godhead—the Father, Son, and
Holy Spirit.

John presented Christ's credentials to us in his gospel.
"In the beginning was the Word, and the Word was with
God, and the Word was God. He was in the beginning with
God. All things came into being by Him, and apart from
Him nothing came into being that has come into being. In
Him was life, and the life was the light of men" (John 1:1-4).

Prayer — Jesus Christ lived a sinless life, and died on the
cross of Calvary for my sins. I worship the King of Kings!

Where Is the Promise of His Coming?

Know this first of all, that in the last days mockers will come with their mocking, following after their own lusts, and saying "Where is the promise of his coming? For ever since the fathers fell asleep, all continues just as it was from the beginning of creation." For when they maintain this, it escapes their notice that by the word of God the heavens existed long ago and the earth was formed out of water by water; through which the world at that time was destroyed, being flooded with water.
2 Peter 3:3-6

If you aren't into eschatology, or the study of events to come at the end of time, perhaps you won't share my appreciation of this verse. However, here's Peter, over 2,000 years ago, letting us know that the earth we know will someday be destroyed. How will this happen?

"But the present heavens and earth by His word are being reserved for fire, kept for the day of judgment and destruction of ungodly men" (2 Peter 3:7).

How can a loving God destroy the very men and women and their world which He created? Look at how much time He provided for them to repent. From the time Noah received the order from God to build the ark until the rain began, a span of 120 years had elapsed. Certainly this was time enough for everyone to hear the prediction and take appropriate action.

Prayer — Today I will repent of my sins. And, if I'm not entirely sure I've done so, today I will claim Jesus to be my Savior and Lord.

God Stands by His Word

"Behold, I am going to send My messenger, and he will clear the way before Me. And the Lord, whom you see, will suddenly come to His temple; and the messenger of the covenant, in whom you delight, behold, He is coming," says the Lord of hosts. Malachi 3:1

God always keeps His promises. Through Moses, God had warned the nation of Israel that if they refused to obey, they would be taken into captivity. In 586 B.C. this prophecy was fulfilled.

God spoke through the prophet Jeremiah, giving the exact duration of this captivity as seventy years. This is the number of years Israel remained in Babylon.

Today's Scripture reveals two specific messages. First, a messenger will precede Messiah, announcing Him to Israel. This would be John the Baptist (Luke 1:76).

Next, the Messiah will "come to His temple." Three specific times stand out from the rest. At the time of His circumcision a prophecy was given about Christ being the appointed child by Simeon (Luke 2:34). When He was twelve years old he became separated from Mary and Joseph when they were preparing to leave Jerusalem. They found Him in the temple, astounding the learned scholars about His knowledge of Scripture (Luke 2:42-51). The third time Christ stood in the temple and read from the Book of Isaiah the very prophecy concerning His coming. Then He said, "Today this Scripture has been fulfilled in your hearing" (Luke 4:21).

Prayer — Jesus Christ, God's promise to the world, has come! Thank You for Your Word of Truth.

Hold to God's Truth, Not to Visions

You have died and your life is hidden with Christ in God.
When Christ, who is our life, is revealed, then you also will be
revealed with Him in glory. Therefore consider the members of
your earthly body as dead to immorality, impurity, passion, evil
desire, and greed, which amounts to idolatry. For it is on
account of these things that the wrath of God will come, and in
them you also once walked, when you were living in them.
Colossians 3:3-7

Some Christian testimonies really stir your heart. Some are from individuals who have turned from lives of debauchery and waste to become true seekers of God.

Our churches are comprised of redeemed sinners. "For all have sinned and fall short of the glory of God, being justified as a gift by His grace through the redemption which is in Christ Jesus; whom God displayed publicly as a propitiation in His blood through faith" (Romans 3:23-25).

Paul's message is that Christ in us should cause a change in our lives. For we have been delivered from the "wrath of God." This metamorphosis should make a visible difference in how we are living our lives. For Christ has set up residence within us.

There cannot be any detours or distractions from the truth. "Let no one keep defrauding you of your prize by delighting in self-abasement and the worship of the angels" (Colossians 2:18).

Prayer — Let me be cautious of bypassing the Word of God and the Spirit of God to substitute visions of angels for the Gospel.

Christmas Joy

*And we have seen and bear witness and proclaim to you the
eternal life, which was with the Father and was manifested to
us—what we have seen and heard we proclaim to you also,
that you also may have fellowship with us; and indeed our
fellowship is with the Father, and with His Son Jesus Christ.
1 John 1:2-3*

The countdown to Christmas has begun. Are your cards in
the mail yet? What message have you extended to friends
and family? Illustrations of cats in floppy red Santa caps or
snowy winter scenes cannot effect a change in the lives of
those who do not know the Christ of Christmas. For only
the Word of God has the power to reach into searching
hearts and bring hope.

Where will you find joy this Christmas? It's not in
brightly colored packages under the tree. And unless your
loved ones know the Lord, jubilation probably won't be present at your family gatherings either. For we cannot partake
of this commodity apart from Christ.

Consider today what printed message you will send to
loved ones this Christmas. . .a message of hope about Christ
the Savior, or a scene in which He is nowhere to be found?

Prayer — Dear Lord, thank You for the knowledge that
Jesus is still the "reason for the season."

The Revelation of Jesus Christ

The Revelation of Jesus Christ, which God gave Him to show
His bond-servants, the things which must shortly take place;
and He sent and communicated it by His angel to His
bond-servant John, who bore witness to the word of God and
to the testimony of Jesus Christ, even to all that he saw.
Revelation 1:1-2

After God gave Malachi the prophesies concerning Messiah's coming, He remained silent for over 400 years. And then He spoke to us. . .through His blessed Son, Jesus Christ. John, the gospel writer, became the recipient of today's Scripture revelation while he was exiled on the Isle of Patmos in A.D. 95. It was given to John by Christ. Thus, the canon of Scripture was complete.

To those seeking to add further revelations to what God had pronounced as complete, God has issued a warning. "I testify to everyone who hears the words of the prophecy of this book: if anyone adds to them, God shall add to him the plagues which are written in this book" (Revelation 22:18). So, if someone comes to your door and tries to hand you "another gospel" or "further revelations," you don't even need to read it to be assured that it is false.

Prayer — Lord, let me pray for an understanding of these truths, known as the Revelation, presented by Christ to John. Help me to hear and heed Your Word.

Christ Eliminated All Ethnic Barriers

There is no distinction between Greek and Jew, circumcised and uncircumcised, barbarian, Scythian, slave and freeman, but Christ is all, and in all. And so, as those who have been chosen of God, holy and beloved, put on a heart of compassion, kindness, humility, gentleness and patience; bearing with one another; just as the Lord forgave you, so also should you.
Colossians 3:11–13

To say we love Christ and yet maintain deeply rooted prejudices against others is inconsistent with everything He taught. For Christ came to reconcile all peoples to Himself, not separate us into factions.

Above all, God wants us to be harmonious in worship of Him and also in working with Him. "Now may the God who gives perseverance and encouragement grant you to be of the same mind with one another according to Christ Jesus; that with one accord you may with one voice glorify the God and Father of our Lord Jesus Christ. Wherefore, accept one another, just as Christ also accepted us to the glory of God" (Romans 15:5-7).

Prayer —Lord, let the true peace of Christmas, which is Christ, be found in my heart as I am obedient to Your command to love one another, just as You have loved me (John 13:34).

The Father Has Bestowed a Great Love

See how great a love the Father has bestowed upon us, that we should be called children of God; and such we are. For this reason the world does not know us, because it did not know Him. Beloved, now we are children of God, and it has not appeared as yet what we shall be. We know that, when He appears, we shall be like Him, because we shall see Him just as He is. And every one who has this hope fixed on Him purifies himself, just as He is pure. 1 John 3:1-3

Have you ever looked into the mirror and thought, *I wish I had a new body?* Well, Christ has one reserved for you in heaven. This body is imperishable, undefiled, and will not fade away (1 Peter 1:3-4).

While we don't know when Jesus is coming again, we do know that our new bodies will coincide with this event. "When Christ, who is our life, is revealed, then you also will be revealed with Him in glory" (Colossians 3:4).

Yet the gift of our new bodies is only one aspect of the Father's incredible love for His children. His love prompts His children to purify themselves just as He is pure (1 John 3:3). They also abide in Him and practice righteousness (1 John 3:6-7), for they have been born of God (1 John 3:9; John 3:7).

Prayer — Lord, as I prepare to celebrate Your birth, the greatest gift I can lay beside the manger is an act of my will that makes me Your child. Yes, I have been born again.

He Is Coming with the Clouds

Behold, He is coming with the clouds, and every eye will see Him, even those who pierced Him; and all the tribes of the earth will mourn over Him. Even so. Amen. Revelation 1:7

Cecil B. DeMille was known for his extravagant movie productions. Who can forget his version of Moses parting the Red Sea? However, the appearance of Christ in the clouds will surpass every event which has ever taken place on earth. This future event will be a worldwide phenomenon in which every eye will see Him. And the hearts of those who refused to examine the evidence and refused to know Him will ache with the agonizing pain of conviction that it's simply too late. The purpose for His appearance this time will be to judge the world of its greatest sin, the rejection of His great gift of salvation.

Those who are "unprepared" for this global happening will be in shock! "For the Lord Himself will descend from heaven with a shout, with the voice of the archangel, and with the trumpet of God; and the dead in Christ shall rise first. Then we who are alive and remain shall be caught up together with them in the clouds to meet the Lord in the air, and thus we shall always be with the Lord" (1 Thessalonians 4:16-17). It doesn't get any better than this!

Prayer — Father, when humans have failed me I tend to blame You for their choices. Please break down the barriers in my heart that I might worship Your Son this Christmas.

How the Church Was Born

We give thanks to God always for all of you, making mention of you in our prayers; constantly bearing in mind your work of faith and labor of love and steadfastness of hope in our Lord Jesus Christ in the presence of our God and Father.
1 Thessalonians 1:2-3

If you're looking for a new church home, you need to ask yourself some important questions. Is there well-grounded Bible teaching coming from the pulpit? Is attendance consistent? Do many seem eager to assume responsibility for teaching?

God meant for His Church to be dynamic. For this is the place where His believers still gather to worship and grow. Paul and his little band of followers, as well as the rest of the apostles, gave their lives to start churches founded and grounded in the Word of God. Their purpose was to see that the souls of repentant sinners might be regenerated, nurtured, and then sent out to begin other congregations.

Paul wrote 1 Thessalonians to encourage these believers. From this large group of faithful followers in Thessalonica would spring other small churches in the surrounding areas.

Upon arriving in Thessalonica, Paul spoke in the synagogue for "three Sabbaths" (Acts 17:2), knowing his listeners' attention would be riveted on the Word of God. During that time the groundwork for this thriving church was laid.

Prayer — Lord, help me to spread the Gospel to those yet unsaved around me.

Spirit of God or Spirit of Antichrist?

The eyes of the Lord are toward the righteous, And His ears are open to their cry. Psalm 34:15

When those inevitable disagreements occur between husband and wife, they are often accompanied by a time of lost fellowship and an intense sense of isolation. Yesterday found me sitting alone on a huge boulder in the mountain retreat where we were camped. I cried out to God for intervention, that He might "fix this man," but God seemed absolutely silent. After forty minutes or so I got up and returned to our campsite, knowing that God would somehow work out this rift.

This morning I read the following Scripture: "For the eyes of the Lord are upon the righteous, and His ears attend to their prayer, But the face of the Lord is against those who do evil" (1 Peter 3:12). The Spirit of God heard my cry and took my petition before the Father who answered my prayer, for I have confessed belief in Him.

If you have discarded the commands of God, then you are not God's child. "You are from God, little children, and have overcome them; because greater is He who is in you than he who is in the world. They are from the world; therefore they speak as the world, and the world listens to them" (1 John 4:4-5).

Prayer — Lord, guide me in this last hour, that I continue to spread the Gospel and not walk away.

God's Message to the Churches

" 'But I have this against you, that you have left your first love.' " Revelation 2:4

One of my favorite questions to ask couples over dinner is "How did you meet?" Each story invariably presents a set of impossible circumstances that had to be orchestrated in order to bring this man and woman together. As these details are relayed, a glow begins to come back into the eyes of those remembering. There is nothing to compare with that "first bloom of love."

This is the kind of love which God desires from us. That on-fire, totally consuming, single focus of our attention. His call to the church at Ephesus then was that they remember their first love—and rekindle their purpose to seek Him first.

His message, however, to the church at Smyrna was very different. " 'I know your tribulation and your poverty (but you are rich). Do not fear what you are about to suffer. . . Be faithful until death, and I will give you the crown of life' " (Revelation 2:9-10).

Throughout history, God's church has suffered persecution. But here is a message of hope to all for whom cruelty is a constant companion: "Remain faithful, God's reward is at hand."

Prayer — O Lord, may Your Light be the fire in my soul!

Precise Instructions to the Beloved

Therefore encourage one another, and build up one another, just as you also are doing. But we request of you, brethren, that you appreciate those who diligently labor among you, and have charge over you in the Lord and give you instruction, and that you esteem them very highly in love because of their work. Live in peace with one another. And we urge you, brethren, admonish the unruly, encourage the fainthearted, help the weak, be patient with all men. See that no one repays another with evil for evil, but always seek after that which is good for one another and for all men. Rejoice always; pray without ceasing; in everything give thanks; for this is God's will for you in Christ Jesus. Do not quench the Spirit; do not despise prophetic utterances. But examine everything carefully; hold fast to that which is good; abstain from every form of evil.
1 Thessalonians 5:11-22

Paul had been hindered several times from returning to this body of believers. Thus, this encouraging letter provides his spiritual last will, recording a priority list of ways in which we can "live out the Gospel of Christ."

For God equates love with obedience. When Christ returns for His believers we are to be found walking in His statutes. "For you yourselves know full well that the day of the Lord will come just like a thief in the night. . . But you, brethren, are not in darkness, that the day should overtake you like a thief. . .so then let us not sleep as others do, but let us be alert and sober" (1 Thessalonians 5:2, 4, 6).

Prayer — Lord, let me be found obediently living Your call and commission.

Those Born of God Obey Him

Whoever believes that Jesus is the Christ is born of God; and whoever loves the Father loves the child born of Him. By this we know that we love the children of God, when we love God and observe His commandments. 1 John 5:1-2

When our children disobey, we feel not only extreme disappointment but a sense that they don't love us. For if they did, they would understand that our instructions are meant to guide them over the rough terrain of life. This is exactly how God feels when we fail to follow Him. For He equates love with obedience.

" 'If you love Me, you will keep My commandments' " (John 14:15). How on earth can we accomplish this task? By the power of God's Spirit within us! " 'And I will ask the Father, and He will give you another Helper, that He may be with you forever; that is the Spirit of truth' " (John 14:16-17).

How can we know for sure that the Spirit of God indwells us? "And the witness is this, that God has given us eternal life, and this life is in His Son. He who has the Son has the life; he who does not have the Son of God does not have the life" (1 John 5:11-12).

Prayer — Lord, if I'm wandering without purpose, please bring me close to You. Help me make room in my heart for the Babe of Christmas!

The Rainbow Surrounding Christ

Behold, a throne was standing in heaven, and One sitting on the throne. And He who was sitting was like a jasper stone and a sardius in appearance; and there was a rainbow around the throne, like an emerald in appearance. Revelation 4:2-3

God promised Noah that He would never again destroy the world by a flood. As a reminder, God set a rainbow in the clouds (Genesis 9:13-16). Now we see that there is also a rainbow in heaven, but it's not the half-bow we're used to seeing. This rainbow is a complete circle because in heaven all things are whole and finished. Yet the most amazing thing about this prism of color is that it surrounds Christ.

We know this because there He is "sitting on the throne," which is the posture of judgment, and He is being worshiped. " 'Holy, holy, holy, is the Lord God, the Almighty, who was and who is and who is to come' " (Revelation 4:8). In this passage Christ is referred to as the Creator. "And He is the image of the invisible God, the first-born of all creation. For in Him all things were created, both in the heavens and on earth, visible and invisible, whether thrones or dominions or rulers or authorities—all things have been created through Him and for Him. And He is before all things, and in Him all things hold together" (Colossians 1:15-17). Jesus Christ, God Almighty, who resides in heaven and sits on the throne of judgment, is surrounded by the rainbow.

Prayer — Lord, thank You that the Babe of Christmas will one day judge the whole world.

When Will Christ Rapture the Faithful?

Now we request you, brethren, with regard to the coming of our Lord Jesus Christ, and our gathering together to Him, that you may not be quickly shaken from your composure or be disturbed either by a spirit or a message or a letter as if from us, to the effect that the day of the Lord has come. Let no one in any way deceive you, for it will not come unless the apostasy comes first, and the man of lawlessness is revealed, the son of destruction, who opposes and exalts himself above every so-called god or object of worship, so that he takes his seat in the temple of God, displaying himself as being God.
2 Thessalonians 2:1-4

Paul and Timothy had founded the church at Thessalonica. For a time these Thessalonians remained strong. But then came persecution so severe that they were shaken to their roots. If these trial-filled days comprised their last moments on earth, where was the hope of being "caught up in Christ"? Had they somehow missed it all?

Paul wanted to dispel their misconceptions and correct several weaknesses in this church.

Before the antichrist bursts onto the world scene, there will be a great falling away from the truth: "Some will fall away from the faith, paying attention to deceitful spirits and doctrines of demons, by means of the hypocrisy of liars seared in their own conscience as with a branding iron, men who forbid marriage and advocate abstaining from foods, which God has created to be gratefully shared in by those who believe and know the truth" (1 Timothy 4:1-3).

Prayer — Even so, come Lord Jesus!

The Father Has Commanded Us to Love

The elder to the chosen lady and her children, whom I love in truth; and not only I, but also all who know the truth, for the sake of the truth which abides in us and will be with us forever: Grace, mercy and peace will be with us, from God the Father and from Jesus Christ, the Son of the Father, in truth and love. 2 John 1:1-3

A foundation of any small-group home Bible study should be the love members display toward one another. It was just such a group which John addressed in this letter.

As a church elder, John reminded these believers that God didn't consider loving one another an option. John further expounded on this concept, viewing it from God's perspective. "And this is love, that we walk according to his commandments" (2 John 1:6).

John shows us the process by which the Word of the Lord can penetrate our hearts. First, we are to know the truth, (2 John 1:1-3) for it is by God's grace that we can love others.

Next, John admonishes us to walk according to His commandments (John 1:4-6).

Lastly, we must abide in the truth, who is Christ (2 John 1:7-11). Jesus said, " 'I am the way, and the truth, and the life; no one comes to the Father, but through Me' " (John 14:6).

Prayer — Jesus Christ. . .heralded by a star, proclaimed by angels, announced by the shepherds, and given by the Father to a world in need of a Savior. O, come let me adore Him!

Jesus Alone Is Worthy

*And I saw in the right hand of Him who sat on the throne a
book written inside and on the back, sealed up with seven seals.
And I saw a strong angel proclaiming with a loud voice, "Who
is worthy to open the book and to break its seals? . . ." And I
began to weep greatly, because no one was found worthy to
open the book, or to look into it; and one of the elders said to me,
"Stop weeping; behold, the Lion that is from the tribe of Judah,
the Root of David, has overcome so as to open the book and its
seven seals." Revelation 5:1-2, 4-5*

As the Lamb stood to receive "the book," an awed hush fell
over His celestial audience. For He alone was worthy, because
He had met God's requirements to redeem the earth. The
prize was His. "And when He had taken the book, the four
living creatures and the twenty-four elders fell down before
the Lamb, having each one a harp, and golden bowls full of
incense, which are the prayers of the saints. And they sang a
new song, saying, 'Worthy art Thou to take the book, and to
break its seals; for Thou wast slain, and didst purchase for
God with Thy blood men from every tribe and tongue and
people and nation'" (Revelation 5:8-10).

The judgments of God comprise the book. These are a
series of progressively worsening catastrophes, deserved by
those who have consistently rejected God, salvation in
Christ, and His Word.

Prayer — Lord, I know I can't truly celebrate Christmas
unless I know that Jesus Christ is God in the flesh, born to
die on the cross for my sins. Because of His sacrifice I will
be able to celebrate forever with Him in heaven.

Jesus Christ, Our Hope

To Timothy, my true child in the faith: Grace, mercy and peace from God the Father and Christ Jesus our Lord. As I urged you upon my departure for Macedonia, remain on at Ephesus, in order that you may instruct certain men not to teach strange doctrines, nor to pay attention to myths and endless genealogies, which give rise to mere speculation rather than furthering the administration of God which is by faith. But the goal of our instruction is love from a pure heart and a good conscience and a sincere faith. 1 Timothy 1:2-5

Paul wrote this letter to encourage Timothy in his own leadership role, knowing that the worst thing this young believer could do was to try and emulate Paul instead of Christ. For Paul held no doubt in his mind concerning Timothy's call from God. "This command I entrust to you, Timothy, my son, in accordance with the prophecies previously made concerning you, that by them you may fight the good fight, keeping faith and a good conscience, which some have rejected and suffered shipwreck in regard to their faith" (1 Timothy 1:18). Paul continues with this powerful admonition: "Do not neglect the spiritual gift within you, which was bestowed upon you through prophetic utterance with the laying on of hands by the presbytery" (1 Timothy 4:14).

Timothy is his "true child in the faith," for Paul had led him to Christ and never ceased to pray for his spiritual growth.

Prayer — Lord, show me how to use my special gifts.

Jesus Christ Came in the Flesh

Any one who goes too far and does not abide in the teaching of Christ, does not have God; the one who abides in the teaching, he has both the Father and the Son. If any one comes to you and does not bring this teaching, do not receive him into your house, and do not give him a greeting; for the one who gives him a greeting participates in his evil deeds. 2 John 1:9-11

There is no greater evil than to fail to recognize who Jesus Christ is, God in the flesh. God has tried from the beginning of time to build a bridge to humankind. He gave men and women His laws and yet they failed to obey. Then the Lord sent His prophets. But the people refused to listen. And finally, He sent Jesus, to show us how to live upon the earth. And instead of responding to His offer of salvation, men nailed Him to a cross.

Today's Scripture warns against false teachings. The apostle Paul also issued an urgent caution: "Now I urge you, brethren, keep your eye on those who cause dissensions and hindrances contrary to the teaching which you learned, and turn away from them. For such men are slaves, not of our Lord Christ but of their own appetites; and by their smooth and flattering speech they deceive the hearts of the unsuspecting" (Romans 16:17-18).

Prayer — Lord, strengthen my faith so that I can love those who don't know You, so that I can reveal the true identity of Your Son.

The Lamb Breaks Three Seals

Behold, a white horse, and he who sat on it had a bow; and a crown was given to him; and he went out conquering, and to conquer. . . And another, a red horse, went out; and to him who sat on it, it was granted to take peace from the earth, and that men should slay one another; and a great sword was given to him. . .and behold, a black horse, and he who sat on it had a pair of scales in his hand. And I heard as it were a voice in the center of the four living creatures saying, "A quart of wheat for a denarius, and three quarts of barley for a denarius; and do not harm the oil and the wine." Revelation 6:2-6

Each of these four horsemen represents a different judgment that will come upon the earth. The first rider, on a white horse, has a bow, but notice he doesn't have any arrows. His initial objective is to conquer peacefully. Also, "a crown was given to him." But his crown is merely a "victor's crown," not a kingly crown; he receives authority from another. But don't be deceived by that white horse: this man is evil.

The next rider, on a red horse, is granted permission to "take peace from the earth." This speaks of war. While he displays a semblance of dominance and control, such power will have a set duration.

The third rider, sitting atop a black horse, holds "a pair of scales in his hand." This reveals that famine will accompany the war. And when this verse describes "a quart of wheat for a denarius," it evokes the Jewish custom of measuring out bread by weight, which signifies that food is scarce (Leviticus 26:26).

Prayer — Lord, please help me understand Your Word.

Order in Our Prayers

First of all, then, I urge that entreaties and prayers, petitions and thanksgivings, be made on behalf of all men, for kings and all who are in authority, in order that we may lead a tranquil and quiet life in all godliness and dignity. This is good and acceptable in the sight of God our Savior, who desires all men to be saved and to come to the knowledge of the truth.
1 Timothy 2:1-4

The demands of this world, and the pace at which our technology is racing, can sometimes overwhelm us, causing feelings of panic, powerlessness, and even paranoia. Is there a solution that brings life back into perspective? Yes. And God calls it prayer.

Our human sense of ineptness—we simply aren't equal to the task of being in charge of the universe—causes us to react to pressure. So, we've got to release the hand controls back to God. And when we practice this on an individual level, the prayers we offer within our congregations become more effective.

Prayer isn't some mystical entity to be attained by a few saintly little ladies in the church. Instead, it is an act of worship on the part of the created toward the Creator. Prayer is simply "talking to God" about everything that affects our lives.

Prayer — Spirit of God, fall afresh on me that I might lift my voice in petition to You.

Welcoming Other Believers

The elder to the beloved Gaius, whom I love in truth. . .
Beloved, you are acting faithfully in whatever you accomplish
for the brethren, and especially when they are strangers; and
they bear witness to your love before the church; and you will do
well to send them on their way in a manner worthy of God.
3 John 1:1, 5-6

Gaius, a strong and cordial believer, was dearly loved by the apostle John. We see in today's Scripture that John refers to him as "beloved." Gaius extended a hand of loving fellowship to all who came to worship.

But it was the truth to which Gaius was a witness that had molded this extraordinary life, one centered on obedience to God. Gaius provided genuine hospitality. And evidently this included opening his own home, heart, and pocketbook to others, that the Word of God might go forth.

If only we all might have such pure motives for assisting others, that they might receive God's Word and see His love flowing all around them. Such a practical ministry of serving God gives honor to God, is a penetrating witness to the lost, and is a way of demonstrating obedience to God.

Prayer — Father, my church will likely be filled this Christmas with people who may only "press the flesh with the faithful" once or twice a year. May I give these inquiring minds a warm reception.

Three More Seals Are Opened

*And when He broke the fourth seal. . .I looked, and behold, an
ashen horse; and he who sat on it had the name "Death"; and
Hades was following with him. And authority was given to
them over a fourth of the earth, to kill with sword and with
famine and with pestilence and by the wild beasts of the earth.
And when He broke the fifth seal, I saw underneath the altar
the souls of those who had been slain because of the word of
God, and because of the testimony which they had maintained;
and they cried out with a loud voice, saying, "How long, O
Lord, holy and true, wilt Thou refrain from judging and
avenging our blood on those who dwell on the earth?"*
Revelation 6:7-10

Jesus Christ, now seated in heaven, opens these seals. With
the ashen horse comes massive death and destruction. Men
and women have been given ample time to repent. However,
man's favorite response to God has been to ignore Him.

In this vision John viewed two personages. First came
death, the rider of the pale horse, and Hades followed him.
Although death claims the body and Hades the soul, only
Jesus Christ holds the keys of death and Hades. " 'Do not be
afraid; I am the first and the last, and the living One; and I
was dead, and behold, I am alive forevermore, and I have the
keys of death and of Hades' " (Revelation 1:17-18).

These judgments are the result of war. The punishment
is warranted in recompense for those who have been martyred upon the earth (Revelation 6:11).

Prayer — God of power and might, I repent before You.

Phoebe: Fit for Leadership

It is a trustworthy statement: if any man aspires to the office of overseer, it is a fine work he desires to do. An overseer, then, must be above reproach, the husband of one wife, temperate, prudent, respectable, hospitable, able to teach, not addicted to wine or pugnacious, but gentle, uncontentious, free from the love of money. He must be one who manages his own household well, keeping his children under control with all dignity (but if a man does not know how to manage his own household, how will he take care of the church of God?); and not a new convert, lest he become conceited and fall into the condemnation incurred by the devil. And he must have a good reputation with those outside the church, so that he may not fall into reproach and the snare of the devil. 1 Timothy 3:1-7

An overseer refers to one who held the primary responsibility of directing the work of the church. Such a man was to lead a blameless life, that his character would never be in question (1 Timothy 3:2).

Although this passage may appear directed toward men, it applies to women as well. For the position of deacon, referred to as a servant who assisted the apostles, Paul singled out Phoebe, a deaconess, for special recognition. "I commend to you our sister, Phoebe, who is a servant [same Greek word as *deaconess*] of the church which is at Cenchrea. . .for she herself has also been a helper of many, and of myself as well" (Romans 16:1-2).

Prayer — Jesus, let me live my days with these godly characteristics in mind. And when You call me into leadership I'll be ready.

God's Bond-Servants Are Sealed

And. . .another angel. . .cried out with a loud voice to the four
angels to whom it was granted to harm the earth and the sea,
saying, "Do not harm the earth or the sea or the trees, until we
have sealed the bond-servants of our God on their foreheads."
And I heard the number of those who were sealed, one hundred
and forty-four thousand sealed from every tribe of the sons of
Israel. Revelation 7:2-4

After centuries upon centuries of enduring Israel's disobedience and broken promises, God still loves His people. And
He's about to preserve for Himself "a remnant" of the nation
who will survive the atrocities of the tribulation.

The Book of Revelation describes seven seals, seven
bowls, and seven trumpets filled with judgments that become
progressively more severe.

Eventually, the antichrist will amass a huge army to come
against Jerusalem. And then God's timetable for His kingdom
on earth begins to count down. "And the angel. . .swore by
Him who lives forever and ever, Who created heaven and the
things in it, and the earth and the things in it, and the sea and
the things in it, that there shall be delay no longer, but in the
days of the voice of the seventh angel, when he is about to
sound, then the mystery of God is finished, as He preached to
His servants the prophets" (Revelation 10:1-7).

Prayer — Jesus Christ, the Alpha and Omega, is the King of
Kings and Lord of Lords. And He's coming back! Hallelujah!

Paul's Ministry Comes to a Close

*Paul, an apostle of Christ Jesus by the will of God, according to
the promise of life in Christ Jesus, to Timothy, my beloved son. . .
I constantly remember you in my prayers night and day,
longing to see you, even as I recall your tears, so that I may be
filled with joy. For I am mindful of the sincere faith within
you, which first dwelt in your grandmother Lois, and your
mother Eunice, and I am sure that it is in you as well.*
2 Timothy 1:1, 3-5

One of my favorite full-time jobs was keeping a database for
a large magazine publisher. However, as time went on I
became more convinced that the Lord was calling me away to
begin my own ministry of writing. Training my replacement
hurt my soul to the core.

As I read Paul's second letter to Timothy, I can identify
with his anguish at letting go. Paul had to make sure that
Timothy, who suffered from bouts of insecurity, remained
strong in the faith. For Timothy would now "carry the torch
of faith" and continue bringing the Gospel to all who would
listen.

Paul praises Timothy, reminding him of the heritage of
belief passed down to him from his mother, Eunice, and
grandmother, Lois. And Paul, the ever-present spiritual
mentor, expresses his love by referring to Timothy as "my
beloved son."

Prayer — Use me, Lord, to do Your will.

Jude, a Bond-Servant of Jesus Christ

*Beloved, while I was making every effort to write you about
our common salvation, I felt the necessity to write to you
appealing that you contend earnestly for the faith which was
once for all delivered to the saints. For certain persons have
crept in unnoticed, those who were long beforehand marked out
for this condemnation, ungodly persons who turn the grace of
our God into licentiousness and deny our only Master and
Lord, Jesus Christ. Jude 1:3-4*

It's Christmas Eve and you probably have a busy day ahead.
Has the luster of it worn off, replaced by the worldly pressures that overshadow Christ's birth?

Jude writes to exhort the "saints," those who are sanctified or "set apart" by God, reminding them that they share
salvation in Christ. The church had been infiltrated with
persons who had "crept in unnoticed." The believers had
become complacent, no longer aware of those who intended
to destroy the body of Christ.

Therefore, Jude says, "Now I desire to remind you. . . ,
that the Lord, after saving a people out of the land of Egypt,
subsequently destroyed those who did not believe. And
angels who. . .abandoned their proper abode, He has kept in
eternal bonds under darkness for the judgment of the great
day" (Jude 1:5-6).

Anytime the church's purpose is undermined, Satan
himself is the instigator of such evil. The church will forever
be buffeted by these demons who attempt to thwart the
message of Christ crucified from being disseminated.

Prayer — Jesus, remind me today to set aside time to be
with You.

Happy Birthday, Jesus!

*And Joseph also went up from Galilee, from the city of
Nazareth, to Judea, to the city of David, which is called
Bethlehem, because he was of the house and family of David, in
order to register, along with Mary, who was engaged to him,
and was with child. And it came about that while they were
there, the days were completed for her to give birth. And she
gave birth to her first-born son; and she wrapped Him in
cloths, and laid Him in a manger, because there was no room
for them in the inn. Luke 2:4-7*

Joy fills our hearts as we celebrate Christmas. But are we
mindful of the sacrifices surrounding this tiny Savior's birth?
First, Christ, the Son of God, willingly left heaven's throne,
took on a human body, and grew to manhood so He could
die on the cross.

Next, consider Mary, a young girl filled with dreams of
Joseph, the man to whom she'd just been betrothed. An
angel announced to Mary that she had been chosen as the
mother of the Messiah (Luke 1:35). Putting her own desires
aside, she accepted God's plan.

God also sent an angel to prepare Joseph's heart.
"Behold, an angel of the Lord appeared to him in a dream,
saying, 'Joseph, son of David, do not be afraid to take Mary
as your wife; for that which has been conceived in her is of
the Holy Spirit. And she will bear a Son; and you shall call
His name Jesus, for it is he who will save His people from
their sins'" (Matthew 1:20-21).

Prayer — Father, Your Word is all I need today: " 'Behold, a
virgin will be with child and bear a son, and she will call His
name Immanuel' "(Isaiah 7:14).

Titus, Appointed by Paul

*Paul, a bond-servant of God, and an apostle of Jesus Christ,
. . .to Titus, my true child in a common faith: Grace and peace
from God the Father and Christ Jesus our Savior. For this
reason I left you in Crete, that you might set in order what
remains, and appoint elders in every city as I directed you.*
Titus 1:1, 4-5

After Paul had made sure that Timothy was well-grounded
and could help guide the church at Rome in the faith, he
turned his attention to Titus, in Crete.

Paul's letter to Titus is similar to the one he wrote to
Timothy. The qualities for choosing leaders is so critical
that Paul makes sure nothing is left unclear.

Ever present is Paul's concern that these people of Crete
might stray from the faith, as they're surrounded by godless
people. "To the pure, all things are pure; but to those who are
defiled and unbelieving, nothing is pure, but both their mind
and their conscience are defiled. They profess to know God,
but by their deeds they deny Him" (Titus 1:15-16).

Therefore, he admonishes the older people to hold fast
to the truth. "Older men are to be temperate, dignified, sensible, sound in faith, in love, in perseverance. Older women
likewise are to be reverent in their behavior, that they may
encourage the young women to love their husbands, to love
their children, to be sensible, pure, workers at home, kind,
being subject to their own husbands, that the word of God
may not be dishonored" (Titus 2:2-5).

Prayer — Lord, have I lived my life this year in a way that
pleased You?

God's Voice of Truth

*"And I will grant authority to my two witnesses, and they will
prophesy for twelve hundred and sixty days, clothed in
sackcloth." These are the two olive trees and the two lampstands
that stand before the Lord of the earth.*
Revelation 11:3-4

The world will be for a time under the control of the
antichrist and the outcome appears hopeless. God appoints
two witnesses who speak forth His word for 1, 260 days. The
"saints of God" have been taken to heaven and the Holy
Spirit has been taken out of the world. Those choosing to
remain in unbelief become terrified of the two witnesses, for
their God-given power is truly awesome! "And if any one
desires to harm them, fire proceeds out of their mouth and
devours their enemies; and if anyone would desire to harm
them, in this manner he must be killed. These have the power
to shut up the sky, in order that rain may not fall during the
days of their prophesying; and they have power over the
waters to turn them into blood, and to smite the earth with
every plague, as often as they desire" (Revelation 11:5-6).

Finally, "the beast that comes up out of the abyss will
make war with them, and overcome them and kill them"
(Revelation 11:7). Their dead bodies will lie in the streets of
Jerusalem for three and a half days and no one will be permitted to bury them. The earth dwellers have a great celebration.
Suddenly the two witnesses are taken up to heaven in a cloud
as their enemies look on in disbelief (Revelation 11:8-12).

Prayer — Lord, what a powerful God You are!

The Marriage Supper of the Lamb

"Let us rejoice and be glad and give the glory to Him, for the marriage of the Lamb has come and his bride has made herself ready." And it was given to her to clothe herself in fine linen, bright and clean; for the fine linen is the righteous acts of the saints. And he said to me, "Write, 'Blessed are those who are invited to the marriage supper of the Lamb.'" And he said to me, "These are true words of God." Revelation 19:7-9

At the beginning of Christ's ministry on earth, John the Baptist presented Him as the Lamb of God. " 'Behold, the Lamb of God who takes away the sin of the world!' " (John 1:29) And now John the Apostle reveals Christ again as the Lamb. But this time He is preparing a supper in which His bride, "the Church," will be in the presence of the Lamb. This scene will take place in heaven, where the believers finally see Christ face-to-face.

However, this is not the kind of "supper" one would expect. For instead of a banquet, it is the Church's viewing from a heavenly vantage point God's judgment upon the earth. "And I saw the beast and the kings of the earth and their armies, assembled to make war against Him who sat upon the horse, and against His army" (Revelation 19:19). This is not the same ashen-colored horse we saw at the beginning of the Book of Revelation. This rider is Jesus Christ, accompanied by the armies of heaven, ready to execute righteous judgment. And after the battle is over, Satan is bound for a thousand years and death and Hades are thrown into the lake of fire (Revelation 20:2, 14).

Prayer — Come, Lord Jesus!

The Eternal Gospel

*"And I saw another angel flying in midheaven, having an
eternal gospel to preach to those who live on the earth, and to
every nation and tribe and tongue and people; and he said
with a loud voice, 'Fear God, and give Him glory, because the
hour of His judgment has come; and worship Him who made
the heaven and the earth and the sea and springs of waters.'"*
Revelation 14:6-7

Following the Resurrection, Jesus prepared to leave this earth
and return to heaven. Before going, He delivered a message
to His disciples and charged them with a mission: "Go therefore and make disciples of all the nations, baptizing them in
the name of the Father and the Son and the Holy Spirit,
teaching them to observe all that I commanded you; and lo,
I am with you always, even to the end of the age" (Matthew
28:19-20).

This great commission is extended to all who choose to
believe in Christ. In looking for creative ways to present the
Good News to the children who visit my home, I filled a
large, handmade bag with age-appropriate books and videos.
How eagerly the kids seek out this "grandma bag," ready to
discover more about the Lord.

Prayer — Lord, while there is still time, please provide
imaginative ways in which we can speak forth Your Word of
Truth to all those whom we love. We are grateful that You
will "never leave us or forsake us" (Hebrews 13:5).

Some Will Be Singing

"And they sang the song of Moses the bondservant of God and the song of the Lamb, saying, 'Great and marvelous are Thy works, O Lord God, the Almighty; righteous and true are Thy ways, Thou King of the nations.'" Revelation 15:3

Those who are victorious over the adversities of the last days on earth will have much to celebrate. This victorious number will include many Jews who come to believe in Christ as their Messiah. And in true Isrealite fashion, they will express their jubilation in song, just as King David did. For the covenant God made with His people stands for all time: "He has sent redemption to His people; He has ordained His covenant forever; Holy and awesome is His name. The fear of the Lord is the beginning of wisdom; a good understanding have all those who do His commandments; His praise endures forever" (Psalm 111:9-11).

Occasionally, I attend Sabbath worship services with a nearby Messianic congregation, for they truly know how to celebrate. Their joyful music resounds as they sing praises extolling the attributes of their faithful God. And this represents only a minute glimpse of the glorious sounds to come, when they will someday worship the Lamb in heaven.

Prayer — Lord, You alone are worthy of our worship. I praise You with all my heart, and look forward to the day when I will worship You in heaven.

We Shall Behold Him

*And there shall no longer be any curse; and the throne of God
and of the Lamb shall be in it, and His bond-servants shall
serve Him; and they shall see His face, and His name shall be
on their foreheads. Revelation 22:3–4*

A year ago we began a journey together in the Garden of
Eden with Adam and Eve. The tree of life stood in the midst
of that garden and God presented these two humans with
the opportunity to "live forever." But they turned down that
offer, choosing instead to commit the first sin of disobedience and defiance toward their Creator. Thus began our long
journey back to God.

But there in the garden God also promised Adam and
Eve that He would send a Redeemer (Genesis 3:15).

Isaiah prophesied that the Redeemer would be born of
a virgin (Isaiah 7:14), and the prophecy was fulfilled (Luke
2:4-7). Isaiah also said that this Redeemer would die on the
cross for our sins. Again, the prophecy was fulfilled (Isaiah
53:1-12).

God is presenting you with a chance for a fresh start.
Today you can take the first step on the road, with all its
inevitable trials, that leads to Jesus. Will you choose to
behold Him. . .face-to-face?

———————

Prayer — Lord, give me the courage to put the old year and
all its mistakes behind me. Let me grasp Your strong hand
of forgiveness so that in Christ I might have not only a new
year, but a brand-new life. Amen!

INDEX

January

February

March

April

May

June

July

August

September

October

November

December

Inspirational Library

Beautiful purse/pocket-size editions of Christian classics bound in flexible leatherette. These books make thoughtful gifts for everyone on your list, including yourself!

When I'm on My Knees   The highly popular collection of devotional thoughts on prayer, especially for women.
Flexible Leatherette $4.97

The Bible Promise Book   Over 1000 promises from God's Word arranged by topic. What does God promise about matters like: Anger, Illness, Jealousy, Love, Money, Old Age, and Mercy? Find out in this book!
Flexible Leatherette $3.97

The Quilt of Life   Ninety devotional stories center on the popular topic of quilting.
Flexible Leatherette. $4.97

My Daily Prayer Journal   Each page is dated and features a Scripture verse and ample room for you to record your thoughts, prayers, and praises. One page for each day of the year.
Flexible Leatherette $4.97

Available wherever books are sold.
Or order from:

Barbour Publishing, Inc.
P.O. Box 719
Uhrichsville, OH 44683
www.barbourbooks.com

If you order by mail add $2.00 to your order for shipping.
Prices subject to change without notice.